Ranches,
Rowhouses,
AND
Railroad Flats

Ranches, Rowhouses,
AND
Railroad Flats

AMERICAN HOMES:
How They Shape our Landscapes
and Neighborhoods

CHRISTINE HUNTER

W. W. NORTON & COMPANY
New York · London

For Lou, Peter, Jonathan, and Gregory

The author is grateful for the talent and patient help of Elizabeth Newman, who drew many of the illustrations.

This book was initially undertaken through the author's receipt of the 1992 Arnold W. Brunner Grant from the American Institute of Architects New York Chapter.

Additional support was provided by a grant from the Graham Foundation for Advanced Studies in the Fine Arts.

The text of this book is composed in New Baskerville
with the display set in Papyrus and labels in Mr. Hand
Manufacturing by Courier Companies
Book design by Charlotte Staub
Composition by Ken Gross
Acknowledgments for permission to use copyright material are on page 327.

Library of Congress Cataloging-in-Publication Data

Hunter, Christine (Christine M.)
    Ranches, rowhouses, and railroad flats : American homes : how they shape our landscape and neighborhoods / Christine Hunter.
        p.   cm.
    Includes bibliographical references and index.
    ISBN 0-393-73025-5
    1. Architecure, Domestic—United States. 2. Architecture—Environmental aspects—United States. 3. Architecture and society—United States. I. Title.
NA7205.H78   1999   98-34933
728'.0973—dc21   CIP

W. W. Norton & Company, Inc.,
500 Fifth Avenue, New York, NY 10110
    http://www.wwnorton.com
W. W. Norton & Company Ltd.,
10 Coptic Street, London WC1A 1PU

0 9 8 7 6 5 4 3 2 1

Contents

Introduction

home *n.* 1. the place where one lives. 2. the place where one was born or reared. 3. the natural environment of an animal, plant, etc. *Webster's New World Dictionary*

The word [ecology] comes from two Greek words meaning "study of the home." In a broad sense this is just what ecology means.... It is the study of how plants and animals relate to the land, to other living things, and to their total environment.

John Vosburgh, *The Land We Live On*

When I was growing up the rooms inside my home were so familiar to me that I never thought about them very hard. In describing my own bedroom I would have first listed the things in it, the furniture and other important possessions. Then I might have talked about the blue and yellow flowered wallpaper I'd chosen myself, or the views from the windows. I probably never would have gotten to its size and overall shape, where the door was, and how the room fit, like a puzzle piece, into the rest of the building. And I truly didn't know, because I couldn't see it, what held the room up, or what the whole house was made of.

My parents lived in the same place from the time I was born until the day I turned twenty-five. By American standards it was a very old house, the original structure probably built around 1800. I was told that it had been the main house of a farm that later became the campus of the college where my father taught. The house had thus started out in rural Pennsylvania, but by our time it was firmly ensconced in the suburbs of Philadelphia, with no commercial agriculture in sight.

Though it had been undermaintained for quite a while, I liked our house and was comfortable there. Knowing that it was so old gave me the chance to imagine things that might have gone on in it long ago. (One of my sisters claimed to have seen, in an inaccessible part of the attic, a coffin-sized box that she was sure contained a dead Civil War soldier.) What I thought of as problems were not its spaces or appearance but its technological weaknesses: fuses that blew unpredictably, hot water that suddenly went cold when someone else turned on a faucet, leaks from the third-floor bathroom that streaked my bedroom walls, and all the small mammals and insects that shared the building with us, partly because it still had sections of the original dirt-floored cellar.

Our house sat at the back of the campus, neither part of the main quadrangles of classroom buildings and dormitories nor along the two lanes of homes that had been built by the college as faculty housing. Around it were three other houses, newcomers, built in the years immediately before and after World War II. Each of these had been constructed by individual faculty members, largely through their own labor, under a special arrangement stipulating that the homes would revert to college ownership when their builders moved out. Along Featherbed Lane (unpaved until the 1950s) there were no street numbers and, to my knowledge, no formal property lines, as all the land belonged to the college. The distance between houses varied from perhaps 75 to 150 feet, and seemed to allow each family plenty of space for its own outdoor uses, with informal dividing clumps of brush and trees as well.

This group of four disparate homes was bounded on one side by a large parking lot, hastily built (also during the 1950s) to accommodate a sudden surge in cars on campus. It was ugly and a little raw around the edges but great for practicing bike riding. On the other side was the college dump, where we unearthed odd pieces of bric-a-brac and where small fires occasionally broke out, bringing sirens, fire trucks, and a crowd of onlookers to an otherwise quiet spot. Separating our homes from the back edge of the campus and the beginning of private suburban lots was a several-hundred-foot swath of largely unused and overgrown land. A dirt road off the parking lot gave access there to garden plots that the college rented out to staff and interested neighbors.

Overall, it was an amiable and idiosyncratic setting in which to grow up, providing a friendly community with some other children, though not nearly as many as in surrounding towns of the era, and lots of space for independent exploring at a young age.

While I was conscious of how my neighborhood differed socially from the wealthy and conservative suburbs where many of my elementary and high school classmates lived, I lacked a real frame of reference for analyzing it physically.

Around age twelve, when my immediate surroundings began to feel oppressively familiar, I discovered the pleasures of riding the commuter train and exploring center-city Philadelphia. To me at that time it offered both a welcome anonymity and far more to see and think about than the towns just outside the campus gates. By high school, when I rode in and out of the city daily, I knew the views from the train window almost as well as those around my house. Again, however, I would have been hard put to explain the buildings I traveled past in clear physical terms. Because of what I heard and read, what might be called the social landscape was far more vivid; I was aware of the economic and racial segregation of the city and its suburbs, and could see West Philadelphia's blocks of abandoned factories and burned-out homes. But I didn't really see the pattern of houses changing from rows to pairs moving out toward the city boundary, nor did I compare the repeating clusters of small stores around each station with newer and larger shopping areas. The landscape was completely familiar but arbitrary; I had explanations only for how bits and pieces of it had come into being.

When I moved away to college and began to study architecture, I took a class where we were each asked to draw from memory a plan of our childhood home. It was a wonderful assignment, one that should be given not just to future architects. What I produced wasn't very accurate in terms of feet and inches, but it gave our house a whole new order in my mind. The home that I had always thought of as somewhat rambling and patched together actually had an extremely simple organization. The original part of the house had four square rooms on each floor, divided by a hallway that ran straight though the building and included stairs at the back end. Each room opened directly off this hallway and was roughly the same size and shape. This meant that the kitchen was larger and the living room smaller than those in many more modern homes. It also meant that there were lots of doors to slam when I got annoyed at other people in my family.

When my turn came I sheepishly pinned up my drawing in front of the class and was told by the professor that the home I had grown up in was a "Palladian farmhouse." Andrea Palladio, the Italian Renaissance architect, designed symmetrical, beautifully proportioned country homes or *villas*, for his wealthy clients. I doubt that the Pennsylvania farmer who built our house knew a lot about Palladio, but he did manage to inherit and build according to a certain tradition of laying out a freestanding house. In any case, whether or not it was historically accurate, suddenly my home had a label.

Seeing and discussing the plans drawn by classmates also gave me a new basis for comparing our house with other dwellings, including the three right around it. These I had always thought of as products of the eccentric personal preferences of the neighbors who had built them, which was to some degree true. But I now also realized that they all had integral garages with doors leading directly inside, unlike ours, which was a concrete block structure, perhaps fifty years old, separate from the house. None of the other houses had a wide, roofed porch spanning the front façade, the most distinctive and welcoming feature of our house, which would otherwise have been originally a plain roofed cube with identical windows on all sides. Each, however, did have a more spacious living room than ours, with what were known as picture windows, distinct from those in other rooms, looking out on a landscaped yard. While our house had three stories and the neighboring house built just before the Second World War had two, both of those from the early 1950s were so-called ranch houses, with living areas and bedrooms spread out on a single ground floor. In other words, though all four houses been conceived and laid out by amateur builders for their own individual use, each design was also very much the product of its time in the use of land and in the underlying patterns of family life, technology, and transportation.

After my siblings and I grew up, my parents moved to a newer and smaller home off campus. Over the last twenty years the college continued to expand, and what was once its haphazard and underdeveloped back end was transformed into a carefully designed extension of the formal campus environment. In retrospect I see that the small neighborhood that seemed so fixed and inevitable to me in childhood actually lasted only a couple of decades; it was in fact changing continually during that time as well.

The old dump, of course, disappeared first, while I still lived there in the 1960s, perhaps because of more stringent township regulations on waste disposal. The clumsily placed parking lot is gone as well, resodded and now a green quadrangle surrounded by new academic buildings. (New parking lots, presumably better planned, were built closer to the edge of campus.) Our old house was renovated, with upgraded wiring and plumbing and a new cellar floor, as a center for the study of religions. The freestanding garage behind it was demolished. One of the neighboring ranch houses was made into the college security office, while the other two houses are still used as faculty homes. A high wooden fence, however, was erected around the one that faces the new quadrangle, to give it privacy in what is now a clearly institutional setting.

Thus, though the house still looks much the same from outside, I imagine earnest students and teachers sitting around a conference table and discussing philosophy in the room where I once slept, played, and fought with my sisters. For no particularly good reason, as I certainly don't begrudge the college the right to alter its buildings, this makes me slightly uneasy. Not that I want to be living there any more, but it would be nice to think that other people were.

On the other hand, knowing how many Americans have seen the homes where they grew up disappear altogether, I'm glad the house is still standing. It is largely luck, I realize, that has allowed it to endure; similar houses built on neighboring farms in the early 1800s were no doubt torn down to make way for new development. I also think, however, that its survival has something to do with its original straightforward design. The eight similar main rooms did not provide the house with dramatic spaces or long interior vistas. (Had I designed such a plan in architecture school, I would probably have been told to work harder at differentiating the various parts of the home and to think more sculpturally.) But their basic comfortable proportions, and the fact that they all opened off a central hall, wide enough for furniture or for use by many people at once, gave the house a flexibility that made it adaptable—as a home, a school building, and perhaps something else in the future.

Since moving away from my parents I haven't lived in any other freestanding single-family houses. My own children are growing up in homes that are physically very different from the one where I was raised, first an apartment on the fourth floor of a sixteen-story building, and now a brick rowhouse on a city street with other attached houses and apartment buildings. Both were built in the late 1920s, which makes them old compared with most homes in the United States but still at least a century younger than the Palladian farmhouse. Both were a part of developments that housed many families; neither was individually built by its original occupants. Because of urban land values and construction costs, rather than their inherent form, each of them was built with some-what less interior square footage than the old farmhouse. My hus-band and I have had to think harder than my parents did about where to put all our possessions in order to keep the space we have livable for everyone in the family. Our shelves go from floor to ceiling and we store something under every bed. But both have been great homes, and there are times now when I miss our old apartment much more than I do my parents' house.

The biggest differences between the home I grew up in and the ones I have lived in since are not the rooms themselves, nor the things in the rooms—they are the connections: to the ground on which the buildings sit, to the rest of the outdoors, and to other homes and nonresidential buildings. Because they are growing up in dense city neighborhoods, my children experience a surround-ing built environment that is more complex than the one I knew. There are sidewalks as well as streets, and subways, buses, and taxis as well as private cars. Within a few blocks are stores, restaurants, offices, factories, schools, and parks.

This complexity both limits and adds to their freedom growing up, as it also affects the daily lives and choices of all our neighbors. Most city toddlers and preschoolers are strictly trained never to open the front door by themselves and always to stop at the corner, waiting to cross the street with adult help. However, once children reach an age when they're allowed out on their own, which varies greatly from one family to another, the physical nature of their neighborhood determines what they can get to independently.

Generally, Americans today are far more fearful for their chil-dren's safety in all neighborhoods than they were in the 1950s. This is a troubling shift, with causes that are a complicated mixture of physical and social changes. The results are simpler to understand. Few kindergartners, for instance, walk even a short distance to school by themselves, a common practice only forty years ago. Though I sometimes wish my children could have the same early and casual freedom I did, I know that that freedom occurred in a place and a time that have both changed.

In our present neighborhood, however, I enjoy seeing the satisfaction that my children get from each successive step of the independence we are comfortable allowing them: first walking down the sidewalk to a friend's home on the block, then crossing the street for a solo trip to the corner deli; later going by themselves to a park or pizzeria a few blocks away, and eventually learning to navigate bus and subway routes in order to go farther afield. This gradually increasing freedom, I hope, is helping them to become street-smart travelers as well as familiar with both the beauties and the eyesores of their immediate environment. I like to theorize, though of course I will never have proof, that it is a healthier progression than being driven everywhere and then suddenly released to total independence behind the wheel at age sixteen.

What do my children think of their home and neighborhood? Their answers are specific and anecdotal, as mine would have been when growing up. They like and name individual stores, local events such as street fairs, and particular friends living nearby. Our rowhouse is good because it has several different places to play, including a basement and a back porch. What's bad about the neighborhood is that it has too much litter and that cars are stolen (a topic of endless discussion among adults on our block). While they like to be able to do things on their own, in most cases my children don't agree that walking someplace is better than being driven.

Simply because of the complexity and variety of their surroundings, my children do have a broader frame of reference than I did; they have experienced a wider range of homes as well as other types of buildings. Some ideas they come up with would never have occurred to me at their age. If he won the lottery, my middle son proposed when he was eight, he would buy the apartment building on the corner and install all his cousins and grandparents from far away, as well as us and his friends' families, to live in separate homes under one roof. At the same time these kids have the accurate sense that the homes in their neighborhood are not what most

Americans aspire to. Where we live is okay, acknowledged the same son on another occasion, but added, "When are we going to live in a *real* house, like Aunt Barbi?"

The word *home* has many strands of meaning that are tightly wound together in our minds. We define it first by our emotional connections. Home is where our family is or where, if we live on our own, we have a kind of privacy not found anyplace else. Whatever our social living arrangements may be, this place has a physical form and is sited within a specific larger context, or neighborhood. Furthermore, it includes not just a set of spaces, or rooms, built out of certain materials, but also a set of mechanical services and connections to the natural world. Today in most wealthier nations we take for granted that homes will have, among other things, electrical wiring, clean running water, fresh air, and mechanical heat when necessary.

In the United States, more than in many other countries, these sheltered spaces, services, and connections take the form of houses. The primary dictionary meaning of *house* is "a building to live in—specifically, a building occupied by one family or person." This definition says nothing about what a house should look like; it could be anything from an igloo or a sod hut to a thirty-room mansion. The most basic American image of a *real* house, however, is similar to the small green house of a Monopoly game: a cube with a triangular roof on top. As a Monopoly game progresses, more and more of these houses are "built" on the playing board, and they get increasingly close together. When a property is filled up with houses, the next step is to get rid of them and substitute a hotel, which earns more for its owner.

Monopoly, of course, is a game about money, not architecture, and doesn't allow any consideration of the various ways that homes can be grouped and attached. But neither do the laws and customs that govern the building of many American communities. It is deeply entrenched in our thinking that a detached house in the middle of a large plot of land is the most desirable form of dwelling.

Whether or not we think of them as equally valid or livable, there are three basic arrangements for homes—*freestanding houses, attached houses,* and *apartments*—all of which were built in North

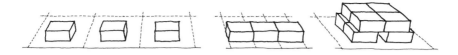

I-1. The three basic arrangements for homes.

America before the United States was formed. Because of minimum building code requirements and standardized methods of construction, the sheltered spaces, or rooms, inside these three types of homes are now quite similar. However, the exterior appearance, connection to the outdoors, and amount of energy needed to make these inside spaces comfortable are not. And as these three forms are grouped into neighborhoods, with each other and with other man-made structures, they create differing outdoor environments with varying effects on the rest of the natural world.

Many consequences of the ways that we have built our homes and neighborhoods in the United States are well documented: the energy consumed in heating and air-conditioning, the miles driven in gasoline-powered cars to get to work and to accomplish everyday errands, the gallons of water used indoors and for maintaining grass and shrubs around our buildings. Others may be harder to quantify precisely—for example, the ways in which our building, outdoor paving, and replanting practices alter flooding patterns or destroy the health of local rivers and lakes. Overall, however, there is no lack of data connecting the buildings and landscape around us with serious environmental issues. But we tend to focus our attention elsewhere; it seems easier to be concerned about the destruction of the Amazon rain forest or the disappearance of tigers in Asia than to look closely at the homes and neighborhoods that we ourselves build and inhabit. We don't think of human habitats as comparable to those of other animals; books on birds' nests are not on the same library shelf with books on houses.

The problem posed by this separation made between "natural" and "man-made" environments has been pointed out recently by writers from a variety of disciplines. The environmental historian William Cronon, in his essay "*The Trouble With Wilderness*" (1995), wrote:

15

Idealizing a distant wilderness too often means not idealizing the environment in which we actually live, the landscape that for better or worse we call home. Most of our serious environmental problems start right here, at home, and if we are to solve those problems, we need an environmental ethic that will tell us as much about using nature as about not using it.[1]

Despite widespread agreement that we need to expand the focus of popular environmentalism to include our coexistence with the natural world in our everyday surroundings, there is scant material available to help accomplish this task. A great deal of beautiful writing describes plants and animals in wilderness settings and human expeditions to distant or underdeveloped regions. Nature documentaries are both popular as entertainment and effective in generating concern for at least some threatened species and habitats. The dramatic tension of such films is often created by the threat of bulldozers and builders; once these arrive, however, the battle is lost. Choices about what to build are not part of the plot.

Writings about the environmental implications of building design address a comparatively small audience. A growing number of architects, landscape architects, engineers, and planners are concerned with developing new approaches known as *green architecture* and *ecological* or *sustainable design*. Their writing, directed mostly at other practitioners and students, is often largely prescriptive, describing only a few recently completed building projects. Most of what exists or is currently being built, especially in the United States, they condemn wholesale. The introduction to *Ecological Design*, by Sim Van der Ryn and Stuart Cowan, for instance, is unequivocal:

The house, the habitat we are most familiar with, seemed to be a good place to start this first generation of ecological design. The rural or village homestead was once the center of a largely self-sufficient system that produced a family's livelihood, its food and fiber, and its tools and toys. Over a period of several hundred years, this homestead has become an anonymous mass-produced dwelling unit, its inhabitants members of a faceless consumershed, the house itself totally dependent on outside resources to sustain its inhabitants.[2]

Such blanket criticism of the design and human value of millions of existing diverse homes is not limited to those with environmental concerns. There is a long tradition of writing about architecture from a more traditional aesthetic and cultural viewpoint that also dismisses, in broad terms, most of what gets built. This approach helps make a strong case for whatever new design solutions are being advocated, but does little to help us differentiate among buildings actually out there along the street.

Part of the reason that we don't think more analytically about the everyday buildings and other man-made structures around us is simply that we are not trained to do so. From a young age we study more about the nonhuman environment, both inanimate geological forms and the forms of living things, than we do about the structures and mechanical systems on which we've come to depend so heavily.

Learning to differentiate among and categorize plants and animals has always been a fundamental part of human education, formal and informal. This process of taxonomy starts early in life, as toddlers begin to name the animals they see around them or in pictures, and it continues through school, forming a large part of the basic science education that is included in all elementary and secondary curricula. Initial classroom teaching introduces children to concealed aspects of familiar living things, the bones and organs of animals and the root structure of trees. It also gives them ways to identify and classify that which they do see, differentiating insects from spiders by the number of their legs, and plants by the shape of their leaves. In higher grades, the mastery of ever more detailed classifications is not simply a matter of rote memorization but a basis for understanding how different life forms are connected and mutually dependent. Thus, to take but one obvious example, the form of an animal's mouth, teeth, if any, and digestive organs are related to what he eats, and when, where, and how he moves around and reproduces are related to who eats him.

Even for those of us who never use this taxonomic education in any professional way as adults, it has lifelong importance. To begin with, it helps to develop an understanding of and frame of reference for our own bodies, what's inside us and how we resemble and differ from other creatures. When we venture into the outdoor world, it also enriches our vision; the more categories we have for what's around us, the more we see. If we learn to identify many types of trees and smaller plants, for example, then a forest no longer appears as an undifferentiated swath of green, and individual places within it develop distinct characters. This is important for navigation and survival in some situations, but also simply increases our enjoyment of hiking there. Our perception of the precise and intricate geometries of living things provides a balance and contrast to the seemingly more random forms of the nonliving landscape, the mountains, sand dunes, and clouds that are part of patterns too large to comprehend from ground level.

As our knowledge of specific plants or creatures grows more detailed, particularly our understanding of their role in the larger ecosystem, we also typically put more value on them, both aesthetically and scientifically. Knowing the Latin name or the classification of a plant or insect may not keep us from viewing it, for our immediate purposes, as a weed or a pest. But the more we appreciate about its physical structure and role in its native habitat, the less likely we are to consider it ugly or worthless.

In contrast to this continuing attention to plant and animal life, which is an accepted part of our formal schooling, we get very little training in differentiating and analyzing the buildings and other man-made structures that make up so much of our daily environment. Blocks and "housekeeping areas" disappear from the classroom after kindergarten. From then on, the buildings discussed, usually in social studies, are those of faraway or preindustrial cultures: longhouses, igloos, Greek temples, perhaps traditional Japanese homes. Elementary school classes may study and visit local landmarks notable for their beauty or historic importance, but never the ordinary houses, apartment buildings, offices, and stores that form the bulk of what we drive or walk past regularly. At more advanced levels of education, architectural and landscape design, engineering, and planning are studied mainly by those who plan to become practitioners. Within a broad liberal arts curriculum, art history, not required but offered as an elective, does include the history of architecture. Most of the recent buildings studied, however, are those few designed by well-known architects, the intellectual equivalent of local landmarks.

Though we don't study them in school, we do of course have names for most of the buildings that we pass every day, and in some cases we may even be familiar with their particular structural system, materials, and layout. One reason that the local built environment is not much emphasized in our formal education is that in many places and for much of history it has seemed self-evident. Why study something abstractly when we can figure it out intuitively by walking around with our eyes open? In communities, small or large, where most homes and other utilitarian structures are built to common designs out of local materials and depend on nearby sources of water and heating fuel, most residents may fully understand both the formal logic and the technology of their built surroundings. Under these circumstances it may indeed be more enriching to study the buildings of other places and eras.

In the United States, however, we have built so rapidly and so extensively, with such continually changing technological standards and design ideas, that most of us lack this intuitive understanding of our surroundings. Our homes become "old" sometimes faster than we do, not just as a result of shifting fashions but because of more profound changes. As neighborhoods develop over time, many come to include a mix of buildings and streetscapes that can be hard to decipher.

During the early 1900s, for example, electric streetcars, or trolleys, invented only in the 1880s, were the latest and most convenient form of local transportation. Extending outward from towns and cities all over the country, new neighborhoods were built on either side of the major streets where streetcar tracks ran. What developed were blocks of closely spaced homes, attached in rows or pairs in some communities and freestanding in others. Laid out with small front- and backyards, they allowed many families to live for the first time beyond walking distance of the factories and other businesses where their breadwinners worked. Food and other daily needs were supplied by small stores within easy walking distance, usually located along the same major street where the trolley ran.

Only thirty years later the trolleys were disappearing, in some cases replaced by new rubber-wheeled, gasoline-powered buses but more often, of course, giving way to the growing predominance of the automobile. New homes built on empty lots or blocks adjacent to these neighborhoods were laid out differently in order to include driveways and often garages.

Because many people living in existing homes also began to buy cars, by necessity or choice, they made what modifications they could to accommodate them. Where there was sufficient space for parking, and even sometimes where there wasn't, pavement replaced grass and shrubs in the original small front yards, or garages were added alongside the houses. What had initially been a regular pattern of continuous sidewalks and planted yards crossed by narrow entry walks now became more chaotic and less green. As the street and front yards filled with cars and there were fewer neighbors out walking, front steps and porches became less inviting. The focus for outdoor socializing began to shift to the rear of the house, and new decks and patios were built in back-yards. (This change was also made possible by other technological inventions, such as electric washers and dryers, which eliminated some of the more mundane uses, for example, hanging laundry, for which private rear yards had previously been required.) Some local stores still prospered, but others no longer could compete with larger businesses that provided parking and drew customers from a wider area.

By the 1950s and early 1960s, when most trolley tracks had been removed and streets paved over, it was not easy to look at some of the neighborhoods they had spawned and understand the logic behind the varied buildings and often conflicting uses of outdoor space. Though for the most part the homes were still sound, often more sturdily built than newer ones, many blocks had a jumbled or random appearance that led to their being dismissed as run-down. As both popular opinion and government economic policies favored the building of brand new neighborhoods that accommodated cars more comfortably, this label became a self-ful-filling prophecy. A great many of the children raised in the older streetcar neighborhoods moved to newer ones as they grew up. The homes they left were in some cases taken over by other families, often less prosperous, but in others condemned or torn down for other uses.

Starting in colonial times, Americans have built and left behind their homes and workplaces more rapidly than people in many other countries. This behavior pattern reflects not so much our inherently wasteful nature as our lack of limitations. Throughout much of our history we have had both land and building materials in seemingly inexhaustible supply, and hence at relatively low cost. Especially as technologies have shifted, it has often been cheaper to build new buildings on open, undeveloped land than to alter and upgrade existing ones in more crowded locations. In nations with less land per person, even those that are quite prosperous, greater thought must be given to modifying or replacing existing structures in the same locations, and new technologies often spread more slowly.

The conditions that have allowed Americans to continually build anew have often favored experimentation and creative thinking. At the same time, however, they have led us to to devalue that which is already there. Nowhere has this tendency been more pronounced than in the area of homebuilding. An amazing formal variety of homes has been built in this country, but many of them no longer exist or remain relatively unknown. Because we learn little about local neighborhood history in school, much of the information that we do get comes from the real estate industry, the builders, the brokers, and the manufacturers of modern materials. The floorplans and photos in magazines and newspapers are those of what is on the market and currently fashionable; existing older homes, unless they are very costly, are not given the same visual play.

Thus, unlike our view of what we classify as nature, our perception of what's worthwhile in the built environment tends to be slanted toward the new and the pristine. We have learned to value old-growth forests and understand the ecological importance of rotting logs and even boggy wetlands, but find it harder to see the inherent worth or potential longevity of a mixed block of rundown rowhouses, especially if they have been altered over the years and no longer look "historic."

The intention of this book is to provide a framework to help readers look more closely at their homes and neighborhoods. It is an introductory examination of the three possible forms of housing and the ways in which each has been designed and built in the United States. These homes, so familiar to us that we barely see them, are the basic building blocks of our communities. While there are lots of building types, the sheer number of homes—their overall mass and presence on the landscape—far outweighs that of other built structures. Where and how these homes are constructed and connected is closely related to everything else that we build, from stores, offices, and factories to schools, highways, and parks.

In order to provide a basis for comparing the three forms of housing, the first few chapters of the book cover the evolution of spatial and legal standards for American dwellings. The central section then discusses the inherent geometric and environmental qualities of each form and presents examples showing how each has been built in the United States. The final chapter examines how these forms have been combined, with or without other building types and public spaces, into neighborhoods, and how our thinking about what a neighborhood should contain has changed along with our homes and means of transportation.

Assembling this material has meant, in some cases, putting down on paper concepts and accepted design practices that are so taken for granted today that they are rarely discussed. Answers to seemingly simple questions, such as why windows must legally open only in certain kinds of spaces, can be surprisingly hard to find; rules are embedded in the fine print of building codes when they should be important environmental issues. In other cases I have distilled information from established and far more detailed works, particularly historical studies of individual cities and styles of home-building. I hope that this overview of American homes is useful not only to readers with a casual or professional interest in architecture but also to those with wider environmental concerns. Understanding the truly broad range of "real" homes that we have built so far in this country is critical to making wise choices for the future.

1

WHAT WE ALL NEED TO SURVIVE:
Fundamental Requirements for Human Dwellings

> Many creatures create a large proportion of the environment
> in which they live. The most extreme example is the termite,
> but each species of termite builds a predictable form of termi-
> tarium. In no species is the exact form of the built environ-
> ment less predictable and more variable than in man.
>
> Paul Shepard, *The Only World We've Got*

Human beings are not physically adapted to live on most parts
of the earth without relying on some combination of shelter and
clothing. Other animals, of course, also need and build shelters
for themselves or their young, creating structures that range from
the rigid geometry of a beehive, made from a substance produced
by the bees themselves, to the seemingly more casual though still
structurally sound bird's nest, which uses found bits of material
that vary from site to site. And many creatures who don't actually
build nonetheless modify their environments in a deliberate way,
like the hippopotamus who excavates a mud wallow where he can
stay comfortable in the heat.

What sets humans, as a species, apart from all these animals is
the great variety of homes that we build or modify. Although we
may feel that our needs are specific and that only one type of
dwelling is appropriate, in fact we are amazingly adaptable. Our
homes vary not only across climates and geographic settings but
also within and among cultures and throughout history. As our
numbers have increased we have devised technologies, notably
long-distance transportation, water supply, and electrical systems,
that allow us to inhabit an ever wider range of locations on the
planet. Many people believe that this extension of our range is
endless and that they or their children will have the opportunity
to live in some future form of space colony.

Ranches, Rowhouses, and Railroad Flats

Whether or not we ever establish viable communities in space or on other planets, our extending range of habitation here on earth is a major reason that we have had such a profound impact on the global environment. The influence of human life is everywhere, even in the locations we try to preserve as pristine and "natural." To cite just one example, fish and plants disappear from mountain lakes inaccessible even to hikers because of emissions from smokestacks hundreds of miles away. Conversely, however, human influence never amounts to total control. The areas we classify as our built environment, intended for our own habitation, are home to countless other life forms and subject to the same nonhuman forces as the places we call wild. Insects colonize our basements and eat their way through our wood structures. Birds learn to recognize our backyards as resting points along their routes of migration. Rain freezes, thaws, and cracks the joints of even the shiniest sealed mirror-glass skyscrapers.

If in fact there is no clear and absolute distinction between wilderness areas and human-dominated environments, does this mean that we should look at all our surroundings under a single light, analyzing the landscapes of our cities and suburbs in the same way that we do our national parks? We have, for instance, arrived at some understanding of the required size and physical nature of a healthy habitat for a grizzly bear population. Might we, through careful observation and analysis of what we have built already, come to a similar understanding of our own absolute requirements for space or shelter? Many such attempts to create universal laws for the design of human homes and communities have been made; they are applied today both as building and zoning laws and in ancient design guidelines like the Chinese system of *feng shui*. Though all these prescriptions are based on some degree of useful knowledge, they of course differ widely from one another. The reality is that we are so adaptable and inventive that the variety of our homes and communities exceeds our ability to evaluate them scientifically. It is not just that the huge number of buildings now in existence differ from one another in form, construction, and use, but that they have ranged even more widely through time. Any attempt to make sense of our current living and building habits, or to consider the future, has to include some study of history, with all its unscientific guesswork and dependence on limited points of view. Every building has both a physical and a cultural logic, neither of which can be ignored.

This is not to say that we lack absolute requirements that must be met for our health and survival, only that these requirements may be met through a limitless variety of homes. While we may be more adaptable and inventive than grizzlies and most other creatures, there are still fundamental needs that all our dwellings must fulfill and that, indeed, constitute the most basic purposes of architecture, "the art or science of constructing edifices for human use."[1] It's useful to list and analyze these as a basis for considering how we've come to build homes in the United States.

SHELTERED, VENTILATED SPACE, WITH ROOM TO LIE DOWN

Sharks don't sleep at all, and horses can sleep standing up, but human beings, in order to stay healthy and sane, need to sleep in a reclining position on a daily basis. Though we may doze off in an armchair or spend an occasional night on a plane, our bodies relax most fully when lying down. As a group we are diurnal, active during the day and getting most of our sleep in one concentrated stretch at night. This pattern is apparently so innate that people who do adapt to other schedules over long periods, working through the night or sleeping only in very short stints, suffer measurable health consequences.[2] Thus, a human family needs at least enough sheltered space so that everyone can lie down and sleep at one time. Whatever form this shelter takes, it must protect them from weather that would interrupt their deep rest, such as rain, snow, or high winds. At the same time, it must permit enough fresh air to enter and circulate so that they can breathe comfortably.

Of course just a tiny percentage of homes, even over the course of history, have been built solely for sleeping. The vast majority accommodate a wider range of daytime and evening activities, both work and recreation. Inside these shelters we therefore need to be able to see, through some combination of direct or reflected sunlight and artificial sources of illumination like candles and lightbulbs. Most of the time, though not always, the same openings that provide ventilation also admit sunlight, but a comfortable balance between the two varies greatly with climate.

Major factors that affect the form and materials of a well-lit and livable shelter are average temperature and its daily or seasonal variation, humidity, the strength of local winds, and the presence or absence of shade trees. At two extremes are very cold northern regions, where the air holds little moisture, and tropical areas that are perpetually hot and humid. In the first we may enjoy all the direct sun we can get but need protection against cold winds and want only a minimum of fresh air to prevent stuffiness. In the second a constant breeze is crucial for comfort, so any shelter should let in as much air as possible, but only low levels of filtered or reflected light.

Traditional designs that successfully meet these three sometimes conflicting needs—shelter, ventilation, and light—have developed over long periods of time, no doubt through trial and error as well as individual inspiration. They are carefully modulated according to climate, natural setting, and available materials, and show an incredible range of solutions, even within similar areas. People in Arab desert regions, for example, live in courtyard houses with thick masonry walls and small windows as well as in portable tent structures with very different thermal characteristics.

Modern buildings tend to vary less according to climate and setting, depending more on mechanical systems for comfort and livability. Nearly identical aluminum-sided, single-story ranch houses probably exist today in Houston, Texas, and outside Buffalo, New York, but the owners' utility bills and use of windows no doubt differ greatly.

Beyond sleeping, the specific activities that make up our home lives and the amount of space we use to accomplish them vary in ways that can't be explained solely in terms of climate and relative wealth. Of course more of daily life takes place outdoors in warmer regions, and richer societies or individuals build larger dwellings. But there are also variations, even among affluent modern communities with similar levels of technology, that reflect deep-seated cultural differences in the very concept of *home*. In *House Form and Culture* (1969), an analysis of traditional home design around the world, the architect Amos Rapoport proposed that human homes range along a continuum between "two traditions of concentrated settlement":

> In one the whole settlement has been considered as the setting for life, and the dwelling merely as a more private, enclosed, and sheltered part of the living realm. In the other the dwelling has essentially been regarded as the total setting for life, and the settlement, whether village or city, as connective tissue, almost "waste" space to be traversed, and secondary in nature.[3]

This distinction provides a useful way to think about homes in the United States, both in comparing them to those of other countries and in understanding the causes of national environmental problems. In general, we expect an ever-growing amount from our homes but far less from the "connective tissue" between them. The technology and consumer goods that have become available sooner here than elsewhere in the world enable us to enjoy at home a succession of amenities previously available only in more public places. Indoor plumbing eliminated the public wells or pumps that had been gathering places in earlier communities. Telephones made it possible to stay abreast of local news and gossip without venturing into local stores or cafés. Refrigerators and freezers reduced the frequency of trips for groceries. Outdoor playsets in backyards replaced public sidewalks or playgrounds. And radios, televisions, VCRs, and desktop computers each in turn expanded indoor home entertainment options, competing with theaters and other kinds of commercial entertainment. Today, in America, the term *good neighborhood* frequently describes an area that consists almost exclusively of streets and private homes (though well-funded schools are still a requirement). Restaurants, stores, even parks are often thought better located some distance away.

Under these circumstances, the physical design and contents of our homes take on enormous importance. With few, if any, other types of building on the immediate landscape, their exterior appearance becomes critical in how the neighborhood is judged socially. And the range of leisure activities and entertainments we expect to be able to enjoy within them leads to a perpetual feeling that they need to be larger. Today the increasingly affordable technology of computers and modems is enabling more of us to work there as well, increasing still further our desire for additional space, and also the degree to which homes become "the total setting for life."

It is easy but misleading to assume that our standards are universal among similarly wealthy societies. Customs regarding such basic habits as entertaining strangers, where children play, how much independence they have, and whether or not families eat together still vary widely and have an effect on dwelling and neighborhood form. In many other countries, for instance, socializing with friends and business acquaintances routinely takes place away from home in restaurants, cafés, or tea shops. These establishments are often more casually intermingled with homes and other building types than they are here. Homes, therefore, do not have to contain the range of public and private eating spaces, kitchens, breakfast nooks, family rooms, and formal dining rooms that are included in our dwellings as they get larger and more expensive.

A mundane but telling example of the high expectations we have in America for our homes, and the low standards we set outside them, is the dispersal of bathrooms in the built environment. Ever since the widespread introduction of indoor plumbing, the number of bathrooms within individual homes has been steadily growing. Both developers and realtors today emphasize the importance of multiple bathrooms in raising a private home's market value. In the public realm, however, there are barely enough bathrooms to meet the requirements of a fit adult who plans ahead. The needs of small children, pregnant women, and many elderly people are underserved, so that one of the constant refrains of parenthood is reminding kids to use the bathroom before venturing out of the house. Even when they are built in such essential places as playgrounds, we seem to consider nonresidential bathrooms among the most expendable of amenities and close them down readily because of deterioration, security problems, or budget cuts. It is a startling contrast for an American to travel in a place with very different residential and community traditions. For example, South Korea is modernizing rapidly and building countless Western-style buildings, including homes, but in both new and old sections of the country public bathrooms are readily available and seem to be considered a routine part of the infrastructure, like streetlights and signs.

TEMPERATURE MODIFICATION

Human beings need to maintain a body temperature close to 98.6°F in order to survive; our naked bodies can adjust only to temperatures within a certain range of this. If we lived solely in places where the air temperature always stayed in this range, however, we would be confined to a narrow band around the globe. There are three basic ways to protect ourselves against natural conditions under which our bodies cannot maintain this state. Clothing usually keeps us warm but can also deflect the sun's rays and protect us against wind and precipitation. Shelters, by their materials and design, can create an interior climate different from that outside. Lastly, the direct manipulation of sources of energy changes the air temperature or radiates heat directly to our bodies. Building a fire outdoors and huddling around it will warm us up for a while, but the heat rises and dissipates very quickly; it is far more economical and long-lasting to heat or cool the air or locate radiant elements within an enclosed shelter. Most of us stay comfortable through a combination of all three of these methods, though the balance between them can vary tremendously.

In the United States, relative to most other countries, heating fuels—first wood, then coal, natural gas, and oil—have been plentiful and therefore inexpensive. The same is now true for electricity, widely used for air-conditioning as well as some home heating. As with ventilation, discussed in the previous section, we have consequently tended to rely on mechanical heating and cooling to keep us comfortable, rather than on design and materials that are particularly effective in moderating the climate.

SPACE AND FUEL FOR COOKING

Even in warm climates where no additional heat is needed for comfort, a home has to have some provision for cooking, though again this is not always indoors. Before the early nineteenth century, a single fireplace or stove in most homes provided both space heating and a place to cook. Today, in the United States and other wealthy countries, these functions are almost always separated, except when people are camping out or the system used to heat the indoor air is inadequate.

Providing for either indoor cooking or space heating always creates the risk of fire or suffocation, and complicates the design of a simple shelter. Any solution, whether it's a hearth under a smokehole, a fireplace and chimney, or a boiler with piping and radiators, must include additional ventilation, which should be separate from that which admits fresh air for breathing.

SECURITY

Security for ourselves and our belongings can be provided by a built structure, such as a wall, by a location in the the natural environment, or by organized social action (a night watchman, police force, or reliable system of flood insurance). Many animals show an instinctive preference for homes in locations that afford them protection against carnivorous enemies or other dangers, and some scientists have theorized that humans also innately prefer sites similar to those where early man evolved:

> [T]he African savannahs in which early humans flourished . . . [were] . . . a mosaic of open grassland, scattered copses, and denser woods near rivers and lakes. The wide vistas provided the necessary space to plan distant moves, while the trees and prominences offered places from which to track moving animals. Such prospects also afforded visual surveillance of other human groups who were competitors for food and mates.[4]

Though we may well retain some inborn inclination for this type of landscape, we of course spread long ago into diverse regions that are nothing like the African savannah. It is interesting to speculate that some of the modifications we make to other landscapes may be attempts to recreate the security and comfort of our original habitat. Usually, however, there are also more pragmatic or immediate explanations for these changes, as well as examples of contradictory building practices. For example, the American fashion for unenclosed, grass-covered front lawns might stem from the feeling of security created by an open vista, but in many other countries outdoor yards are commonly surrounded by high walls to create privacy, thus limiting views from the house to the street.

Part of our decision to create new homes anywhere involves the inherent safety of the site, but in most cases we rely much more heavily for security on our abilities to design and build. Like the continuum described by Amos Rapoport for the distribution of daily activities, there is a continuum of security measures ranging from those provided for an entire community to those provided for individual homes. A walled medieval town provided group security through a built enclosure, but probably not much for individual dwellings except those of the wealthiest citizens. Southwestern pueblo villages built high against the sides of canyons also provided common security through both natural location and design, but no family homes had lockable doors or windows. At the other extreme is a solitary home in a rural setting, without a telephone and far from any police station. Here all safety is related to the design and location of the house itself, which must keep out animals and human intruders, and survive or avoid floods, lightning storms, and landslides.

In this country, where we expect our homes to fill so many social and material needs, security is a major and sometimes politically explosive concern. We have in place extensive public and private social systems to protect them, police and fire departments as well as many types of insurance. These are intended both to prevent dangerous situations from occurring and to minimize the effects of those that happen nonetheless. Police surveillance is meant to deter crime, building codes and on-site inspections to reduce the risks of fire, and graduated insurance rates and availability to encourage building in safe locations. Because fire and police protection are locally funded and administered, their effectiveness varies widely among different communities. Insurance protection for homes is provided by a complicated mixture of private companies and government programs. Disaster relief, an example of the latter, while important from a humanitarian standpoint, is often administered in a way that encourages the perpetuation of dangerous situations. The pressure to rebuild established communities is tremendous and understandable, even when logic argues for doing things differently a second time.

Our actual home-building practices are full of contradictions. Though we worry about burglary and violent crimes, the design of American freestanding houses and yards is far more open than those in many other parts of the world, most often without walls and gates along property lines, and with many windows easily accessible from outdoors, particularly in single-story homes. However, there has been a recent increase in the number of *gated communities*—enclosed developments where access to streets as well as individual homes is restricted by a guard or electronic entry system.[5] Their growing popularity indicates that residents at least feel more secure, but many critics are troubled by their implied social segregation and by the removal of streets from the public realm.

The relationship of home and neighborhood design to crime is a loaded topic on which opinions differ widely; only a few studies have attempted objective comparisons of home forms or neighborhoods, and it is hard to make broad generalizations from their conclusions. The continual development of new neighborhoods in the United States has allowed many wealthy and middle-class people simply to move away when they felt their homes were not secure, rather than working on social or physical solutions to the problem. Poor families, of course, rarely have that choice, and therefore endure a great deal more crime.

We respond differently to the risks of natural disasters than we do to those of burglary or violent crime. This country has vast acres of buildable land, much of it in areas not prone to violent storms, earthquakes, floods, or sweeping fires. Nonetheless, locations where such events are virtual certainties, on some periodic basis, are built up with homes both modest and expensive. Sometimes these are in communities whose original site presented danger but also compelling economic opportunity, such as the old ports of San Francisco, with its repeated and much-studied earthquakes, and low-lying Galveston, Texas, vulnerable to hurricane damage. On a smaller scale, many towns and cities develop in a local pattern where wealthy neighborhoods, with names ending in "heights," "hills," or "bluffs," sit on higher ground, and working-class neighborhoods are found in the flood-prone and more humid valleys. Both these circumstances, while not ideal, are predictable and can be found around the world.

Less predictable, and perhaps more common in America than elsewhere, are expensive homes built in very risky locations along fragile and shifting ocean beaches or on dry hills vulnerable to wind-driven fires. Generally, of course, these are areas of spectacular beauty, and our systems of property insurance and government-financed disaster relief reduce the financial losses involved when homes are destroyed. But it is striking that these areas are rebuilt nonetheless, especially after major devastation that is almost certain to recur and even when plenty of other beautiful and safer sites are available. At a minimum, this raises questions. Do we have a cultural tendency to discount the risks of nature, perhaps because of our confidence in technological solutions? Or is it a universal human response to see crime as more terrifying than natural disasters, even when the statistical risk of harm or even death may be the same?

FRESH WATER

The final two requirements for human homes, access to fresh water and some means for sustaining a living, are just as critical as the first four but often considered less directly related to the act of building. Basically they come down to the needs of all living creatures for food and drink. With our elaborate modern networks for transporting water and food, and our complex economic system of exchanging goods and labor, we now inhabit many areas of the earth where local resources alone could not sustain a human community. But our inventiveness has not reduced the importance of these two requirements, or, on close analysis, their connection to the actual design of our homes.

For the earliest humans, a reliable source of fresh water within walking distance was essential to any habitation. Those studying our responses to different types of natural landscapes speculate that this critical need to find and live near water is one reason that certain of its qualities are so aesthetically pleasing to us today. Clear glassy lakes and flowing streams may seem inherently more beautiful than brackish swamps because for millions of years they were necessary for survival.[6] As people developed the understanding and technology to dig or drill wells and to build aqueducts, dams, and underground piping, the geographic range of their homes increased, and sources of water were no longer a visible presence in or near every village or home compound.

Today the bodies of water that we seek out for contemplation or recreation are rarely the source of what comes out of the tap; most are not even clean enough to drink directly. While piped, potable water is virtually universal in American homes, the complex networks that supply it are unseen, so that the environmental and political problems connected with them can seem unreal and hard to grasp. It was no doubt easier to conserve when we could look down into the well, or at the exposed edges of a lake bed, and gauge the situation directly. And even where water was plentiful in earlier eras, transporting it by hand also ensured more careful and limited usage.

ACCESS TO LIVELIHOOD

For most people, access to livelihood means a home that is convenient to where they work. Farmers must live on or close to land where they can grow crops, a fisherman must live near the water, and a factory or office worker must be able to get to and from the job with at least enough time left over to eat and sleep. No matter how elaborately and solidly they are built, individual homes as well as entire communities are abandoned when sustaining a living becomes impossible. Thus in America there are ghost towns where mines closed, the surrounding land became unprofitable for farming, whatever gold that once existed was removed, or the mills and factories that were the main employers shut their doors. It's unsettling and eerie to visit such places and realize how much care and resources were put into homes that lasted sometimes only a few decades.

The physical meaning of being close to work has changed profoundly over the last two hundred years, with a dramatic effect on the forms of many homes. Long-distance trains, successive forms of public rapid transit, cars, and even airplanes have all extended the geographic range and variety of places that people could live. In the United States, which has always had more land relative to its human population than most other countries, these changes have often meant an increase in the size of lots possible for individual homes. Sometimes they have also allowed places that might otherwise have become ghost towns to be reinhabited in new ways, as dying farming villages, for instance, have become new suburbs or exurban towns.

An oversimplified example of the relationship between transportation mode and home form is that of a single large factory with several thousand workers situated on an undeveloped plain. If all of them must walk to work, the amount of land available for individual homes is obviously much less than if each can get in a car and drive for twenty minutes (the time equivalent of a one-mile walk.)

In the real world, of course, there are countless other factors, including competing land uses, zoning laws, neighborhoods separated by income and race, and roads in some places but not others. Overall, however, changing technology in the United States has meant that we have been able to build towns and cities with homes progressively more spread out across the ground as well as spaced farther apart from one another. The middle-class craftsman and his family, who lived and often worked in a narrow two- or three-story city rowhouse at the beginning of the nineteenth century, walked almost everywhere. A hundred years later, a comparable skilled workman was able to take the streetcar to his job, now in a larger business up to several miles from home, and live with his family in a one-and-a-half or two-story detached house on a lot twice as wide. By the middle of the twentieth century the same family could live in a single-story home, with a larger footprint but not necessarily more indoor space than the two-story house, on a property that had doubled again in size and had plenty of space for parking the cars they now needed to get around.

Just because these moves have become physically possible does not mean that all Americans have made them; many have chosen to stay put or locate anew in older neighborhoods, and others, perhaps greater in number, have been excluded from the new ones by poverty or race. Moreover, unlike the theoretical example, as changing transportation technology has enabled people to move faster, their travel time to and from work has not always stayed constant. In the widely dispersed patchwork of homes, highways, and businesses that now covers much of our nation, the one- or even two-mile walk hasn't necessarily been replaced by a twenty- or even forty-minute ride. As businesses relocate, jobs become less secure, and more families include at least two wage earners working in separate places, the amount of time that Americans spend commuting to and from work grows erratic. Overall, however, it has been increasing, with real and troubling effects on many families' lives.

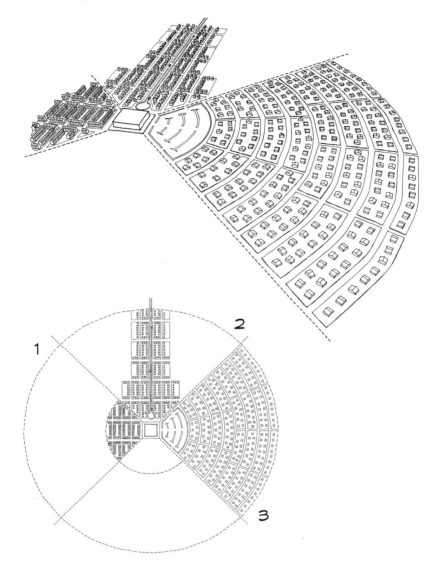

1-1. The plan and perspective sketch show three alternate arrangements for the same number of homes accessible to a central workplace. Each type of home has the same interior floor area, but sits on a different size lot. In the pedestrian quadrant (1), houses are narrow and attached, three stories tall, spreading in all directions. Clustered within walking distance of a streetcar line (2), they are two-story and detached, with small front- and backyards. When cars are used to get to work, homes can again spread evenly (3), covering more ground with only a single story each. Note that workplace parking occupies almost as much land as the homes in the pedestrian quadrant.

There is, of course, an ancient alternative to establishing a permanent home close to what is, it is hoped, also a permanent means of survival. Nomadic peoples who move to follow work, graze crops, or hunt often create portable homes—gypsy caravans in Europe and the tent structures of desert herdsmen in the Middle East are two examples. Cultures in which a nomadic way of life has developed over a long period often have distinct priorities regarding dwellings and possessions, both of which, if too cumbersome, inhibit movement and seasonal adaptation. Before Europeans came to this continent, many Native American tribes were also nomadic or seminomadic, moving between summer and winter habitats and varying the areas where they hunted, fished, and grew crops so as not to deplete soil or animal populations. The European idea that land could be individually and permanently owned, along with the built structures sitting on it, came directly into conflict with this long-standing way of life.[7]

Today in the United States all land is owned, either by private individuals, corporations, government, or Native American tribes. Every piece of property has restrictions on its use, so anyone living a traditionally nomadic existence eventually runs afoul of the law. Even in our large national parks the duration of camping permits is limited. The structures that we build and classify as legal homes are assumed to be permanent and must include a specific set of spaces and connections, among them indoor bathrooms and kitchens with an approved means of waste disposal.

At the same time, there have always been and still are many Americans whose means of survival involve travel on a regular or frequent basis. Cowboys, salesmen, corporate business employees, migrant farm laborers, truck drivers, workers in certain types of specialized construction—the list is long and includes jobs that are romanticized and sung about as well as many that are taken for granted, some very lucrative and others paying barely a subsistence wage.

Though we don't officially recognize nomadic homes as such, numerous forms of buildings and social institutions have been devised throughout United States history to house those who travel with their work. These have included boardinghouses, minimal cabins put up by farmers for migrant workers, portable shelters bought and set up in movable camps by railroad companies, trailer parks, camping vehicles, motels, and, at the upper end, especially today, a network of expensive hotels with special suites for business travelers. Many of these accommodate only the traveling worker and not his or her family. For the most part they are not classified with, or located among, the buildings we consider permanent homes. Boardinghouses, which were widespread in the nineteenth and early twentieth centuries and filled many needs, are no longer legal in most residential neighborhoods. As house trailers became mobile homes and then "manufactured housing," they gained legal status but lost real mobility, and no longer serve the market of those whose work involves moving regularly.

Our need to be close to different kinds of work still requires a variety of living arrangements, but we don't always acknowledge these solutions as "homes." Over the last two hundred years, with advancing technology and material prosperity, we have developed a legal definition and standards for the term *home* that go far beyond most of the basic requirements discussed in this chapter. Partly as a result of these standards, most Americans now live in dwellings that are larger, safer, and have more mechanical conveniences than those in other parts of the world. But as our definition of home has grown more complex, it has also become less flexible. Of all our basic needs, it is perhaps this last one, a viable physical connection between home and work, that remains most problematic.

2

Toward Minimum Standards for American Homes

Plants cannot grow in the dark, neither can children. . . . When you rent a flat make sure that all the rooms are light and have plenty of air.

from *For You,* a 1914 pamphlet of the Charity Organization Society, Tenement House Committee[1]

The most basic requirements for human dwellings can be met by structures ranging in size and complexity from single-room huts without running water, mechanical heat, or electricity to modern apartments in thirty-story elevator buildings. In the United States today, however, our definition of an acceptable and legal home isn't as broad. Over the last two hundred years we have developed a clear set of technological and social expectations. Homes in this country must now have indoor plumbing and other specified mechanical services, as well as a series of separate walled spaces, each intended for distinct uses that conform to our cultural notions of family life.

For the most part we are not actually required to use these spaces according to their named functions; it's mothers, rather than governments, who try to prevent eating in bedrooms. But some uses, especially many kinds of productive work, are now illegal within our homes, and certain spaces are restricted because of their size and ventilation. Thus closets and bathtubs are not legal places for sleeping, though in a crowded situation or to a child they might sometimes seem like quiet and comfortable locations.

These requirements, or minimum standards, for an American home have developed slowly and sporadically; they still do not exist as a single set of laws. In this country the regulation of all kinds of buildings has historically been the job of local and state governments. Most building codes and zoning ordinances are still enacted and enforced at those levels. Over the last sixty-five years, however, since the Great Depression of the 1930s, the federal government has become increasingly involved, through a variety of programs and laws, in setting building standards relating to issues that have become national concerns. Many federal environmental laws now affect construction practices, and the broad Americans with Disabilities Act (ADA), passed in 1990, has complex implications for the design of private buildings that were previously subject only to local control.

One reason for this patchwork of regulation is that there have always been conflicts between almost any proposed limitation and the American concept of individual property rights, implying that owners should be able to do (and build) whatever they wish on their own private land. Our laws have remained piecemeal in part because they are not supposed to be comprehensive. The reality today, however, is that virtually all land, and any new home, is subject to numerous and varied restrictions. Even for a seemingly straightforward building project, a block or two of new houses that look just like an earlier subdivision half a mile away, it can take a whole team of professionals—architects, lawyers, engineers, zoning consultants, and environmental scientists—to interpret the applicable regulations.

BASIC REGULATION

The earliest formal laws related to building were enacted in young, growing communities to protect public safety and health. Among the first were those mandating the proper construction and maintenance of fireplaces and chimneys; as early as 1683 the government of New York City was appointing "viewers and searchers of chimneys and fire hearths"[2] to inspect for violations. Despite such regulations, periodic fires throughout the eighteenth and nineteenth centuries devastated substantial sections of many American cities. Without extensive water supply networks or modern communication systems, effective firefighting was close to impossible. Flames spread rapidly from one property to another, especially because most buildings were made of wood, the cheapest and most widely available construction material.

Ordinances requiring the use of fireproof masonry for exterior walls were generally passed only after particularly destructive blazes, and even then were not always well enforced.

One of the most catastrophic events of the nineteenth century was the 1871 Great Fire of Chicago, which destroyed 1,688 acres that included many residential neighborhoods as well as the entire commercial downtown of a booming city less than forty years old.[3] Chicago rebuilt itself even faster than it had grown originally, but now carefully designated its busiest and most built-up sections as *fire districts*, within which all buildings had to meet current standards for fireproof construction. Other localities required the use of masonry walls when buildings were above a certain height or within a certain distance of each other, or were built right up to the edges of a property.

As they grew beyond a size where informal cooperation and social pressure were effective, towns and cities also regulated waste disposal; individual households couldn't pollute a common water supply by dumping rubbish or wastewater. Continuing population growth and the changing, more concentrated nature of industry, however, meant that by the early 1800s, in spite of such restrictions, some communities had damaged or outgrown their original local sources of water and began to construct permanent long-distance supply networks. Even after both water supply and sewer pipes were in place, however, nothing required that private homes connect to them.

Except to the extent that they endangered neighboring buildings, the construction and internal layout of individual homes were not considered a matter for government control until the second half of the nineteenth century. Up until then, most houses, both freestanding and attached, were simple and standardized arrangements of only a few rooms. The middle-class houses going up in towns and cities by around 1800 were rarely built by their occupants, more often being erected one or two at a time by speculative builders, or "housewrights," for sale or rent. (Contrary to popular myth, it was not until after World War II that a majority of Americans became homeowners.[4]) But even though homes had already become a commercial product, their materials, construction, and layout were based sufficiently on common local traditions and limitations that formal control was not felt to be necessary. If

2-1. Small attached houses, such as these in Baltimore from about 1800, had similar floor plans and facades although they were built only one or two at a time and before the advent of extensive legal regulations.

the homes of poor families were less safe and standardized, more likely to be rickety self-built structures or deteriorating older dwellings, they were seen as the best that could be done under the circumstances, and not generally in need of public regulation.

TAMING THE NEW INDUSTRIAL CITY

The widespread public concern that led to more regulation of dwellings was the result of the interrelated changes in manufacturing, trade, transportation, and scientific technology collectively known as the Industrial Revolution. On the one hand, these developments allowed middle-class American houses to grow larger and more complex, in both form and technology, so that standards for what constituted an acceptable home rose steadily. On the other, they caused an explosive growth in nineteenth-century cities, creating serious environmental problems and an actual decline in the livability and safety of many poorer homes. Increasingly large factories and mills clustered together near transportation access (ports and, later, rail lines) and employed many people at once, all of whom needed to live nearby.

2-2. This drawing of late-nineteenth-century homes in a poor neighborhood of Chicago shows two common practices of the era: *backbuilding* (one house added behind another on a single lot) and below-grade *basement dwellings*, dank and subject to flooding. What appeared to be a small individual house from the front was actually a complex housing at least five families.

Without legal requirements for open space on private property, these new industrial neighborhoods quickly became densely built up. Existing houses were divided into smaller units and new ones filled in older backyards. Dank cellars were rented out to the poorest or most recently arrived workers. Even as businesses grew larger, a great deal of paid work was also done in these homes, such as piecework for the garment industry. Many families, whose households often included unrelated boarders, spent both working and sleeping hours in dark, underventilated dwellings consisting of two or three small rooms.

In these overcrowded conditions infectious diseases spread rapidly, leading to periodic outbreaks of cholera, typhoid, smallpox, and other illnesses that killed many people. Some data available for New York City, for instance, indicate that death rates in that city rose substantially between 1810 and 1859, even as the metropolis was prospering and growing economically.[5] While earlier plagues in crowded European cities had been considered fatalistically as acts of God, nineteenth-century doctors were just beginning to understand the nature of infectious disease and to appreciate the importance of sanitation and adequate ventilation in reducing its spread. Enough public records were now maintained so that correlations could be made between poor housing conditions and the high incidence of certain illnesses.[6] Most specific agents, such as the lice that carry typhus, had not yet been identified, but health problems were associated generally with an unsanitary, dank atmosphere. An 1875 newspaper quoted an engineer of the time:

> [W]e are practically saturating ourselves and everything about us with deadly miasmatic emanation. . . . [T]he made and undrained land on which so many thousands of our homes are built, is packed with miasm. . . . [W]e live and sleep in an atmosphere stifling with sewer gas.[7]

It was not just overcrowding, lack of sewers, and inadequate ventilation that caused health problems for these rapidly growing city neighborhoods. The new factories themselves were the source of a multitude of pollutants. Constant noise and dirty air from coal-burning furnaces were almost universal, but specific neighborhoods had additional hazards. Though Chicago, for instance, prided itself on being less crowded than New York and other East Coast cities, the environmental conditions around its meat processing plants were among the worst. One such neighborhood was Packingtown, inhabited mostly by Eastern European immigrants, where open-air heaps of aging animal parts and other waste stank and bred swarms of flies, so that residents had to keep their children's bodies fully covered even in summer; disease rates were, of course, very high. The neighborhood was also crisscrossed by grade-level unfenced train lines carrying freight cars full of hogs and cattle; pedestrian train deaths, especially of children, were common.

The epidemics that swept through American cities throughout the nineteenth century disproportionately affected low-income families in overcrowded and underventilated homes, but they also killed many middle- and upper-class city dwellers. Thus, out of what might be called enlightened self-interest, improved living conditions in the poorest neighborhoods began to be seen by more affluent citizens as important to safeguarding their own health.

Economic changes in the industry of home-building itself also led to public pressure for regulation. As the century progressed, the incredible demand for homes in growing industrial centers created profit-making possibilities from the construction of small, closely spaced rental dwellings for the working class. Speculative builders had a new market of factory wage earners who could not possibly afford the escalating cost of urban land and therefore had no opportunity to build for themselves. The exact forms of these new homes varied from city to city, as did the dates of their flourishing, which depended on the particular history of a local economy. But whether they were known as *house courts* (Los Angeles), *alley dwellings* (Washington, D.C.), or *tenements* (Chicago and New York), they were often very lucrative for their owners.

Compared with the way most homes are built in the United States today, the scale of development was still extremely limited. For the most part, only a few houses or small apartment buildings were erected at a time, and the majority of owners had other professions or businesses, investing in home-building as a sideline. It was in the second half of the nineteenth century, however, when the systematic development of homes for low-paid industrial workers became a thriving commercial enterprise, that the image of the evil landlord profiting from his tenants' misery was established. Not everyone vilified the owners; many middle-class white Americans blamed the tenants themselves, who were often foreign-born or African-American, for poor neighborhood conditions. But even with many points of view about underlying causes, the rapid changes in both workplaces and homes in the late 1800s led more people to see their dangers as being man-made rather than inevitable, and therefore capable of being changed.

As industrialization transformed the American landscape and immigrants flocked to take advantage of the work opportunities, private reform groups were established in virtually every city to address the interrelated problems of public sanitation and housing conditions. They had earnest intentions and long names: the

Washington Sanitary Improvement Company, the Boston Cooperative Building Company, the New York-based Association for Improving the Conditions of the Poor. Most focused initially not on increasing government control of home design but on privately financed experiments to show that better laid out and healthier homes for working families could also be built at a profit. The hope was that thoughtful businessmen would see the long-term advantages of improved design, even if the immediate return was lower, and follow suit. In the late 1800s and early 1900s some very interesting homes and neighborhoods were built this way, all over the country; a few will be examined in later chapters. But while these model tenements and other innovative developments demonstrated that more livable homes in the crowded city were indeed possible, they had little effect on the vast majority of dwellings being constructed. Increasingly, private housing reformers realized that only government regulation would force changes in currently profitable building practices. Using the new art of documentary photography as well as dramatic eyewitness accounts of urban slum life, they did everything they could to galvanize public opinion and pressure state legislatures or local city councils to act.

Public health and housing were not the only aspects of poor industrial neighborhood life of concern to middle- and upper-class Americans. Reformers came with many agendas. Some focused on providing social services and education both to non-English-speaking immigrants and to poor, often minority Americans; in Chicago Jane Addams established Hull House in 1889 as the first of many settlement houses around the country. Others, often with religious connections, focused more exclusively on curbing what they saw as rampant immoral behavior, particularly drinking and prostitution. In the sensationalist journalism of the day, all these concerns were often linked, suggesting that crowded and inadequate housing conditions caused moral decay, which of course titillated public interest. In 1856 a New York State Assembly Committee spent a week inspecting tenement houses and found "idiotic and crippled children suffering from neglect and ill treatment; girls just springing into womanhood, living indiscriminately with men of all ages. . . ."[8]

The notion that tenement neighborhoods bred immorality was closely related to contemporary claims that properly designed houses in a more rural setting would create moral families. The fact that adolescent girls in small colonial town- and farmhouses with extended families had also slept in cramped conditions and shared beds was not raised, probably because mid-nineteenth-century American citizens did not see their own ancestors as comparable in any way to the vaguely threatening foreigners now crowding the cities. A century later, more middle-class citizens of the United States would trace their ancestry to a tenement beginning than to any home in the original thirteen colonies. Referring to a historically inaccurate nineteenth-century symbol for humble but virtuous American origins, tenements are now sometimes characterized as "urban log cabins."

Despite the widespread efforts of reformers and often lurid press coverage, the economic forces that had brought new urban slums into being were not easy to affect. But after what were sometimes many unsuccessful tries, most major cities by about 1905 had legislation in place prescribing basic requirements for the design of new homes. Except for corridors and closets, windowless rooms were no longer permitted, and windows had to open onto outdoor spaces of certain minimum dimensions (which varied greatly from city to city). This meant, effectively, that neither houses nor apartment buildings could cover their entire lots, because side yards, rear yards, or internal courts had to be left open to the sky to allow for ventilation. Property owners could no longer add backbuildings or unlimited rear extensions, either for their own use or to maximize their rent rolls. Indoor plumbing—at least cold running water and a toilet connected to a hygienic sewage system—also became mandatory. Fire safety provisions now went beyond the early laws intended only to keep fires from spreading to neighboring property. They prescribed measures such as fire escapes or a second set of interior stairs to protect the lives of those who lived inside.

The effects of these new housing laws were complex. For the most part they did not require the demolition of existing structures that failed to meet their standards, especially if the buildings already in place were still economically viable (that is, full of rent-

paying tenants) and posed little fire threat to neighboring properties. Smaller changes, such as the addition of fire escapes in multistory buildings, often were required, and the gradual extension
of city sewer systems and, eventually, electric lines did reach many
older buildings. But the now familiar streetscapes of older slum
housing remained largely intact. Even new buildings did not
always conform to enacted standards, as many city governments of
the era were notoriously corrupt, with inspectors wide open to
bribes. Gradually, however, enforcement of the laws became sufficiently consistent so that blatant violations in new structures were
rare, and the safety and comfort of working-class homes built in
the early twentieth century improved greatly over the preceding
decades.

Though these first laws regulating housing design were aimed
at improving homes for poor and working-class city dwellers, they
set a precedent that was extended within a few decades to include
standards, within a given jurisdiction, for all homes and other
building types as well. As the scale of home development continued to grow, and fewer families had any contact with those who
actually built the structures they lived in, Americans of all income
groups came to rely on these government-enforced standards, or
building codes, to ensure safety, prescribe long-lasting materials for
concealed structural and mechanical systems, and set basic criteria for design. Many of the minimum dimensions and material
thicknesses set by code were also adopted by manufacturers of
building components. An 8-foot ceiling height, for example, is
now not just the lowest generally permitted by law but also the
long dimension of standard sheetrock panels. Building a home
with higher ceilings today therefore requires extra labor and material costs for cutting and fitting. "Minimum" standards thus greatly
affect the design and construction not only of the least expensive
dwellings but of most middle-class homes.

By limiting *coverage* (the portion of an individual lot a building
could occupy) and requiring higher levels of technology, the new
laws also changed the underlying economics of building. On small
lots it was difficult to meet the new requirements for side and rear
yards while still creating a large enough structure to make a profit,
so the scale of development, especially for multifamily dwellings,
increased to larger parcels of land. These, naturally, required

more capital up front, limiting the possibilities for small investors. As new amenities, such as indoor bathrooms, modern heating systems, and electrical wiring, were incorporated into basic requirements, the square-foot cost of construction also rose.

Homes that met new standards for better ventilation and more advanced technology were most often built not in the same crowded neighborhoods with older nineteenth-century homes but further out along new transportation lines, where land was not as costly. For the more prosperous and established residents of tenement neighborhoods, they provided previously unavailable opportunities to move up and out. But for many poorer people, private builders no longer put up affordable new homes. Moreover, the older homes where they continued to live, with smoky gas lighting and shared toilets in the hall or backyard, were now officially *substandard* and subject to possible condemnation. New laws created a legal rationale for *slum clearance* without guaranteeing better options for those whose homes might be destroyed in the process. Thus, though they were undoubtedly necessary to ensure improvements in new construction, the earliest housing laws did not always help those who actually lived in the worst conditions.

ZONING

As local laws regulating the design and construction of individual buildings were enacted across the country, a new and far broader type of legislation was also being considered. Many Americans, not just social reformers, were alarmed by the rapid and seemingly uncontrollable growth that was transforming so much of their built surroundings. Quiet neighborhoods in expanding cities were suddenly altered by the construction of new factories or large stores, often leading residents to relocate. New forms of high-rise office buildings, known as skyscrapers, appeared, made possible by the technologies of steel construction and elevators. These put adjacent buildings and streets into shadow and flooded the sidewalks with workers at rush hours and lunchtime. In many ways, especially as the scale of building increased, individual property owners were making design decisions that greatly affected their neighbors, who unfortunately had no say in the matter. Even the prosperous sections of towns and cities seemed unstable in nature and chaotic in appearance.

This rapid change and the juxtaposition of disparate building sizes and uses was compared unfavorably to older and more elegant European cities, whose less democratic governments had for years exercised far more control over what could be built and where. During the early 1900s, many American architects and other civic activists were involved in the City Beautiful movement, which took its inspiration from across the Atlantic and promoted the coordinated improvement of public buildings and open spaces in the classical style. A new profession called city planning, distinct from architecture and engineering, was just beginning to be recognized. "A City Without a Plan is Like a Ship Without a Rudder," proclaimed a 1910 treatise on the subject that continued:

> The most important part of City Planning, as far as the future health of the city is concerned, is the districting of the city into zones . . . in which buildings may be a certain number of stories or feet in height, and cover a specified proportion of the site. . . .[9]

As proposed in the United States, this process of zoning gave municipal governments the power to regulate the uses of the land within their boundaries and to limit as well the size and location of new buildings. Its goals were to keep incompatible building types apart from one another, prevent rapid change in established areas, reduce real estate speculation, and create an orderly plan for growth, thus assuring all citizens of a more gracious and livable environment. Given the raw and constantly changing nature of so many communities at the time, it is easy to understand why these goals seemed desirable both to wealthy residents and businessmen and to reformers interested in poorer neighborhoods. The concept of zoning had widespread support.

At the same time, however, there seems to have been remarkably little public debate regarding the significant new power over private land that zoning authority would give to local governments, with only the vague criterion of "public interest" to guide their decision making. The earlier and harder-fought building laws had addressed the much more tangible issues of individuals' health and safety. Fire escapes saved families' lives; operable windows and greater open space around homes allowed them to breathe air with more oxygen and fewer bacteria. Zoning legislation was often promoted as preventing unsafe conditions at a larger scale—the glue factory invading the residential neighborhood was invoked repeatedly. But it also allowed government to dictate separations, especially those between homes and small businesses, and between different forms of homes, that were really based on aesthetics and social preference rather than science or public safety. In candid moments, even prominent members of the new city planning profession were skeptical about the logic behind certain divisions; at a 1926 national conference, one questioned "whether a grocery store next door to my house is going to seriously affect the health of my children. There have been mighty healthy kids raised over grocery stores."[10]

New York City, the most built-up and fastest-changing metropolis in the nation, passed the first *zoning ordinance* in 1916. It was a complex document that divided the entire city into geographic zones of allowable uses: manufacturing, commercial, and residential. In most of these it also established maximum building heights. While existing building laws had prescribed side and rear yards or courtyards to allow for light and ventilation, the new law dictated front yards, or *setbacks*, as well in all but the most built-up areas. These were intended to create a uniform and less congested appearance along the street. Residential districts, while all of a single use, were further broken down by the size and forms of homes. The most restrictive permitted only freestanding single-family houses on large lots, while others allowed houses on smaller lots, and still others rowhouses or apartment buildings. Previously, the ground floors of both houses and apartment buildings had sometimes housed retail stores and other small businesses. Under the new law, such uses could be included only in new residential buildings along major commercial streets. Most new blocks of homes would now contain nothing else.

Over the next twenty years, legislation similar to New York's was adopted in most American cities. By 1936, 85 percent of all municipalities had some form of zoning ordinance.[11] Implementation by local governments, however, typically fell far short of the goals expressed by zoning's original supporters, especially those interested in housing reform. Too often, the designations of land use reflected the financial and social interests of the most influential local property owners rather than being part of a comprehensive and public-spirited plan. As urban historian Kenneth Jackson noted much later, "In theory zoning was designed to protect the interests of all citizens by limiting land speculation and congestion. . . . In actuality zoning was a device to keep poor people and obnoxious industries out of affluent areas."[12]

Although zoning ordinances did not directly address or change the minimum standards for American homes, they had a tremendous effect on where homes could be built and what form they could take. Because individual municipalities had no obligation to include a full range of possible land uses in their zoning categories, or even, within the residential category, homes for those in a variety of income groups, they simply omitted those they didn't want. If a town's ordinance didn't permit anything smaller than a 2,000-square-foot house on a one-acre lot, it was not necessary to state overtly that working-class families were not welcome. Where wealthy homeowners could afford high taxes to pay for their own services such as schools and policing, they also zoned out all industry and large businesses not wanted as neighbors. Major property owners in large cities were more often interested in the commercial use of their land, and hence much larger areas were zoned there for industry, offices, stores, and sometimes large apartment buildings.

As numerous towns and cities drew up separate zoning maps, the net result was a pattern of economic stratification and homogeneous neighborhoods. Those with smaller and less expensive homes were far more likely to be bordered by or to include factories and "undesirable" businesses. In many ways, of course, these new maps just codified what already existed and might have been enforced by other means such as deed restrictions. But by mapping substantial areas of undeveloped land and strictly predetermining their use, zoning ordinances made subsequent development far less varied than it might otherwise have been, and certainly discouraged experimentation in home design and neighborhood layout. After the introduction of zoning laws, developers of large tracts were rarely able to build a variety of sizes and forms of homes within a single area—for example, mixing smaller and less expensive semiattached houses with larger freestanding ones

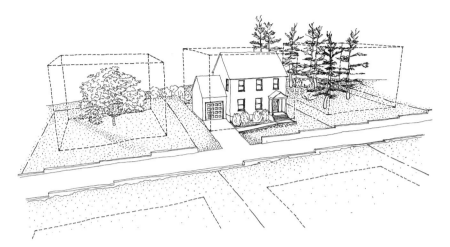

2-3. Zoning laws typically prescribe the minimum size of a building lot (indicated with long and short dashes) as well as a smaller envelope (dashed lines), within which the building itself must sit. Such regulations often disregard the physical characteristics of the land and make it almost impossible to preserve preexisting natural features, such as old stands of trees, on small lots. The sketch shows the restrictions that govern many neighborhoods of freestanding houses, where minimum setbacks for front-, side-, and rear yards are all prescribed, as well as a maximum building height. Zoning within dense cities may allow larger and more continuous buildings, but these are still subject to complex setbacks and height limitations.

in the same style. Such mixed or unconventional developments now required a formal variance from zoning boards or municipal officials, a lengthy and expensive procedure that didn't (and still doesn't) always result in approval.

In many neighborhoods, zoning laws also reduced the choices that Americans could make about how to use their homes. Patterns of use commonplace in earlier eras now became illegal. A middle-class widow with grown children and an empty house could no longer take in boarders or open a shop on the first floor to help pay her bills. Apartments could no longer be added above garages or older carriage houses, even for adult children or aging parents. These new restrictions, inspired by fears of unwanted change and instability, actually made it harder for some people to stay in their homes over long periods of time because they could no longer adapt them to meet their own changing needs.

Compliance with the first zoning ordinances was uneven, as it had been with building laws. Initially, many people in existing homes simply ignored the new restrictions on residential areas. At a national planning conference in 1937, a report on Milwaukee, Wisconsin, noted that:

> There were large numbers of land uses developing in violation of the classifications established under the zoning law. During the twenties, and then under the strain of the depression, small businessmen gave up establishments like beauty parlors, barber shops and real estate offices and conducted their businesses in their homes, which were in zoning districts where such uses were prohibited. It was estimated that some 80 percent of these violations had occurred after Milwaukee passed its ordinance in 1920.[13]

By the end of World War II, however, when new home construction skyrocketed, zoning laws were firmly entrenched and much more consistently enforced. The notion that homes should be physically separate from all paid workplaces (except those of domestic servants) was now rarely questioned.

Zoning was only one of many forces that drastically changed the American landscape after the war, but its environmental and social implications are still important today. Across undeveloped land it creates a kind of shadow landscape, which has a legal reality that can't be ignored. It affects our thinking about how we and our neighbors should be able to use or modify our homes, issues that affect all our neighborhoods on an ongoing basis.

NEW TECHNOLOGY AND STANDARDS IN THE COUNTRYSIDE

For several decades, building and zoning laws did not apply outside of metropolitan areas. Even some codes enacted at the state level were limited to communities over a certain size. Though plenty of unhealthy and dangerous conditions existed in small-town and rural homes, they caused less public concern. If a single farmhouse burned down or disease spread because of a polluted town water supply, these were isolated local tragedies and not necessarily cause for legal action. Adequate light and fresh air were less often issues in uncrowded places, and the houses of poor families in the country were far more likely to be self-built than those in the city.

As the technology of middle- and upper-class homes in cities and suburban towns progressed rapidly in the decades before and after the turn of the twentieth century, however, their counterparts in more rural areas did not keep pace. Even prosperous farmers and small-town professionals remained without electricity and often without modern plumbing, which required electric pumps to bring well water indoors. While a concentrated customer base made it lucrative for private utility companies to install power lines in urban areas, there was no such profit to be made from the large investment required to wire dispersed homes in the countryside.

By the 1930s and the beginning of the Great Depression, a wide gulf existed between the technological standards of urban and rural dwellings. It was not just a matter of the wiring and plumbing built into the physical envelope of a home. Middle-class life in urban areas was being transformed by a whole host of new electrical appliances: radios, which revolutionized home entertainment, electric stoves and irons, washing machines, and, eventually, refrigerators. Magazines, advertising, and popular fiction glorified these new laborsaving devices and predicted even more amazing inventions to come, making country dwellers feel increasingly backward.[14]

During the Depression the federal government became involved in many aspects of development that had previously been undertaken almost solely by private business. One major initiative of this kind was rural electrification. Starting in 1933 with the Tennessee Valley Authority (TVA) and followed by the wider-reaching Rural Electrification Administration (REA), publicly funded programs began to compete directly with private industry in both the generation and distribution of electrical power. While wiring individual homes was only one aspect of these efforts, which also aimed at modernizing and improving the productivity of American farms, underlying them was a social conviction that the fifty-year-old technology was now a basic need of all citizens. As President Roosevelt said in defending the new national involvement, "Cold figures do not measure the human importance of electric power in our present social order. Electricity is no longer a luxury, it is a definite necessity."[15]

In addition to electrical plants and power lines, the national government invested heavily in building highways and bridges. To some extent these also helped farmers by improving their connections to markets and reducing social isolation from the rest of middle-class America. At the same time, however, they literally paved the way for the transformation of farmland into new residential neighborhoods for those who worked in the city. The combination of convenient highway access and widely available electric power would make it possible, when the economy strengthened, to build equally modern homes almost anywhere in the country.

PUBLIC HOUSING

Still another federal initiative during the Depression, smaller and far more controversial, was direct government funding of new home construction for poor families. This had long been urged by housing reformers who had seen, decades earlier, that neither the educated self-interest of private builders nor the enactment of public regulations would by themselves create safe and modern homes for many low-income Americans. But the use of public funds for individual home construction was (and still is) seen by many as socialistic and dangerous to American traditions of free enterprise. It was only when the private home-building industry had all but collapsed that government intervention had enough support to proceed, and its stated purpose at the time was as much to generate employment in the building trades as to erect needed homes.[16]

Under the first major federal housing program of the Depression, fifty-one apartment complexes were built in thirty-six cities around the country.[17] Many of them were well designed by architects who had worked earlier for housing reform organizations and been involved in the struggle to enact effective building laws. Though the government funds invested were far less than those involved either in rural electrification or the extensive highway- and bridge-building projects of the same era, nonetheless they set an important and visible new precedent. Up until the early 1930s a growing body of laws, at least in urban areas, prescribed changing limits and standards for the structures that could be built and occupied as homes. But nothing guaranteed that they would be built, especially at a price affordable to all Americans.

For decades, despite rapid and continuous home construction, a severe housing shortage had existed for the poorest families.

While some of the politicians who approved government-funded home construction during the Depression may have thought of it as a temporary program to be discontinued in a healthier economy, this was not to be the case. The concept of direct government intervention to build *minimum-standard homes* for those who can't afford to buy through the private market remains controversial but has not disappeared. Moreover, just as the earliest building laws intended to bring light and air into poor industrial neighborhoods were expanded in scope to include the regulation of all dwellings, so the precedent of public funding to build and rent homes to low-income families led fairly quickly to a variety of government programs that directly or indirectly aided the construction of middle-class homes as well.

The effects of government financial involvement in the development of new homes have been just as complex as those that followed from the first comprehensive regulations. Thanks to the indirect aid of federal mortgage insurance programs and tax deductions for homeowners, a great many Americans have been able to purchase homes they could not otherwise have afforded. Others, usually less affluent, have rented larger, safer, and better-designed dwellings than any available to them on the private market. But while expectations for what actually constitutes a minimum-standard dwelling are entrenched, the shortage of such homes actually affordable to low-income people is still acute. In recent years the problem has been getting worse, with growing homelessness and overcrowding in many parts of the country. And the private building or financing of homes for poor people has all but disappeared.

POSTWAR DEVELOPMENT AND NATIONAL EXPECTATIONS

In the late 1940s, after the Depression and the end of World War II, new power lines and a growing highway system were fast eroding the technological gulf between cities and rural areas. As the connections necessary for fully modernized homes became available throughout the nation, and as suburban development occurred almost overnight in previously rural landscapes, building codes and zoning ordinances extended their reach to what had been largely unregulated areas. Though codes were still individually enacted at the state or local level, there was now a widely accepted set of minimum expectations for an American home. A modest ranch house in rural West Texas, built by a local contractor from a stock plan, might well have the same distribution and sizes of rooms, the same arrangement of outlets and switches, the same kitchen equipment and bathroom fixtures as a two-bedroom elevator apartment in downtown Chicago.

During the thirty years from 1950 to 1980, new homes went up across the United States at an astonishing rate. While in 1930 there had been a total of about 30 million homes in the country and by 1950 some 43 million, the next three decades saw the construction of an additional 50 million dwellings.[18] There were three reasons for this enormous increase. One was a high rate of population growth during the postwar baby-boom years; another was the trend of family members moving apart from each other and setting up smaller households. The average number of people in an occupied home dropped steadily from 4.1 in 1930 to 3.5 in 1950 and 2.8 in 1980. Finally, about 12.5 million older homes, from all previous eras, were demolished during this period and replaced by new ones, not always in the same location.[19] Some were torn down individually as they deteriorated or made way for more profitable uses, others en masse, as multiblock sections of city neighborhoods were condemned for *redevelopment*. In a sense, because of the rapid pace of both demolition and new construction, the nation's built environment was younger in 1980 than it had been forty years earlier.

Most Americans, therefore, now live in recently built homes and neighborhoods. Though we expect a lot from our homes and often work obsessively at improving them (or at least read magazines and contemplate possible projects), there is much about their basic design that we take for granted. With little educational emphasis on the varied history of America's built environment, we tend to see what surrounds us as largely inevitable. When the economic climate is favorable, new local subdivisions seem to follow patterns as predetermined as those of trees with the right soil, rain, and sun; deteriorating older neighborhoods are said to be undergoing a similarly "natural" process of aging. In addition, we associate the comforts and technologies to which we are accustomed with the particular form in which they exist in our neighborhoods. In the United States, of course, this usually means the suburban single-family house, but it can also be the elevator apartment, townhouse complex, or one of a few other standardized modern home types.

As a basis for exploring a wider range of forms, the next chapter will first examine the assembled package of comforts and technologies that has, over the last fifty years, constituted our minimum-standard dwelling. Though it risks oversimplification to neatly pull apart and categorize as complex an entity as a home, we will look first at its enclosed spaces and then at the extended connections of those spaces—to the immediate outdoors, to mechanical and plumbing systems, and to society.

A Basic Home Today

Dorothy lived in the middle of the great Kansas prairies. . . .
Their house was small, for the lumber to build it had to be carried by wagon many miles. There were four walls, a floor and a
roof, which made one room; and this room contained a rusty-
looking stove, a cupboard for the dishes, a table, three or four
chairs, and the beds. Uncle Henry and Aunt Em had a big bed
in one corner and Dorothy a little bed in another corner.

L. Frank Baum, *The Wizard of Oz*

American culture has long idealized spartan homes in the
countryside, associating them with more virtuous lives than those
unfolding in inexpensive homes in the city. Nonetheless, the basic
one-room house to which Dorothy so longed to return would not
have met contemporary Victorian notions of an acceptable family
home, and certainly wouldn't comply with our current legal standards. Despite our admiration for the simple life, we expect a family home today to have differentiated spaces for privacy as well as
a modern technological infrastructure.

The dwelling shown here contains the basic components that
are now expected in an American home for the smallest family
unit—two adults or an adult and one child. Why not look at a
home for just one person as the basic unit? Ever-growing numbers
of people in this country do live by themselves; one quarter of all
homes in the United States were occupied by a single resident in
1996, up from seventeen percent in 1970.[1] In our social, legal, and
architectural expectations, however, there is a big difference
between an acceptable home for a single person and one for a
family. From the days of the first European explorers, American
history was full of individuals fending for themselves, and built
into our thinking is still an assumption of adaptability for people
on their own. They can share bathrooms, cook on hotplates or eat

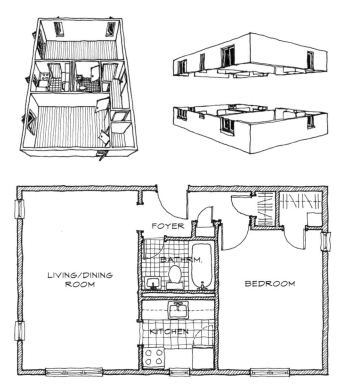

3-1. Conceptually, a floor plan is a horizontal slice through all or part of a building, usually taken about halfway between floor and ceiling looking downward. Walls that are cut are shown with heavy lines, sometimes filled or hatched, as here. Objects below the cut are drawn more lightly; those above it, such as wall cabinets or beams, may be indicated with dotted lines.

out, and socialize away from home. Even a fully equipped modern studio or one-room cottage has an inherently bohemian quality because it combines public and personal areas in ways that defy established conventions. Privacy starts at the front door and doesn't have to extend to an interior separation of spaces.

But if an individualized "room" is minimally sufficient for one person alone, a basic family home is both a more complicated and a less adventurous structure. It must include separated sleeping areas and places for day and evening activities, so that family members can have some privacy from one another. And at least part of this latter living space, or all of it when it's only one room, must have a public face; it must be furnished, decorated, and kept presentable for guests. Going back to Amos Rapoport's idea of a continuum between two settlement traditions, many American neighborhoods, especially those recently built, are composed almost exclusively of private land and dwellings, which are therefore the setting for most activities outside of work or school. Thus our homes often end up accommodating a range of social occasions, from bridge clubs and birthday parties to casual meetings for coffee and the newly formalized children's play dates, all events that in other societies might routinely happen outside of individual dwellings, in tea rooms, bars, cafes, playgrounds, church halls, clubs, or simply out of doors.

SPACES

Most building codes define the requirements for different spaces within a home in terms of minimum linear dimensions or square foot areas. Under New York State's Multiple Dwelling Law, for instance, a bedroom such as the one shown here would have to be not less than 8 feet wide in any direction and contain at least 80 square feet of floor area, barely enough to place a double bed with one long side next to the wall and clearance to walk by on the other. An alternate and more realistic method is to define a minimum set of furnishings needed for each space in order to use it for its stated purpose, in essence a *performance specification*. While the two systems are obviously connected—a typical twin bed takes up about 21 square feet of floor area, and so forth—the second takes crucial design issues much more into account. In addition to its square footage and least dimension, a room's overall proportions, the location and size of its windows, and, most important, its connections to other spaces all determine how fully and comfortably it can be inhabited. Though no one may actually fill a home exactly as shown here or as listed in a given legal standard, using any set of commonly available furniture will reveal a lot about the inherent ability of the space to accommodate other living arrangements as well.

As building codes vary around the country, the minimum sizes of the spaces required in a basic home are not absolute; those shown here are closer to the standards used for government-sponsored public housing than to the smallest rooms permitted by some local laws.

Bedroom

No matter how or where we spend our waking hours, if we don't go home to sleep then we're not really living there. Often less self-consciously designed than the more public spaces of a home, bedrooms nonetheless satisfy its most basic purposes. They provide a quiet and comfortable environment for sleeping as well as privacy, even from other family members, for dressing and for sex. Beds and bureaus or other clothes storage, therefore, are their primary furnishings. Ideally, twin beds should be fully accessible from one side and double, queen, and king-size beds from both, so that no one has to climb over anyone else to get in and out. A night table or some equivalent to hold at least a lamp, a box of tissues, and a pair of glasses is also important, though not always required, for each sleeper.

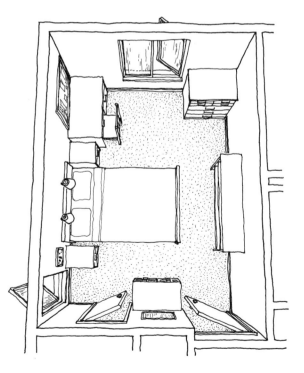

3-2. Bedroom.

When they are large enough, we also work, exercise, and play in bedrooms, and engage in just about any activity that does not involve the whole family. At their most generous, federal guidelines for subsidized homes required space for a number of items such as desks and bookcases, located either in public living areas or in reasonably sized bedrooms. These requirements added a small amount of floorspace that built in some allowance for individual needs.

Children, of course, adapt all kinds of furniture and spaces to their own purposes. When a home includes a designated play area it may or may not be the space they actually use most often, and in homes without any such special provision they will play anyway. But usable floor area and flexible storage inside a bedroom, for toys and other possessions, can give a child independence and control. Lego constructions can stay up and clothes can remain longer on the floor, reducing daily conflict with adult notions of order.

Living Area

In a large and expensive home the *living room*, known a century ago as the *front parlor*, is a highly decorated and rarely used space, with the nicest windows and the best view. Other areas, called *family rooms*, *dens*, or, more recently, at least in real estate ads, *great rooms*, are where daily living actually takes place. But in smaller homes the living area, whether or not it is a separate room, has the symbolic role of a formal parlor and serves many real functions as well. To accommodate an ever-changing stream of activities from entertaining friends to folding laundry, it is usually furnished with a *conversation area*, consisting of padded chairs, a couch, and one or two small tables, all arranged so that everyone faces each other. A set of deep shelves or a stand holding a television and other home entertainment appliances is placed on one side, most often against a wall, to allow a view from the seating. (Not all rooms, whatever their size, make it easy to set up a comfortable arrangement for conversing as well as for watching TV.) In keeping with the formal and public nature of the space, living area shelving and walls are also the most carefully considered areas in a home for display of artwork and photos.

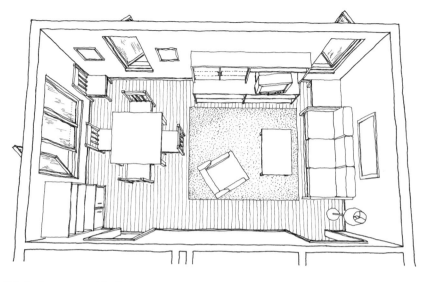

3-3. Living-room with dining area.

Dining Area

Family habits with respect to cooking and eating vary greatly among cultures. If current media accounts of family life in this country are accurate, Americans, overall, eat together at formal sit-down meals less and less often. Nonetheless, a dining table with chairs that seat at least the whole family, and perhaps one or two guests as well, are standard furnishings in our homes. Much less standard, however, is the relationship between dining and cooking spaces. Most building codes and minimum design standards allow the dining area to be part of the kitchen, an alcove off the kitchen, an entirely separate room, or part of a combined living/dining area, as shown here. Historically, a formal *dining room* is associated with a proper middle-class home and an *eat-in kitchen* with a more humble one, but this is actually an area where recent style has gotten less class-conscious and more individualized. Many people now prefer an open kitchen/dining arrangement as more sociable and spacious than smaller separated spaces.

Even for those who rarely cook and sit on the couch to eat their takeout, the dining table is often a central place in the household.

Because of its association with food it generally gets cleared and cleaned more often than desks or side tables, and is therefore an ideal surface on which to spread out and work. Bill paying, homework, sewing, and myriad other projects tend to end up at the dining room table when they theoretically should occur in more specifically designed areas. Its accessibility from several sides can also make the table the most convenient setting in a tight home for games or group discussions.

Kitchen

Food preparation and cooking have moved around within American homes far more than most other domestic activities. In the earliest one- and two-room houses built by European settlers, they took place of necessity in the same room as other daily functions; the fire that warmed the house also provided the heat for cooking, and water was carried in and out in any case. But as families prospered and added to their homes, or built new and larger ones from scratch, kitchens were always among the first spaces to be segregated from other living areas. Though cooking was a central household activity, it posed problems of cleanliness, safety, smell, mess, and, in warm climates, excess heat.

As metal stoves replaced fireplaces for cooking and baking, and water was more commonly piped into sinks, the kitchen routinely became a separate space, usually square and about the same size as other rooms in the home. In addition to its fixed elements it contained an assortment of tables, chairs, and freestanding cabinets. Before refrigerators existed and prepared foods were widely available in supermarkets, storage space for canned goods, vegetables, and other basic supplies was critical, and often extended to separate pantries and root cellars or bins in cool locations.

Starting in the late 1800s the design of kitchens began to be analyzed by early home economists and industrial experts concerned with efficiency and time saving in factory production. These early efforts at creating scientifically designed kitchens rested largely on the premise of enabling a housewife on her own to be as efficient and productive as possible. As cooking was still tedious, time-consuming, and even dangerous, better-designed kitchens were intended to improve women's lives and professionalize their daily housework. A separate motivation for change was the incorporation of new technologies that raised the square-foot costs of construction. Builders needed to reduce the size of homes in order to keep them affordable.

One way of achieving both greater working efficiency and lower cost was to combine the loosely furnished kitchens and separate pantries common in middle-class homes into a less spacious but better organized single room. This new space came complete with fixed counters, cabinetry, and the latest in domestic technology, thus appealing to middle-class women despite its reduced size. Over the first few decades of this century, the built-in kitchen became a standard element of an American home. Smaller than its immediate predecessors, a modern kitchen comes with the house, as fully finished and decorated as the inside of a car.

Today's minimum-standard kitchen requires three appliances: a sink, deep enough for washing pots, a refrigerator with separate freezer space, and either a single stove with rangetop above and oven below, or the two separately. According to commonly accepted rules of layout these are best organized in a *work triangle*, with the sink at the center and counter space immediately adjacent to each component, so that there is always a place to put things down. There is no standard requirement for any place to sit while working, though some larger kitchens do include space for a table. Both the floor and the counters generally have special finishes, glossy and water resistant, designed for frequent cleaning.

Most design standards are clear on what a basic kitchen must contain but flexible regarding the degree of separation between this space and other living areas. Over the course of this century the nature of food preparation has gradually changed, and most of the reasons that kitchens were originally segregated from other areas now don't have quite the same force. On average, cooking doesn't take as long or generate nearly as much mess and lingering smell. We no longer start by plucking the chicken but by unwrapping a neat package of boned breasts ready for slicing. Staples such as ketchup come from the store, no longer simmering for hours with a scent that permeates the entire room. It is easier, therefore, to reintegrate cooking with other household activities in the same space.

Some assumptions regarding the layout of kitchen equipment are also less valid now than they were even fifty years ago. An efficient work triangle makes a comfortable arrangement for a single cook but can be too constrained for several people at once. Now that cooking is easier and more women work away from home, kitchens often become the domain of an entire family. Breakfast is less likely to be a platter of eggs and bacon cooked by mom and brought out to the table than separate dishes of cereal, yogurt, and toast prepared by both children and adults, all bumping into one another. In this type of household a less "efficient" layout with more open access can work better.

As cooking and eating habits get more individualized, kitchens and dining areas are probably the most frequently altered spaces within existing American homes. Changes such as relocating sinks, ripping out and replacing cabinets, and moving walls, however, are too costly to be easily undertaken by families in the most basic dwellings. A more flexible approach to building minimal kitchens might incorporate movable cabinetry, finished on all sides, and fewer fixed walls, so that layouts can be more easily rearranged.

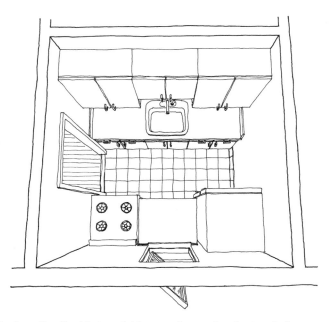

3-4. A typical small galley kitchen, laid out to form a "work triangle."

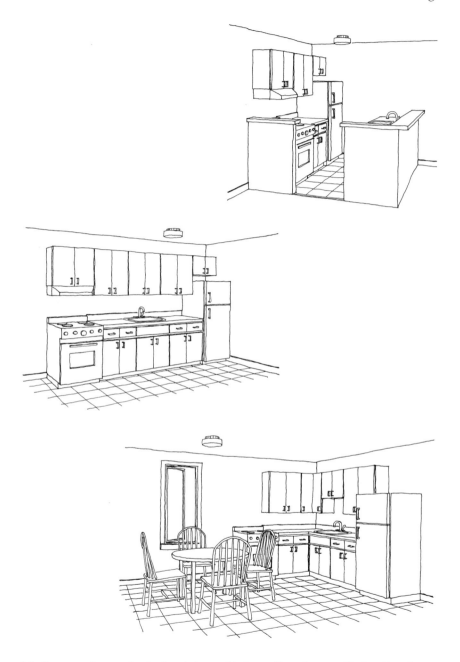

3-5. Common layouts for basic minimum kitchens. Top, the two-sided *galley* , shown enclosed in figure 3-4, is semi-open. Center is a standard *strip*, with stove and refrigerator at either end; bottom is a typical *L-shaped* layout, here part of a larger eat-in kitchen with a window.

Bathroom

Unlike a modern kitchen, which may be either completely open to living areas or closed off by degrees, the bathroom's relationship to other spaces in a home is clear and fixed. It is a separate, closed space, and even its entry door should be as private as possible, never opening directly off the living or dining area. When a home has only a single bathroom it is ideally located next to the bedrooms but accessible from a common hallway.

A minimum-standard full bathroom has three fixtures: a toilet, a shallow sink or lavatory, set lower than the one in the kitchen for easy handwashing, and some means for washing the whole body, either a stall shower or a bathtub and showerhead. These are arranged in a space just big enough to allow one-able bodied person access to each fixture—5 by 7 feet is typical. (With a stall shower or extra-short tub a narrower width is possible, but anything less than 5 feet means that a tall person sitting on the toilet will feel his or her knees hemmed in by the facing wall.) Bathrooms are the wettest place in the house and should have floors and walls, at least around the tub or shower, that are waterproof rather than just water resistant. Though some codes require ceramic tile, others don't prescribe particular finishes. In practice many bathrooms leak, often because of a lack of coordination among those responsible for their construction: plumbers, carpenters, and tilesetters.

Storage in a standard-size bathroom is almost always inadequate, usually just a shallow medicine cabinet above the lavatory and a few towel bars or hooks attached to free expanses of wall area. Sometimes the sink is placed on a base cabinet that at least holds extra toilet paper, but there is rarely a way to accommodate all the clothes, toys, extra towels, and shampoo bottles that accumulate. Before World War II recessed clothes hampers were often set into the wall; these have disappeared in the more streamlined construction of the last fifty years.

Like kitchens, bathrooms are essentially designed and furnished by the builder. Without the expense of major renovation there is little that residents can do to rearrange or customize them to their personal preferences. As the various uses of bathrooms don't really constitute "work," they have not been as carefully

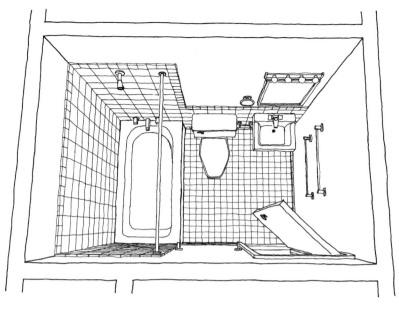

3-6. A 5- by 7-foot bathroom.

analyzed as kitchens according to concepts of factory efficiency, but they are similarly considered a service space rather than a living area. Indeed, the services provided by even the most basic three-fixture bathrooms are real amenities in our everyday lives; it is hard to conceive that most humans throughout history have done without them. Somehow walking everywhere and reading by candlelight are easier to imagine than going back to outdoor privies, or to lugging, heating, and emptying water into a portable tub for a few minutes of warmth and cleanliness once a week.

At the same time, bathrooms do serve as living space, especially for family groups rather than sole occupants. Often the only room with a door that actually closes tight and has a reliable lock, they offer a privacy that can be important far beyond just shielding bodily functions. People lock themselves into the bathroom, among other reasons, to smoke, to cry, to read without interruption, and to pull themselves together when they're angry. For young children, to whom privacy is not so important, bathtubs allow the elemental freedom of waterplay that is not usually permitted anywhere else inside, and only sometimes outdoors.

Small wonder, then, that the average number of bathrooms within newly constructed American homes has been rising. But they are also expensive to build and frequently, because they tend to leak, a cause of structural deterioration. Though the three-fixture, 5-by-7-foot bathroom may be about as spatially efficient as is possible, it is worth noting that in other societies bathing facilities are often separated from toilets, allowing both to be used simultaneously by different family members.

Storage

Belongings that we want to keep close at hand but out of sight can be stored either in large pieces of movable furniture or in permanent closets with doors. The earliest basic homes in this country, like those elsewhere in the world, had simple rectangular rooms without many closets. Wherever they lived, our ancestors stored most of their possessions, which were far fewer than ours, in bulky though often handsome wardrobes and chests. For the many American families on the move in earlier centuries, these must have been very cumbersome to lug from one home to another.

Closets use floor area more efficiently than portable storage because they extend from floor to ceiling and leave free wall space outside in larger rooms for other furnishings. As new building techniques, developed during the early 1800s, made permanent wall construction both faster and cheaper, even modest homes in the United States began to be built with more complicated floor plans, including built-in closets as a matter of course. Today, though few of us feel that we actually have enough storage, several types of closet space are taken for granted as part of a minimum home. Bedrooms are expected to have clothes closets, with hangrods and shelving above them; the same type of closet is typically located near the front entry door for coats. Sheets, towels, and supplies such as the toilet paper that won't fit in the bathroom medicine cabinet are housed on floor-to-ceiling shelves in a linen closet, whose location is more flexible. Ideally, some narrow, tall area for storing long-handled cleaning equipment should be included in one of these, or laid out separately as a broom closet.

What is not standard in a minimum home is any enclosed general storage for the larger items of which everyone seems to have

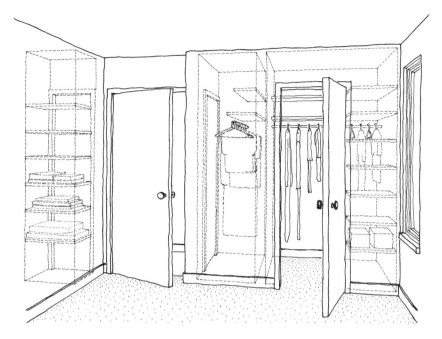

3-7. Built-in storage. In a standard home today this includes a bedroom closet, shown at right with hanging and shelf space, a coat closet (center) and a linen closet (left). Here the latter two open onto the hallway outside the bedroom.

at least some example: a bicycle, a portacrib kept for a visiting grandchild, an air-conditioner or humidifier used only seasonally. Even when two dwellings have the same finished floorspace, additional unfinished areas such as attics, garages, and basements can make one home feel substantially roomier than the other by accommodating these bulky items and leaving designated rooms free to serve their purpose.

Circulation

When any open area is heavily used, by humans or other animals, paths develop according to prevalent traffic patterns. Deer make trails through the forest and children make paths on a grass-covered playground. Within a home, if all rooms are linked directly one to another, the most direct routes from one door to the next essentially become pathways, reducing the area that can be filled with furniture or freed for activities, and eliminating privacy in all but the end rooms. Well-designed entrance halls and

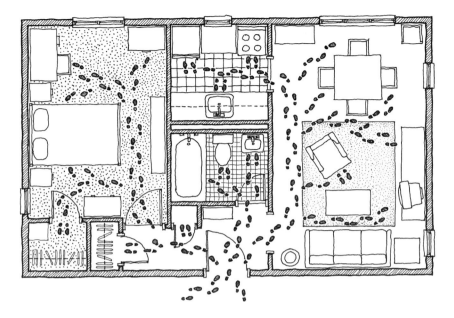

3-8. Circulation patterns.

corridors minimize the circulation area within each room, tying a home together in a way that ensures privacy where desired and allows living spaces to be used as comfortably and fully as possible.

Building codes and other design standards rarely require halls and corridors within dwellings, but they do specify minimum widths for those that are built. Some design standards ask for entrance foyers like the one shown here, recognizing that such a space not only carries circulation but has other functions—a staging area for going in and out of doors, a place to receive strangers without exposing them to the whole home, and a way to shield other rooms from direct blasts of outside air. By prohibiting certain spatial relationships, such as bedrooms opening off of living rooms, many standards also have the effect of requiring at least some corridor space.

In the design of many large building types, especially modern office and apartment towers, public circulation space that can't be rented out to individual tenants is kept to a minimum for economic reasons. Builders want as much of a structure as possible to pay its way. Within individual dwellings there is often the same pressure to minimize circulation space in order to keep down construction costs. As new technologies were added to American middle-class homes early in this century, the need to keep home prices at an affordable level led many builders to eliminate, as much as possible, the entrance halls and corridors that had been standard in earlier floor plans. The front door now often opened directly into the living room and the route to the newly scientific and pared-down kitchen was through the living and dining areas rather than via a separate hallway. To the extent that rooms were enlarged to allow for this traffic, some new homes felt more spacious and relaxed than those with traditional layouts. *Open plans* were promoted as having a modern and fashionable informality in addition to being cost-efficient.

What appeared open and roomy, however, was not always easy to furnish. Builders had not really eliminated the entrance foyer or side corridor; often they had simply run them without walls straight through other spaces. If the main routes to the dining room from the front door and the stairs cut diagonally across the living room in two directions, for example, setting up a comfortable conversation area could be awkward. Today the floor plans of new homes vary in their degree of compartmentalization, but that of a minimum-standard home has to be somewhat open in order for rooms not to be claustrophobic and inflexibly small. This makes well-designed circulation, whether or not it is visibly separated by walls, especially important.

Accessibility and Adaptability

The most recent social development to affect American building design is a growing recognition of the rights of disabled people for full access to the built environment. Over the last twenty-five years, new laws and design standards have been enacted on the premise that all Americans deserve the opportunity to be as productive and live as independently as possible. In 1990 the *Americans with Disabilities Act* (ADA) was enacted at the federal level. It covers virtually all nonresidential buildings: workplaces, commercial establishments such as stores and theaters, and public structures such as schools, courthouses, and train stations. Though previous federal laws required that a percentage of homes built with public subsidies incorporate access for the disabled, most private dwellings, both apartments and houses, are currently exempt from the ADA. Extending its underlying logic, however, many states and localities now require that new apartments, at ground level or in elevator buildings, be *adaptable*: accessible from outside and laid out on the interior so that a person with handicaps can live there with only minor modifications.

Designing buildings for use by people with a wide range of disabilities requires the inclusion of tactile and visual aids for those with limited sight or hearing, and navigational aids, such as wall railings and easily operable hardware, for the physically frail. Many of these can either be included in initial construction or added after the fact. It is the need to provide full access and mobility for wheelchair users that has the greatest impact on fundamental building layout. The most recognizable features of wheelchair accessibility are the gently sloping ramps required instead of stairs at changes in floor level, but other modifications are equally important. Within homes, the traditional layouts and sizes of doors, corridors, and small rooms such as bathrooms and kitchens are based on an assumption of use by only one ambulatory person at a time. As a wheelchair is wider and has a larger turning radius than a person on foot, residential circulation spaces must often be enlarged or reconfigured to ensure that its user can get around comfortably.[2]

A typical 2-foot-wide bathroom door, for instance, must be widened by almost half to allow easy wheelchair access. Inside the bathroom, the usual narrow strip of free floor area where most of us awkwardly dress after a shower, trying to keep dry clothes separate from wet towels, must also be substantially enlarged so that the chair can be rotated and manipulated toward each fixture. Grab bars must be securely fastened to walls and arranged so that the user can transfer safely to and from toilet, shower, and tub. In narrow or two-sided kitchens, similarly, the floor area between counters must be sized and designed not just to allow the wheelchair to enter the room and turn around but to enable safe use of sinks and appliances.

A home that is fully *accessible* to someone in a wheelchair has features, such as lower counter heights and kitchen wall cabinets, that are somewhat uncomfortable for non-wheelchair users, especially

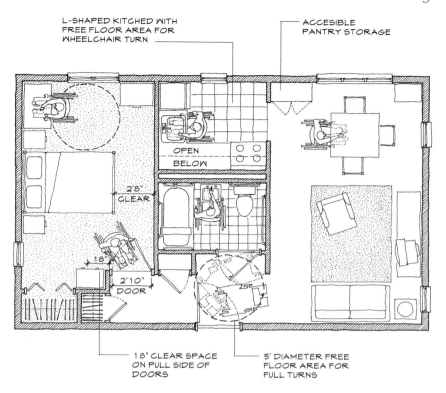

L-SHAPED KITCHED WITH
FREE FLOOR AREA FOR
WHEELCHAIR TURN

ACCESIBLE
PANTRY STORAGE

OPEN
BELOW

2'8"
CLEAR

18"

2'10"
DOOR

18" CLEAR SPACE
ON PULL SIDE OF
DOORS

5' DIAMETER FREE
FLOOR AREA FOR
FULL TURNS

3-9. In a home fully accessible to a wheelchair user, both the fixed architectural elements and the furnishings must allow the wheelchair enough room to pass freely and to turn around where necessary. The 2'-10" minimum door width is larger than the typical residential standard. Sinks and work counters must have open leg-room below; closet and cabinet shelves must be low enough to reach from a sitting position.

those who are tall. In comparison with the tightest minimum-standard homes it will also have areas, in kitchens, baths, and hallways, that seem oddly underutilized. Rather than incorporating all these features from the start, adaptable homes are designed to allow easy and economical alteration for handicapped use when needed.

Increasingly, adaptability is being required by many localities for all homes in new multifamily developments that are wheelchair accessible from outdoors, at grade or via ramps and elevators. Kitchens must be laid out with sections of base cabinet that may be easily taken out to allow greater maneuvering room, or to allow countertops to be lowered. Plumbing connections at the wall must be set to accommodate sinks at different heights. While hallways, bathrooms, and door openings must be somewhat enlarged from the start, the extra floor area can be put to use when not required for wheelchair manipulation, for hallway shelves or removable storage cabinets in bathrooms.

Like other building standards, requirements for accessibility started with a few laws having a limited application but are gradually being extended to include a much greater range of structures. Objections to the growing scope of these standards usually revolve around the extra cost and additional built area needed to comply when the percentage of disabled users is very low or even, in some cases, nonexistent. Why should the law require that private homes be accessible or even adaptable when the occupants are not disabled and will be there to assist any friend or relative who might visit?

Viewed another way, however, making any home adaptable is a kind of insurance for its current residents, enabling them to remain there, if they so wish, under a wide variety of circumstances. As Americans, on average, live longer and more often on their own, many find themselves moving, as they age, out of their homes of many years and into various kinds of specialized dwellings such as self-contained retirement and assisted living communities. While to one degree or another these are designed for accessibility, moving is often traumatic and a community made up only of older people can be isolating.

Families including disabled younger adults or children, moreover, don't fit into these specialized developments, and are often faced with difficult choices. If they can't afford major renovation expenses for their traditional home, they must either move or adjust to conditions where one family member loses more independence than necessary.

As accessibility requirements still do not apply to most individual houses, where the majority of Americans live, they can't be said to be part of a minimum-standard dwelling. But for homes on a single floor that can be reached by ramps or elevators, our standards seem to be moving in that direction. If ground-level apartments constructed by speculative builders must be adaptable, there is no reason why the same should not soon be true of one-story houses.

SPATIAL AND TECHNOLOGICAL STANDARDS

The growing inclusion of adaptability with other requirements for legal homes could reasonably be expected to have the effect of raising spatial standards. If bathrooms, kitchens, doorways, corridors, and the circulation space within rooms must all be slightly enlarged, then the total area of a minimum home should grow, in order to allow the same furnishability of living areas and bedrooms. The logic behind the individual provisions of building codes, however, is not always coordinated. As accessibility standards have concentrated on the design of separate circulation and service spaces, the very low minimum areas prescribed in local building codes for bedrooms and living rooms have remained unchanged. Thus, in New York City, where new elevator apartments are required to be adaptable, a master bedroom may still be as small as 80 square feet, even though it would be difficult to fit any more furniture than a single twin bed in such a space and leave room to manipulate a wheelchair.

In the economic and political climate of the last fifteen years, with deep cuts in government spending, the spatial standards for federally subsidized homes, originally more generous than those of most local building codes, have actually been falling. No longer are there detailed lists of the furniture that must be accommodated in single and double bedrooms, or charts showing the minimum drawer and shelf space in kitchen cabinets gradually increasing with the number of occupants. Instead there are maximums. A federally subsidized two-bedroom home now built for a low-income family, for instance, can contain no more than 800 square feet, into which, depending on exterior constraints and internal layout, one might or might not be able to squeeze the basic furnished areas we associate with an American home.[3]

The odd thing about spatial standards is that while they might seem to be a clear-cut beginning to the definition of an acceptable home, in fact they are far more variable than other criteria. Virtually every locality in the United States has laws that carefully define overcrowding, most often by limiting how many people can sleep in a bedroom. That these are not enforced in many situations is understandable. Most people occupy all the space that they can afford to, and it would be inhumane to deny them what they have without offering a better alternative. Overcrowding is a function of how homes are occupied as much as how they are built. Even our basic standards for how big they should be to begin with in order to be acceptable, however, remain subject to change.

But if spatial standards still fluctuate, technological expectations and standards for a minimum home have risen steadily and are not likely to fall. When private circumstances or public funding sources are constrained, we apparently adapt more readily to reduced living space, even at the expense of personal privacy, than to the omission of amenities such as hot showers and ample electrical power. Our technological dependence may be newer than our social use of the sheltered spaces within our homes, but it is evidently more deeply ingrained.

CONNECTIONS TO THE OUTDOORS

The remaining standards discussed in this chapter cover the physical connections necessary for our health and well being and the technology that we now expect in a minimum home. In addition to containing certain interior spaces, an American dwelling must by law connect to its immediate outdoors, to mechanical, electrical, and plumbing systems, and to the rest of human society. While some homes in this country still fail to comply, overall these more technical standards are quite strictly enforced.

Whether or not a home includes any outdoor land or even sits directly on the ground, it must nevertheless connect in three distinct ways to its immediate environment. Within all buildings, not just homes, people need a continuous supply of well-oxygenated air in order to breathe and a safe route to the outdoors in a variety of emergencies. The third connection, natural light, though no longer required in many other types of buildings, is still considered essential in a dwelling.

Natural Ventilation

If ventilated, sheltered space is critical to all human homes, then why should fresh air even need to be included in a legal minimum standard? The answer is that ventilation, like so many other qualities of the human built environment, exists along a continuum. We will suffocate after exhausting the oxygen in a completely closed space but can adapt to a wide range of enclosures in which the air may be less healthy than that outside. Moreover, it isn't just a question of oxygen content, airborne pollutants, or freefloating germs. There are cultural differences in our standards for fresh air and acceptable lingering smells. Many traditional forms of homes, especially those, like igloos, in harsh climates, have indoor odors as well as smoke that Americans today would find distasteful.[4]

Our present standards for ventilating homes were enacted in response to the overcrowded conditions that developed in nineteenth-century industrial cities. For a given type of room they now specify both the required size of opening to the outdoors, usually as a percentage of floor area, and the minimum dimensions of the exterior space to which this opening connects. Thus a 160-square-foot bedroom might legally require a window that opens to allow a free area of 8 square feet, or 5 percent of the room area, and fronts on an outdoor court or yard at least 10 feet wide.

The first laws regulating ventilation were made before electric fans were widely available or air-conditioning even a remote possibility. Without reliable mechanical means to move air around within enclosed spaces, regulations simply required that every separate space within a home, excepting closets and short corridors, have its own opening to the outdoors. This meant that both houses and apartments had numerous windows in varying sizes corresponding to each room. Operable skylights could be substituted for windows in spaces with no outside wall but a roof above, and were a common feature over the stairwells of attached houses and apartment buildings.

While building codes did not specify any particular arrangement of these openings around the outside of a building, the number required usually gave residents within a home some opportunity to induce drafts, when they wanted them, through cross-ventilation. Opening the kitchen window in the northeast corner and the living room windows on the south-facing front could create a breeze throughout the entire home. Stairwell skylights, though prone to leak, could also draw air upwards out of adjoining rooms if doors were left slightly ajar.

As America electrified and reliable fans came on the market, codes were gradually changed to permit many spaces to be ventilated by means of an exhaust fan attached to a hollow duct extending through the roof or an outside wall. Within homes this arrangement was generally limited to rooms considered to be service space, usually just bathrooms and small kitchens (known in codes as *kitchenettes.*) These changes in law now allowed the inclusion of spaces, such as the first-floor bathroom in a two-story house, that had no exterior walls or roof, so that direct connection to the outdoors was impossible.

Such interior rooms were more likely to be found in apartments than in houses, but for all homes these code changes tended to reduce the total number of windows and often the possibilities for natural cross-ventilation. Exhaust fans, though invaluable for keeping bathrooms dry and quickly getting rid of odors and smoke, are sized to vent only the air from a small room, and will not induce a draft though an entire dwelling. Moreover, they are either on or off, and cannot be adjusted, like windows, depending on the weather.

Code changes permitting mechanical ventilation as a substitute for operable windows were enacted as early as the mid-1920s, but because few homes were built during the Depression and World War II, their effects were not immediately widespread. After the war, when homes were again constructed in large numbers, so many simultaneous and fundamental changes took place both in home design and in overall neighborhood organization that altered ventilation requirements were rarely singled out for comment.

During the 1950s and early 1960s, a period of great technological optimism, low energy costs, and streamlined construction practices, Americans increasingly came to rely on new mechanical devices rather than building design for comfort and convenience. Both houses and apartments built in this period lacked many features that had helped to keep older homes livable in hot weather before electricity. High ceilings disappeared as standardized construction practices made 8 feet an almost universal height. Covered porches, which shaded the interior and provided comfortable outdoor living spaces, were now considered old-fashioned and an unnecessary cost. A reduction in the total number of windows, made possible by interior bathrooms and kitchens, was thus just one of many altered characteristics of new homes.

Most people probably didn't notice these reduced standards for natural ventilation because of the growing availability of air-conditioners. When bedrooms and living rooms could be cooled mechanically there was less need for effective air circulation, and units installed in window openings made them impossible to open and close in any case. But while air-conditioning is now widespread and has helped to foster the recent growth of many southern and southwestern communities, it has never become mandatory. Unlike heating, it is still considered a luxury in the most basic homes. A minimum-standard dwelling must have an exhaust fan in an interior bathroom but does not legally have to have either central or room air-conditioners. As the operating costs of air-conditioning have remained high, it is thus in these basic homes where actual comfort has been most reduced by declining standards for natural ventilation. In all homes, of course, dependence on the consumption of electrical power has grown.

Mechanical ventilation, limited within homes to small kitchens and bathrooms, has been permitted to a much wider extent in other types of structures, such as office buildings and stores. Its effect on architecture in the second half of this century has been profound, helping to make possible the construction of huge buildings with simple overall shapes and lots of windowless interior space. As often as not, we now work, shop, and, in some cases, even go to school in sealed enclosures without operable windows. Within these nonresidential buildings, the cooling, heating, and basic ventilation of most spaces is combined into large central systems that circulate a variable mixture of fresh air drawn from outside and air recirculated from indoors though a buildingwide network of ducts. Because these systems are controlled by building staff, most occupants can do little for their individual comfort and health except to adjust their clothing and complain to management.

The environmental implications of these basic ventilation standards are enormous and perhaps too often overlooked in discussions about the problems of indoor air pollution. Quite apart from the issue of how much energy is wasted in the mechanical ventilation of sealed buildings, many of the toxic or allergic effects of building materials would be greatly reduced or even totally dissipated if the windows could just be opened and the places aired out.

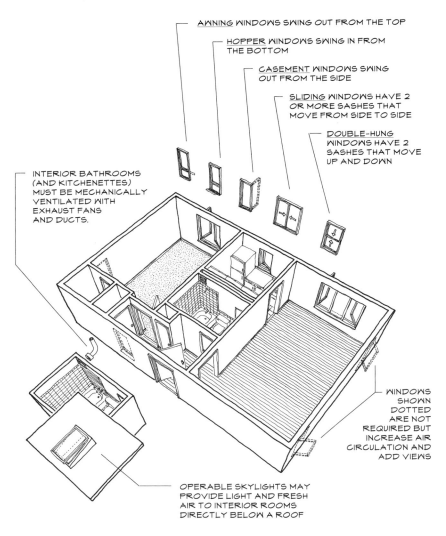

AWNING WINDOWS SWING OUT FROM THE TOP

HOPPER WINDOWS SWING IN FROM THE BOTTOM

CASEMENT WINDOWS SWING OUT FROM THE SIDE

SLIDING WINDOWS HAVE 2 OR MORE SASHES THAT MOVE FROM SIDE TO SIDE

DOUBLE-HUNG WINDOWS HAVE 2 SASHES THAT MOVE UP AND DOWN

INTERIOR BATHROOMS (AND KITCHENETTES) MUST BE MECHANICALLY VENTILATED WITH EXHAUST FANS AND DUCTS.

WINDOWS SHOWN DOTTED ARE NOT REQUIRED BUT INCREASE AIR CIRCULATION AND ADD VIEWS

OPERABLE SKYLIGHTS MAY PROVIDE LIGHT AND FRESH AIR TO INTERIOR ROOMS DIRECTLY BELOW A ROOF

3-10. Windows admit sunlight and fresh air, but not always in the same proportions. Those with two moving sections or *sashes* that slide within the frame can open only to half the total glass area. Windows with hinged sashes that swing out from the frame, like those shown here, provide the same amount of ventilation as light. They are often combined with fixed sashes for additional areas of glass.

In this regard, we should appreciate our homes for the essential differences that now exist between them and other structures. Though residential standards have declined somewhat over the last fifty years, they are still significantly better than those for other building types in allowing us access to the surrounding atmosphere. On a fine, mild day, in any American home, we must still be able to turn off both the heat and the air-conditioning, opening our living spaces to the outdoors.

Natural Light

The same windows that open to allow air circulation also admit sunlight, either direct or reflected, and this *natural light* is a separate and equally fundamental requirement in our homes. Perhaps more than for natural ventilation, our standard for light rests on psychological needs rather than strictly physical ones. *Artificial light*, in the form of candles and oil lamps, goes back much further in history than mechanical ventilation. With the bright electrically powered fixtures of today we have no absolute need for sunlight inside buildings. But while some people now work all day in windowless spaces, at home, fortunately, building codes mandate that they must still have a visual connection to the immediate outdoor world.

Within a home, most codes require windows with glass in all the spaces where natural ventilation is mandatory. The typical minimum area is twice that of the required ventilation opening; when the required free area for ventilation is 5 percent of a room's square footage, the required area of glass is 10 percent. This formula is probably based not on scientifically determined human need but on the common form of the double-hung window, which can never open to more than half of its total glazed area. Other window types have different ratios of glass to maximum opening, making them more appropriate for homes in climates and settings where the two-to-one ratio is not necessarily optimal.

In general, building codes specify only the area of glass for a given room, not its compass orientation or the intensity of the light coming in. A legal home, therefore, might be constantly in the shadow of other buildings and tall trees, or have all its windows on the north side. Historically, many traditional home forms, especially those in extreme climates, had limited fenestration because windows were less effective at retaining or keeping out heat than the wall construction around them. While still a factor in design, this is less critical because of recent advances in the materials and techniques of both glazing and frame construction. Double and even triple layers of glass, with sealed air spaces between them, reduce heat transmission, and modern glass coatings can reflect some rays back outside, reducing heat buildup and glare while still allowing a view out from the interior.

Over the last twenty years many states have adopted separate energy codes that specify minimum insulating values for building exteriors and levels of energy efficiency in mechanical systems. In new buildings, such codes typically require double-glazed windows, which have therefore become standard even in the most basic homes.

Though we still tend to talk of windows as though their main functions were to admit daylight and fresh air, in fact their primary role in many homes may have changed. Now that we rely so heavily on mechanical cooling and heating and have a sophisticated range of interior lights at our disposal, the most important functions of windows may be to orient and connect us, visually and physically, to the outdoors. Through them we can judge the weather, keep watch on the neighborhood, oversee children outside, hear birds, passersby, and car alarms, and focus on either the immediate or the distant view.

Modern buildings, both homes and other structures, include larger areas of uninterrupted glass than their earlier counterparts, often in locations and proportions that make little sense either for energy conservation or the quality of interior light. To some extent this change is due to the greater availability and lower cost of the material itself. Glass can now be manufactured in large sheets of uniform strength and is frequently used because of its exterior visual effects rather than its role in bringing sunlight indoors. In what is perhaps an exercise of collective denial, architects love to talk about transparency and lightness as aesthetic qualities of massive glass-sheathed modern buildings.

This increased use of glass may also be, at least in part, a response to the growing number of hours that we spend inside. With historical changes in work and transportation, and an ever-growing array of in-home entertainment devices, Americans seem to be spending ever more time indoors, within buildings and cars. This is true of both children and adults, and does not appear to be a short-lived or easily reversible trend. Thus, even when the view is mundane and a large expanse of glass compromises our privacy, we have a need to see what's out there, as we are not. The fixed picture windows of postwar homes were maligned by architectural critics, but they have shown enduring appeal, as have the sliding glass doors that tend to jam in their tracks.

Legal requirements for natural light and ventilation distinguish our homes from other modern building types. Though the language of building codes is often awkward and technical, and even straightforward provisions hard to grasp, the codes do make what is actually a poetic and thoughtful distinction between two kinds of spaces: *habitable* and *occupiable*. Habitable rooms, which must have operable windows or skylights, are the sleeping and living spaces in our homes as well as the sleeping spaces in quasiresidential buildings such as hospitals, dormitories, and hotels. (Curiously, a hospital lounge or a dormitory common room is generally not considered habitable space.) Occupiable rooms are those in such spaces as offices, courtrooms, stores, and classrooms, where people may in fact spend as much continuous time as they do in any room of their homes. Theoretically, occupiable rooms must meet the same standards for human comfort and safety, with adequate light levels and a minimum required number of air changes per hour. But when we are occupying rather than inhabiting, these connections may all be mechanical. Implicitly, therefore, our laws recognize that to inhabit a place we must have tangible and sensory connections to the outdoors.

Safe Egress

No matter how completely a structure provides for our needs, we must still be able to leave it in case of fire or other catastrophe, and reach the open air safely. Provisions to ensure safe egress are one of the main concerns of building codes and involve complex interrelationships between building height, materials, and internal layout. As buildings get taller they have to include clearly marked routes back to the ground, and as individual floors grow horizontally beyond a given area there must be two or more alternate routes out, or *means of egress*. The longer these routes, either horizontally or vertically, the more time the building must withstand both fire and structural stresses, such as wind and earthquakes, in order to allow everyone a chance to exit. Structural systems and fire-resistant materials, therefore, are as important as building layout in ensuring safety. The stairwells and sometimes the corridors that make up an egress route are often required to be isolated from other parts of the building, enclosed by fireproof walls and specially rated doors. In recent years, as requirements for handicapped accessibility have increased, codes have been amended to more often require *areas of refuge* along these egress routes, where those who cannot get downstairs on their own can safely wait for help.

Most houses and small apartment buildings in this country do not include heavily fireproofed routes of egress. In them our safety depends instead on getting out quickly and directly. Bedroom and living room windows, therefore, are often required to be designed as secondary fire exits, with a sill low enough and an opening large enough for someone to climb out easily. While we may intuitively fear fire and disasters in tall buildings more than in short ones, in fact the speed with which fire can consume a small home made of light wood framing means that we are not necessarily any safer there than in a more fireproof apartment tower. Design for safe escape is critical in structures of all sizes. The smallest freestanding modern dwellings, mobile homes, were discovered early on to be dangerous in fires because their shallow windows were too small to climb out of; a second door, with no practical function other than as an emergency exit, was therefore incorporated in their standard design.

Because they are essential, egress and fire safety provisions in building codes are carefully studied and continually updated, far more than less critical provisions that may derive largely from historical custom or local construction practices. Compared with many other types of legislation, these *life safety requirements* have been very successful. Though construction inspections are not always complete and some buildings not totally code-compliant, the quickly spreading fires that devastated towns and cities in previous centuries are now rare. Disasters that do occur, especially those in which many people die, are most often in buildings where egress requirements are violated. Unfortunately the way out is also usually a way in, so that security concerns can cause exit doors to be chained shut and windows barred.

MECHANICAL, PLUMBING, AND ELECTRICAL CONNECTIONS

Space Heating

In climates where it gets too cold to survive in the raw, we have three ways to keep going. First, we can put on clothing; second, we can find or construct shelters that, through their design and materials, retain heat from solar radiation and block air infiltration, creating an indoor environment warmer than that outside. Last, we can use various mechanical means, principally the burning of fuel, to warm the air or radiant heating elements around us. These methods, of course, are almost always used in combination, but in the United States, far more than in other parts of the world, we depend most heavily on the third. With plenty of available and affordable fuel, and a tradition of rapid and lightweight home construction, Americans have for the past hundred and fifty years lived in homes that are relatively large and not especially tightly built or fully insulated, but very well heated.

Throughout our history, home design and heating have been closely linked. Early houses built by European settlers were heated first by open wood-burning fireplaces and then by more fuel-efficient cast-iron stoves that gradually replaced them. In both cases heat on the first-floor level was generated by a separate, single-point source in each room, with individual stoves or hearths connected to one or more chimneys for exhaust. Rooms on upper floors, if they didn't have their own fireplace or stove, were warmed by air rising from below or radiating from the chimney. The air temperatures throughout such homes varied considerably, from blazing warmth right by a recently stoked fire to much cooler only a few feet away near the window.

During the last few decades of the 1800s, a new type of heating became available, improving overall indoor comfort and allowing greater freedom in home design. *Central heating systems,* derived initially from steam-generating boilers developed for industrial purposes, are those whereby water, steam, or air is heated in a single boiler or furnace and circulated throughout a building in metal pipes (in the case of steam and water) or larger hollow ducts

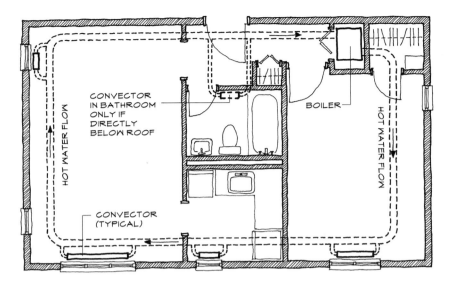

3-11 (a). The selection of a central heating system depends on the size, form, and structural system of a home as well as the choice of fuel. This diagram shows a simple *one-pipe hot water system* for a small single-story house with no basement. The hot water makes a loop, flowing out of the boiler, around, and back in again. Convectors should have valves that allow them to be turned on and off individually.

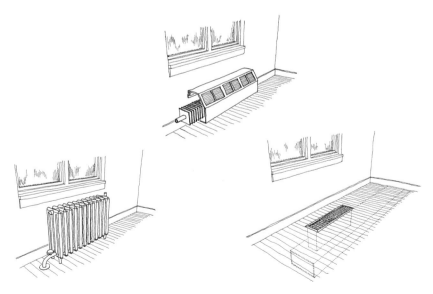

3-11 (b). Common type of convectors for hot water and steam systems are the *fin tube* (top) and the traditional radiator (bottom left). *Grilles* (bottom right), *registers*, and *diffusers*, for warm air distribution, may be located on floor, wall, or ceiling, depending on the duct layout. They can do double duty when there is central air-conditioning.

(for air). The heat is then released to warm the interior through units with a lot of exterior surface, known as *convectors* or *radiators*, or through *diffusers*, grilled openings at the ends of air ducts.

Central heating was a major technological advance in several ways over fireplaces and stoves. First, it improved indoor comfort by making possible the placement of individually sized heat sources at many points throughout a home, especially near openings to the outdoors, such as windows. Flexibility in the size and location of convectors, radiators, and warm air diffusers allowed for more even, better controlled heating. Multiple units around the perimeter of a large room could create an even temperature throughout. A small bathroom or study might have a correspondingly small radiator so that it did not become overheated. Units could be placed in drafty hallways and vestibules to create a roughly uniform temperature within an entire home, reducing the need for doors on every room and permitting much more irregular and open floor plans.

Second, the furnaces and boilers used in central heating systems made more efficient use of their fuel than earlier systems; traditional fireplaces, in particular, send a great deal of warm air right up the chimney. And finally, the new systems were easier to maintain and safer than older ones. They required less frequent stoking and removed the actual combustion process from family living areas, where children could get burned and small objects catch fire.

Installing central heating systems in new buildings was far easier and more cost-effective than cutting holes in the walls and floors of old ones in order to run networks of pipes or ducts. Hence, in the young and still expanding United States, where middle-class and wealthy families were relocating and building new homes at a faster rate than in other industrialized countries, this new and improved form of home heating spread very quickly. By the end of the century, a modest middle-class American home was probably more comfortable on a cold day than the manor houses of English aristocrats, still dependent on fireplaces or stoves.

At the same time, just as in other societies around the world, how warm you were in this country depended on your station in life. Throughout the nineteenth century, in middle- and upper-class houses, servants' rooms were commonly left unheated. Often in the top or attic story, where presumably no one would freeze because of warmth rising from below, they were certainly not a place to linger either in winter or in summer, when they must have been sweltering. Houses and apartments built for or taken over by poorer families also continued to be heated by outdated and primitive methods. Many tenement apartments built in the late 1800s, for example, still relied on a single stove or on shallow gas fireplaces.

Today, at least in theory, all homes in the United States are warm enough inside for shirtsleeves year round. As minimum standards were developed and expanded in the first half of the twentieth century, indoor heating to a high and consistent level went from being a luxury of American middle- and upper-class families to being a requirement for all legal dwellings. Under contemporary codes homes must include or be connected to safe heating systems capable of maintaining a temperature of either 68° or 70°F in any local weather conditions.

In most localities a variety of heating systems and fuels is permitted. The choice of a particular system is closely linked both to climate and to the built form of a home. Modern hot water and older steam systems, still predominant in the Northeast, both use pipes, which take up less space than warm air ducts. The great advantage of a warm air system, now used in more than half of all homes in the United States, is that the same ducts, when connected to the right equipment, can be used to supply both warm and cool air. As an ever-growing number of new homes are built with central air-conditioning, their heating systems are tied in as well.[5]

The choice of home heating fuels varies more according to their historical pattern of cost in different parts of the country. Today about half of all homes are heated with natural gas, but over the last fifty years the percentage that use electricity has been steadily growing everywhere except the Northeast, where rates are much higher. Although electricity is more costly on an ongoing basis than any other fuel, its universal availability means that there are no initial costs such as oil tanks and gas connections.

Even today, not all homes have central heating. Many in mild or hot regions, and a few in colder ones, still rely on small individual unit heaters used only in the winter and powered by either gas or electricity. As might be expected, these do not provide an even level of warmth throughout a room. They have certain safety risks as well, being vulnerable to getting kicked over and to developing small holes in flexible gas connections.

Though requirements for some form of heating are virtually universal, heating to the level set by code is not as critical as ensuring safe egress; it is therefore not as carefully enforced or engineered. Central heating systems, though a great improvement over older methods, vary widely in their reliability and comfort levels. Most public inspection of home heating focuses on boiler, furnace, and chimney safety rather than on even distribution of heat. While there are sophisticated mechanical systems with unified controls for heating, cooling, moisture level, and air quality, these are not installed in modest homes, where we generally depend on more instinctive and homegrown solutions to comfort. If it is only 62°F in the back bedroom, we can always put on a sweater; when warm indoor air is too dry we can place a pan of water on the radiator. As long as the incremental cost of extra fuel is not enough to bother us, we often solve the problem of uneven heat by turning up the thermostat to a level where the coldest part of a home is adequately warm, and then opening the windows a little where it is too hot.

For much of our history Americans had few incentives to heat their homes efficiently or to build homes that didn't require high levels of fuel consumption to be comfortable. With fuel costs relatively low and the price of skilled labor high, homes were quickly built, of lightweight materials whenever possible, without a lot of attention to thermal insulation or weatherproofing. This was true right up through the 1950s and '60s, the period during which so many of our current homes went up.

The early 1970s, however, for economic and political reasons, saw a series of steep hikes in fuel prices. As all Americans found themselves paying substantially more to heat their homes and fill their gas tanks, interest in fuel conservation and energy efficient design grew stronger. Suddenly small cars were popular and the extra cost of double-glazed windows more quickly offset by reduced heating bills.

These energy price increases were a major impetus for ongoing changes throughout the 1970s and 1980s. Manufacturers of building materials, components, and mechanical equipment developed more efficient products. Architects and engineers educated themselves to give greater priority to minimizing energy use. State energy codes enacted during this period added new requirements for insulation and energy-efficient mechanical systems to existing building laws. Technologies that utilize renewable energy sources—sunlight, wind, and hydroelectric power—rather than fossil fuels were explored at both popular and professional levels.

Thanks to the new codes and to growing popular awareness, some of these changes in building products and construction practices became institutionalized. A minimum-standard home constructed today has a better-insulated roof and exterior walls than one built thirty years ago. Typically, it also has a more efficient heating system, though this depends on the particular fuel and equipment. (Electric heat, for example, is still very inefficient and expensive.)

New methods of building more tightly for energy conservation purposes raised unforeseen issues in relation to ventilation. Homes can be damaged by moisture that accumulates in outer walls and is unable to escape, causing rot and other deterioration. And when the air that used to circulate through cracks around windows and doors is sealed out, a home may be fuel-efficient but far more stuffy. Building, however, is rarely an exact science, and widespread efforts to create more efficient buildings have gradually increased the technical expertise available.

More fundamental changes in home design or in the use of so-called alternative energy sources have remained optional and are still outside the mainstream building practices that generally determine how basic homes get built. Since the easing of the political crisis that caused oil prices to climb steeply in the 1970s, government policies, with evident popular support, have focused mainly on keeping fuel prices affordable rather than on encouraging conservation. While many interrelated environmental issues have kept energy consumption habits alive as an abstract topic of concern, Americans are probably less self-conscious now about their day-to-day usage patterns, at home, at work, and in the car, than they were twenty years ago.

Plumbing

Every American home is expected to have an indoor plumbing system that supplies both hot and cold water, pure enough for drinking, to the kitchen and bathroom. In most cases the water source is a common public supply such as a reservoir, but about 15 percent of homes still depend on private wells or other individual sources. The drainage pipes carrying dirty water and wastes out of the home must also connect to a legal sewage system; of these close to 25 percent are private septic or cesspool systems.[6]

At a community-wide scale, water supply and sewage disposal systems are major political and physical undertakings with far-reaching environmental effects. As populations have grown and scientific understanding advanced, the technologies involved in supplying potable water and even more in disposing of wastes have changed. Most fresh water now has to be chemically treated, and very few communities get away, as they once did, with simply discharging raw sewage into the nearest large body of water. But at the scale of a basic individual dwelling, plumbing connections and fixtures haven't changed that much since the late nineteenth century, when running water began to be piped into middle-class homes.

Whether it comes from an individual well or a common main under the street, clean water enters a building through a single pipe. Most American buildings have a *direct supply system* in which smaller pipes carrying cold water to individual fixtures branch off this main supply. A separate branch goes to a hot water heater and tank or, more rarely, runs through the same boiler that provides home heating, before feeding hot water to all fixtures except toilets. In most municipal systems the pressure needed to force a satisfactory flow out of the tap is created by gravity as water moves in large volumes down from reservoirs at a higher elevation. When homes are fed by wells, or in individual tall buildings, including apartment towers, pumps are needed to increase pressure; sometimes they feed water up to a roof tank that holds it temporarily. (In many other countries *indirect supply systems* are far more common. Street mains feed cold water to individual storage tanks or cisterns for every building. These store enough for a day's use and can refill slowly, if necessary, from public mains in the street,

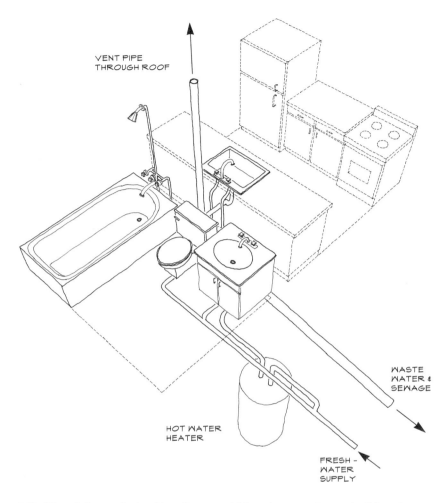

VENT PIPE
THROUGH ROOF

WASTE
WATER &
SEWAGE

HOT WATER
HEATER

FRESH -
WATER
SUPPLY

3-12. The piping and plumbing fixtures within a home or larger building form a closed, connected system that takes in clean water and sends out dirty water, sewage, and some gases.

which may not have adequate pressure at times of heavy use. Indirect systems can cope well with shutdowns and overloads but individual cisterns are more prone to contamination than continuously flowing street mains.)

On the outgoing side of the system, each fixture must be connected back to the soil pipe in such a way as to prevent contamination of clean water or the release of foul gases into the home.

The standard solution to this problem is the *trap*, a *p*- or *s*-shaped bend of piping below each fixture, in which a small amount of water remains as a seal after the rest drains away, blocking gases from escaping. Traps work more consistently if they are separately vented before connecting to the main soil line. Plumbing codes require venting but it is often omitted in illegal installations, especially when bathrooms or individual fixtures are added on the lowest floors of existing buildings, where new connections are difficult.

Plumbing is inherently expensive. Rigid sections of supply and drainage piping must be individually cut to custom lengths and carefully joined to make a watertight system. Codes vary in the materials they allow for different types of piping, some of which are easier to work with than others, but all long-lasting plumbing installations require skill and experience. Drainpipes must be pitched correctly to keep the system flowing and therefore don't always line up conveniently with floors, ceilings, and structural framing. Concealing piping requires planning and takes up floorspace, often in the form of double-walled *chases*, where pipes can run vertically and horizontally.

The number of ways for plumbing to leak is distressingly large—among them improper or corroded joints in piping, worn-out valves, clogged fixtures that back up and overflow, and unsealed openings around bathtub and shower enclosures. Over time, and sometimes right from the beginning, leaks develop within most homes. In 1987 federal government figures on "internal deficiencies" of homes nationwide showed that about 30 percent of all dwellings had water leakage during the previous twelve months, far and away the most common problem listed. This figure did not differentiate between plumbing problems and water coming in through exterior walls, but it was remarkably consistent for all groups of homes, those of the poor and well-to-do, of owners and renters.[7]

Leaks can be frustrating to diagnose and costly to repair. If not corrected they can seriously damage finish materials and even structural elements. For the sake of economy and to minimize problems over the life of the building, therefore, the few spaces within a small home that require plumbing are usually located close to one another, adjacent horizontally or stacked vertically.

Electrical Wiring

[M]other lived the latter years of her life in the horrible suspicion that electricity was dripping invisibly all over the house. It leaked, she contended, out of empty sockets if the wall switch had been left on. She would go around screwing in bulbs, and if they lighted up she would hastily and fearfully turn off the wall switch and go back to her *Pearson's* or *Everybody's,* happy in the satisfaction that she had stopped not only a costly but a dangerous leakage. Nothing could ever clear this up for her.

James Thurber, *The Car We Had to Push*

Electrical wiring in buildings is generally classified with plumbing and heating as a necessary service, but its nature is fundamentally different. While we have an absolute need for access to water and, in most climates, at least a periodic need for heating, an electrical outlet on the wall, in and of itself, does nothing for us. Rather than an actual service, the wiring now required in a basic home is an amazingly convenient, if not always efficient, source of power. Its ready availability inspires us to buy and enables us to operate an ever-widening array of mechanical devices, at least some of which are truly useful.

Heating and plumbing systems are both heard and seen; the wiring in a home is silent and virtually invisible, with little direct effect on building form. Unlike pipes and air ducts, flexible electric cables are narrow enough to fit easily within most standard types of wall and floor construction, and can be run horizontally, vertically, or diagonally without affecting power delivery. With some advance planning, though it does not have to be until well into the construction process, an outlet or fixture box can be placed virtually anywhere that it is needed. Ideally, outlets should be so dispersed and well located that power is available everywhere, as the use of a home varies over time.

Indirectly, of course, the effect of electricity on the forms of our homes is enormous. By making possible safe interior lighting of any desired brightness and by enabling homes to use both fans and air-conditioners, the wiring in our walls allows us to substitute artificial light and mechanical ventilation for those from outside. In fairness, it is not solely a question of substitution but often of real improvement. Electric lights permit us to see more clearly and stay up later than we could in any home without them; air-conditioning and fans can keep us cooler in some climates than could any unwired built enclosure, no matter how well designed. The problem is the extent to which we now design and build homes without regard for their location in the natural environment, so that they are needlessly unlivable without the constant use of electric power. Homes with low ceilings, little or no cross-ventilation, and unshaded windows facing directly into the sun, for instance, can be found in all hot and humid regions of the United States; a century ago they couldn't have existed. Interior bathrooms in which we always switch on the light and fan as we enter are ubiquitous.

Modern electrical codes require outlets on the walls of every space within a dwelling. (The "internal deficiencies" enumerated in the American Housing Survey of 1987 included "rooms without outlet" as well as water leakage.[8]) Also standard are built-in light fixtures, connected to wall switches, on the ceilings or walls of rooms that lack floorspace for tables or standing lamps: bathrooms, kitchens, hallways, and walk-in closets. A common guide for the placement of outlets is every 12 feet, minimum, along the wall, in theory close enough so that any lamp or appliance with a 6-foot cord can be plugged in without an extension cord. As the number of appliances in most homes grows steadily, however, this spacing is probably becoming obsolete. Kitchens in particular already need far more closely spaced outlets, mounted above counter height.

The technology of electrical generation, distribution, and wiring is complex and beyond the scope of this book. At the simplest conceptual level, however, there are similarities between the distribution of electricity to individual homes and the supplying of water from a municipal system. The force of the electricity, its *voltage*, is comparable to the pressure, or *head*, of water, and the amount of current, or *amps*, corresponds to the total flow of water. In the smaller wires or pipes branching off main lines there is greater resistance, or *friction*, which means that the voltage and the water pressure coming into homes are lower than those of the trunk lines under or along the street. Both electrical current and water are usually available to us at a constant level, whether we use them or not. However, if all the end users on either type of network simultaneously turn on their air-conditioners or open their taps, the systems may not be able to cope properly—hence brownouts, blackouts, and sudden drops in water pressure at times of peak loading. [9]

Once water and electrical power have been used within a dwelling, the two networks are no longer comparable. In plumbing systems, the water that enters a home must also leave, and the return side of this cycle is physically more cumbersome and complex than the supply. Part of electricity's appeal is that it is so clean at the point of use. Wastes created by its generation, in the form of heat and fuel byproducts, are concentrated around power plants or dispersed into the atmosphere. The process sometimes causes major environmental problems, but these are not directly connected to the buildings using the power. Most electrical appliances used in homes don't generate dangerous amounts of heat, don't require venting, and are, overall, remarkably safe. While faulty wiring is hazardous and does cause fires, our substitution of electricity for other forms of power has actually reduced the dangers of the built environment; candles, gas lamps, and old-fashioned irons were all more risky than their electrical counterparts. If the stall of Mrs. O'Leary's cow, which allegedly started the Great Fire of Chicago in 1871 by kicking over a lantern, had had an overhead bulb, the disaster might never have happened.

The usage of electricity in American homes has increased steadily throughout this century and is still rising. During the late 1970s and 1980s, as cars became more fuel-efficient and homes better insulated, many standard appliances, such as refrigerators and air-conditioners, were also redesigned for greater efficiency. But even as individual appliances used less power to do their jobs, and despite the rising prices charged by utilities, average household consumption continued to grow every year from 1980 to 1993, while the number of people per household was falling.[10] The BTUs saved in replacing that old refrigerator with a more efficient unit were more than consumed by the new microwave, another air conditioner, a couple of halogen lamps, and the computer.

At present the costs of electricity vary substantially around the country; the utility company that we deal with and the rates we pay are still determined by where we live. Where rates are relatively

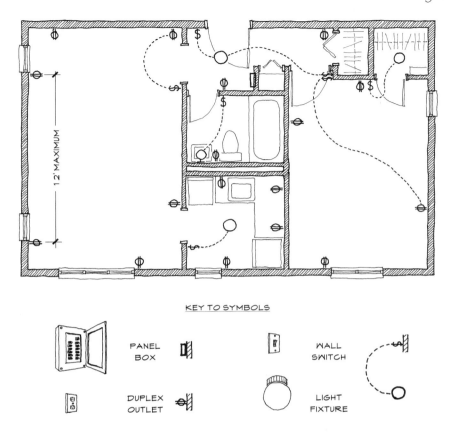

KEY TO SYMBOLS

PANEL BOX

DUPLEX OUTLET

WALL SWITCH

LIGHT FIXTURE

3-13. Electrical wiring snakes its way within the walls and ceilings of a modern home, but we see only the connection points. These should be spaced throughout the home at a maximum distance apart of 12' along the wall. Wall switches may be wired to permanently installed fixtures or to outlets that allow residents to connect table lamps or appliances that can be switched on and off at the wall as they enter or leave the room.

low homes are more likely to use electricity for cooking, hot water, and space heating as well as lighting and appliances, though on a BTU basis it is always far more expensive than natural gas (which is not available everywhere) or heating oil. A process of deregulation already underway but not yet affecting individual homes means that in the future we may be able to buy electricity from competing suppliers, as we now do telephone service. In addition, as photovoltaic cell technology develops and gets cheaper, storing and using solar-generated electrical power may become a more common practice in some areas. All these changes could affect minimum standards for home wiring and electrical use in ways that are hard to predict.

CONNECTIONS TO SOCIETY

In addition to their physical forms and connections, homes have a legal status different from that of any other kind of building. Whether or not we own the home where we live, we have a right to privacy and a freedom of behavior greater there than anywhere else; at home we can take off our clothes, say whatever outrageous things we feel like, and behave in eccentric or even antisocial ways that would certainly get us in trouble in public. The entry doors of rental dwellings must by law have locks that even landlords cannot violate at will. (There is probably no code that actually requires a lock at the entrance to an owner-occupied home, but the same rights exist within.) This separation implies a connection; our homes are in a sense legal extensions of ourselves, protected by our status as members of American society.

A crucial requirement for all homes, then, is identification. Just as we must have birth certificates and social security numbers, part of the process of building any new dwelling is the assignment of a legal address. (Homeless people, with no address, face major obstacles in obtaining services to which they would otherwise be entitled.) Writing is still our official mode of communication, and an address gives us a way to receive mail, though a mailbox does not have to be physically part of or even close to a home. Although we may call other people far more often than we write to them, telephones, and even telephone wiring, are not a requirement for homes. We must be reachable by mail for the census, tax correspondence, and jury duty. Phone service, however, while usually taken for granted, remains, legally, a luxury rather than a necessity.

WHAT'S LEFT OUT OF OUR STANDARDS FOR A BASIC HOME?

When we talk about family homes today in the United States we have a widespread common understanding of their minimum physical components. Any basic home for two people or more should have at least four separate spaces: a living room, possibly including a dining table as well, a separate bedroom, a full indoor bathroom, and a three-fixture kitchen with counters and cabinet space. The living room and bedroom, at a minimum, should have individual operable windows. All spaces should have safe electrical outlets, and the bathroom, kitchen, and any hallways should have built-in ceiling fixtures wired to wall switches. Heating equipment should be such that even in the middle of winter residents can be comfortable in light clothing.

Outside the front door, however, far fewer common assumptions exist. A home might be an apartment whose door opens onto shared indoor or outdoor space, or a house sitting on a discrete piece of property. In either of these cases the adjacent open land could be used as extended working and living space, planted for beauty, or used only for access walks and parking. The house or apartment might connect directly to the public street, which itself might or might not have an adjacent sidewalk and might or might not be paved.

Building codes, which spell out in detail many interior design features intended to keep us safe, are silent regarding most aspects of outdoor safety, even on the private property where a home is built. Children indoors must be protected against exposed wiring and overly steep stairs, but not when outside against open sewers or the omnipresent danger of cars in driveways and streets. While zoning laws do specify many aspects of exterior building design and street layout, these vary widely from one locality to another, and often reflect more concern with visual order than with safety.

Thus, the home illustrated in this chapter could and does exist in a wide variety of outdoor settings far less standardized than its interior. Because the same minimum-standard home could be either a freestanding house, an attached house, or an apartment, the character of these neighborhood settings depends at least in part on the form in which this basic dwelling is built. The next chapters will look briefly at each of these dwelling types, both their general environmental characteristics and their particular pattern of development in this country.

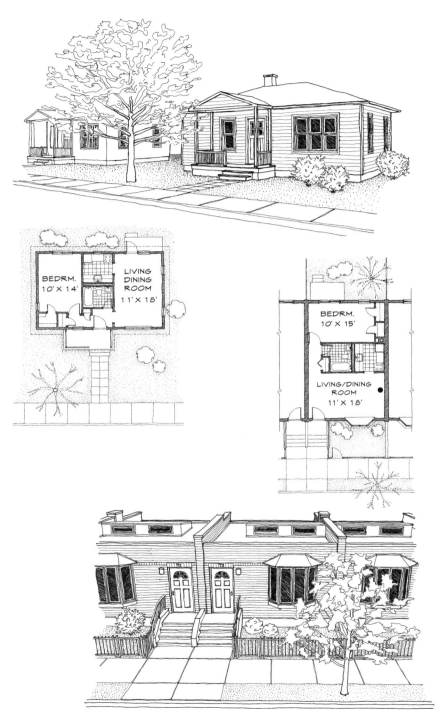

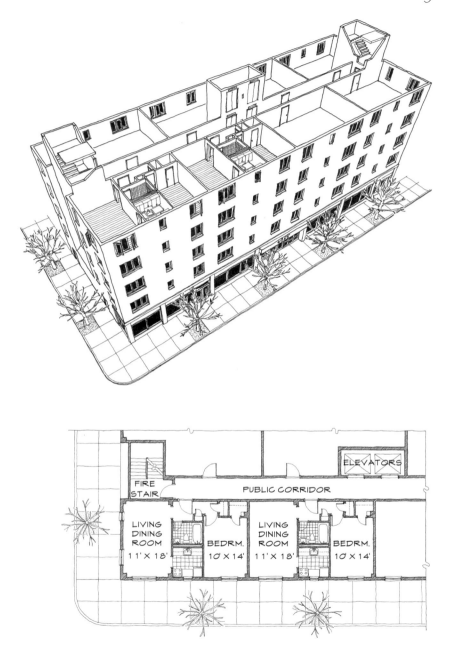

3-14. A basic home with all the spaces and connections that we now require might be built as a freestanding house (opposite, top), an attached house (opposite, bottom), or an apartment (above).

4

FREESTANDING HOUSES

[H]ere they have built competent and decent houses, . . . that every man may have his lodging and dwelling place apart by himself, with a sufficient quantitie of ground allotted thereto for his orchard and garden to plant at his pleasure, and for his own use.

Robert Johnson, description of Henrico, Virginia, in 1612 (quoted in Hugh Morrison, *Early American Architecture*)

An igloo is a freestanding house. So is a 12-by-50-foot trailer in a mobile home park, and so is the White House. In the United States, freestanding single-family houses are the dominant form of dwelling, and many supposedly comprehensive books about American home styles, history, and decorating do not even discuss other forms. This is true for works of architectural and social history as well as for more commercially oriented publications such as patternbooks and magazines. Recent titles as inclusive as *American Shelter*[1] and *The American Family Home 1800–1960*[2] deal only with detached houses, as though all the blocks of rowhouses, twins, and apartments around the country, inhabited both by families and individuals, are neither truly homes nor truly American.

Actual numbers do not justify this exclusion. The proportion of freestanding houses to other forms has varied markedly through United States history. Though the first national Census of Housing was not taken until 1940, other data from earlier years indicate that in 1890 only 41.9 percent of American families who were not farmers lived in detached one-family houses, while another 13.8 percent occupied rowhouses or semiattached units, and 44.3 percent, the greatest proportion, lived in some form of apartment.[3] In this century, while progressively fewer people have actually made their living from the land around them, growing numbers have moved into homes surrounded by open space.

The era of greatest dominance for the freestanding house was the two decades following the Second World War. From 1950 to 1970, site-built detached single-family houses constituted 72 percent of all new home construction, mobile homes an additional 8 percent. Over the following twenty years, however, these proportions changed and the percentage shrank sharply. During the period from 1970 to 1990, only 45 percent of new homes were conventional detached houses, while mobile homes, rechristened in the 1980s as "manufactured housing," increased to 15 percent. Hence, 40 percent of new homes, double the previous level, were now attached houses or apartments.[4]

The focus on freestanding houses, however, reflects more than their prevalence. It stems from deep-seated cultural notions about what makes American life desirable and has been reinforced by laws and governmental policies at federal, state, and local levels. In many neighborhoods a detached one-family house is all that can be built, especially by an individual owner of limited means who does not want to tangle with zoning boards and lawyers.

Many volumes—in fact a whole literature—are devoted to the subject of American freestanding houses: their architectural styles, social meanings, construction, alteration, and furnishings. As an introductory comparison of all three possible housing forms, this book discusses only briefly the stylistic development of freestanding houses. Interested readers will find a great deal of information elsewhere about many, though not all, of the house types discussed here. (Despite the multitude of books about American houses, it is still true that they are unevenly documented, with most attention devoted to those of the wealthy.) Because of gradual changes in family life and dramatic advances in technology, however, the infrastructure and division of spaces within our homes have changed in ways separate from their exterior styles. A Colonial-style house built in the 1960s may have a roof profile, windows, and exterior moldings that resemble one built in the 1700s, but inside and out it is a totally different creature. The latter sections of this chapter examine the coevolution of the exterior forms, interior floor plans, infrastructure, and use of our freestanding houses, to provide a basis for seeing clearly the range of homes and neighborhoods that exist today.

FORMAL AND ENVIRONMENTAL QUALITIES

A freestanding house is surrounded by land, and usually air, on all sides. (Some houses may be dug into the ground on one side or more.) From an environmental point of view, this has built-in benefits as well as drawbacks. One principal advantage is that a home unrestricted by other built structures may be optimally oriented for the movement of the sun, the climate, and the specific conditions of its site. Windows may be designed and located so that they work best for interior light and comfort, exterior views, and cross-ventilation. The house can include covered porches or uncovered outdoor living areas as desired and appropriate to the setting. Because the spread of fire to adjacent structures is less of a threat than for other forms of homes, building codes tend to be less stringent. Thus, the range of materials that can be used to build the house is very wide, and may include those with environmental advantages such as being produced locally or by nontoxic methods.

In practice, of course, other factors frequently override these environmental considerations. Most houses are oriented to the street, with main entrances that are both visible and easily accessible. The location of the front door and the street in turn influence the internal layout. Regardless of compass orientation, the front facade or three-dimensional view of the house from the street is designed as its primary exterior image. That elegant bay window will be put on the front of the house where it adds sculptural interest, even if it faces north and lets in cold drafts. Moreover, the majority of houses in this country are built not singly but in small- or large-scale group developments, with possibly two or three variations or models within each group. On a street that runs east-west, chances are good that identical homes will be built facing both north and south, so that in some the arrangement of openings and overhangs will make sense, from an environmental point of view, and in others it will not.

Even when freestanding houses are not initially well adapted to their sites, however, they can be altered and expanded on any side or from above. That bay window on the front will probably not be removed until it starts to sag or rot, but another might be added where it works better from within the house. Awnings or solid overhangs can be built where necessary to control the light. Sky-

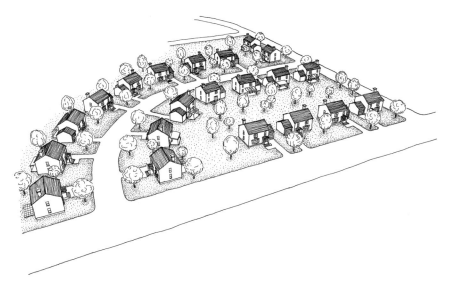

4-1. Houses and the landscaping around them are typically oriented to the view from the public street rather than to the movement of the sun or the direction of local winds. In subdivisions of curving blocks, the result is a random arrangement of homes, with no regard to environmental logic or comfort.

lights can be cut into the roof to light a top floor or a stairwell. In the appropriate settings, solar panels can be installed to cope with some of the energy demands. After living in a house for several years, its residents may have a much stronger sense than the designer ever did about where they would actually use a porch, an outside deck, or additional indoor space. Unless there are strict prohibitions on changes (and often even when there are), houses in large-scale developments gradually acquire more and more individuality. In *How Buildings Learn: What Happens After They're Built*, Stewart Brand observes, "Domestic buildings—homes—are the steadiest changers, responding directly to the family's ideas and annoyances, growth and prospects. The house and its occupants mold to each other twenty-four hours a day, and the building accumulates the record of that intimacy."[5]

While changes take place in homes of all types, freestanding houses offer the greatest range of design options to their residents, especially for expansion. With less stringent building code requirements permitting lighter-weight and often cheaper materials, the actual construction of changes and additions may more readily be undertaken by homeowners themselves. Most local governments honor and encourage this activity by treating single-family houses differently from other buildings. Homeowners undertaking their own work are frequently allowed to proceed with a modest diagram rather than the extensive drawings, filing, and inspection required of large-scale developers or for other building types. However, the changes that people envision when they move into a house sometimes turn out not to be possible; zoning regulations commonly create an invisible inner rectangle on a building lot through minimum size requirements for front-, side-, and back-yards, into which a house cannot extend.

A third potential advantage to a freestanding house is the land on all sides, which, in fact, defines it. The uses of this personal outdoor area and the ways in which it is valued have changed steadily during the several hundred years of United States history. As recently as 150 years ago, all the natural and mechanical connections necessary to a safe, comfortable, and sanitary dwelling had to be local. Every home needed a source of clean water. Dirty water, human waste, and garbage all had to be disposed of close by. Laundry had to dry. Before toys and electronics were widely manufactured and marketed, the outdoors provided most raw materials as well as space for children's play. Even if a family did not farm for a living, they most likely grew vegetables and possibly raised chickens or pigs for their own consumption. If they owned horses and wheeled carts or carriages, these also needed to be housed. Furthermore, in many climates outdoor living, cooking, and even sleeping areas were more comfortable than indoor ones at some times of year; the porch and the yard were often more heavily used than the parlor.

Depending on the community where a house was built, not all of these functions took place on its individual lot. Villages, towns, and cities often had a common well or other water supply, a sewage system, and maybe even a town dump. But virtually every dwelling, whether it was freestanding, attached, or some form of apartment, needed to use its immediate outdoor space, and this naturally gave freestanding houses an advantage.

Many such functional requirements for outdoor areas adjacent to homes were eliminated by the technological advances that gradually became standard features of American dwellings. Indoor plumbing obviated the need to go outside for water or to use a privy. Sanitary sewers carried soiled water away to some distant point of disposal, so that odors and wastes were no longer dispersed into the local atmosphere or absorbed by the soil. Electrical wiring led to the invention of appliances that increased our indoor self-sufficiency. Dryers, for instance, replaced outdoor clotheslines. Refrigeration, both within homes and throughout the food industry, made it easier to have fresh produce on hand without growing it in the backyard. The combination of air-conditioners and television reduced our inclination to sit on the porch on hot summer evenings. Within the last fifteen years indoor entertainment for children, theoretically the heaviest users of backyards, has gone far beyond simple television. Even in the safest, most picturesque neighborhoods, energetic ten-year-olds now spend entire sunny afternoons indoors playing video or computer games. And because of changes in women's work patterns, preschool children, for whom backyards were always more suitable than for older kids, are likely to do more of their outdoor playing at nursery school or day care.

So if there is rarely laundry hanging on the line, only occasional vegetable gardens, few children playing outside, and no one sitting on the porch, how is all the land around American houses now being used? Certainly many people feel strongly about how this land should look, and spend either a lot of time caring for their lawns and plants or a lot of money paying someone else to do so. But the major use of the private land around our freestanding houses now involves another technological innovation of the early twentieth century, one that allowed more Americans to live in them in the first place. Essentially, we now need the land around our homes so that we can house, safely manipulate, and be as close as possible to our cars. Any designer or builder laying out a new house must figure out first where it and its garage can sit, and then where the driveway will go. (Cars have a much bigger turning radius than humans or horses.) If the area on the lot around these elements constitutes usable outdoor space, so much the better, but this is not a necessity.

Of course, just because there are now fewer functions for which we actually need open land around our homes doesn't mean we no longer want it. Most people still enjoy some outdoor living area

—a deck, porch, patio, or planted yard—for at least occasional use. Sadly, however, these are much easier to sandwich into the odd, leftover space than are automobiles, and if they are not very usable then they simply sit empty or become permanent storage spaces. It also takes a longer period of living in a house to see if such outdoor areas really work than it does for driveways.

The final advantage that many Americans might cite in choosing a freestanding house is one of privacy. When it comes to home design this is a hard concept to define with precision. Certainly, if we can neither see any neighbor's house nor hear any other human activity, then we do have an absolute kind of privacy. But even with the vast amount of land in this country, most of us do not have and probably do not want total seclusion. Instead, our family privacy depends both on how our homes are built and on the way we and our neighbors inhabit them. Though an isolated house clearly allows for more solitude than any other form of home, freestanding houses, as they are grouped in typical American neighborhoods, are not necessarily more private than apartments or attached houses.

In Asia, Africa, Europe, and South America, many cultures have developed basic house forms, both freestanding and attached, that feature walled compounds or courtyards clearly defining and enclosing a private outdoor realm. These forms developed over centuries when all dwellings needed outdoor space for many of the functions that we have now brought indoors. Some developed in societies where certain family members, especially women, worked and socialized almost entirely within their extended family, rarely going out in public. From a purely physical point of view, these homes make very efficient use of the outdoor space that is available by enclosing it. A 5-foot-high solid wall with a gate can create enough privacy for household activities to take place between the front of the house and the street. Furthermore, an enclosed outdoor courtyard can also function as an entry foyer, reducing the need for such space within the house itself.

In the United States, by contrast, our yards are most often not walled. Zoning ordinances in some towns and regulations in many private developments specifically forbid fences and walls or restrict their height. The reasons for this significant difference between our house forms and those of many other countries are

4-2. The front courtyard in a traditional Tokyo house (based on drawings made in the 1880s). The entry path was defined by carefully placed paving stones, and the view of the outdoor cooking area was screened from the gate by an angled wall. The one-story wing beyond the grill holds the latrine. Thus many uses, both formal and functional, were accommodated within a small yard right next to the street.

complicated and could be attributed to any number of our cultural and political traditions. However, several factors—physical and economic as well as cultural—certainly play a prominent role. In most parts of this country land has been relatively plentiful and inexpensive, so that its efficient use has not been a priority. To separate different functions and to create some degree of family privacy we have been able to substitute extra horizontal space for vertical divisions or soundproof construction. Our front doors, for example, are typically exposed to the street but set back from it by an area of open land where virtually no household activities occur. This public front yard can be very gracious, effectively adding width to the street and giving residents a full view out while somewhat shielding the view into the house from passersby. But it is too exposed to act as an outdoor foyer, like a walled courtyard, so it does not replace interior entry spaces.

Not just the availability of land but also our standards of beauty affect the way we set our houses along the street. Since the early

1800s we have been heavily influenced by a picturesque and romantic approach to landscape design that places homes and often other buildings as well in a seemingly casual, pastoral setting of carefully arranged plants and broad expanses of grass. Historically, this tradition evolved from the asymmetrical, naturalistic gardens created on English estates in the eighteenth and early nineteenth centuries, and from the work of landscape painters on both sides of the Atlantic. As an image for middle-class homes, it was initially popularized in the United States through the writings of a young landscaping contractor named Andrew Jackson Downing. In two influential books, *Cottage Residences* (1842) and *The Architecture of Country Houses* (1850), he showed plans and sketches of houses and the planting around them, expounding at length on the ability of these dwellings to raise the moral and aesthetic sensibilities of their inhabitants. Though Downing described the homes he advocated as "simple" and "honest," they were far from pragmatic workaday rural homes with farming implements and vegetable plots in full view:

> Especially should attention be paid to disposing the plan so that the kitchen and its offices should be placed upon a screened or blind side, or one that can be concealed by planting. There should be room for a kitchen yard or court, connected . . . to the stable, and all quite turned away from the lawn or entrance side of the house.[6]

The house styles shown in Downing's books remained popular only for a few decades, but the notion of a planted and open front lawn, with all service functions banished to an unseen backyard, has endured. Moreover, the planting patterns first developed in the temperate and humid British Isles have been applied in widely varied regions of the United States, where they are often at odds with the climate and terrain. Virtually every style of American house built in the last century and a half has been shown, for illustration and promotion, standing on its own surrounded by "nature": a carefully designed array of shrubs, trees, and grass. Real estate brochures and the bulletin boards of brokers' offices are lined with photos of individual houses with greenery on all visible sides. Neighboring buildings are not shown, regardless of how close they might be.

4-3. A. J. Downing's 1850 design for a "small Bracketed Cottage," envisioned as a workingman's home. Downing recommended growing vines against the house for "domesticity and the presence of heart." The image of a modest house on its own in a bucolic setting has remained powerful in the United States; for many people it is still an essential part of the American dream.

This tradition is so strong that it is commonly applied even where it does not completely work. As individual houses get closer together, the side yards between them become more and more like alleys or indoor corridors, dark and hard to landscape. Sometimes, of course, these spaces are essential as driveways, but there are also development patterns where they exist simply as separators. If there are windows along these alleys, as is usually the case, sounds can reverberate between buildings, and visual privacy is achieved only with curtains. Were such houses to be attached, with heavy masonry walls between them, they would actually have greater visual and acoustic privacy, but the satisfaction of envisioning each house as a separate and complete entity would be gone.

What are the environmental disadvantages of a freestanding house? Some are fairly straightforward. Any object loses or gains heat through its surface; if two objects have the same volume but a different surface area, the one with more surface will lose its heat

4-4. Even houses built cheek by jowl on narrow lots are typically designed without adjustment for the proximity of neighbors.

faster. Thus, detached houses are inherently less efficient to heat and cool than attached houses and apartment buildings. A freestanding house loses heat on all sides and through its roof. If a house of the same size is attached on one or two sides to another heated building, less heat is lost and not as much fuel required to keep the indoors warm. It will consume even less energy if, in addition to being attached on one or more sides, there is another heated dwelling above it. These same considerations apply in comparing one freestanding house to another, so a compact multistory house is more efficient to heat than a rambling single-story structure.

Though greater surface area relative to volume is an inherent drawback of the freestanding house, other factors affect its energy consumption as well and may in some cases compensate. The insulating effectiveness, or *R-value*, of a building's exterior is also a determinant of its heat gain and loss. Thus, the materials and construction of its roof, outer walls, and components such as doors and windows all count; a well-built house, despite its greater exposure, may in some cases be more energy-efficient than a poorly built apartment of the same size. Thanks to the flexibility of their orientation, freestanding houses can also be deliberately laid out to minimize heat loss or gain. Incorporating passive solar design, which depends on capturing, storing, and recirculating the sun's heat without fans or pumps, is far easier than with more restricted housing forms. In the United States, where detached houses predominate, they have been the focus of most of the research and the products developed since the 1970s to reduce residential fuel consumption.

Less obvious disadvantages of the freestanding house have to do with the process of its construction and the network of services to which it must then be connected. The erection of any building involves a staging area much larger than the site occupied by the final structure. Large machines must be able to get to the property and need plenty of maneuvering room. Materials must be delivered, unloaded, and stored. Workers want to park as nearby as possible. When excavation is required for foundations or basements, it is cheaper to leave the dirt, rocks, and uprooted plant material on the site than to cart it away. Consequently, it is often used to raise the level of low-lying areas, a technique generally known as *cut and fill*, which permanently alters the local topography.

All new building involves this process of change and destruction, but the creation of freestanding houses cuts a particularly wide swath. Because each house has its own staging area, the total amount of land affected by the construction of a group of such houses is much greater than it would be were they simply attached in a row, even with the identical footprint on the ground. The most common practice in building new developments, in fact, is to clear the entire area to be subdivided into individual home lots and replant it, to some degree, after construction is finished. Thus the green surroundings of our freestanding houses, lauded as natural and healthy in defense of suburban living, almost never grow out of the preexisting site. They are purchased and installed by the builder, or the lot is left mostly bare, usually sown with grass, for future residents to plant as they choose.

In addition, as our homes have come to rely less on the land immediately around them and more on services provided from a distant location, the construction and installation of these connections has had a growing impact on the surrounding environment. The length of pipe needed and the amount of earth excavated to connect a freestanding house to a water main are obviously greater than for other forms of homes, and the same is

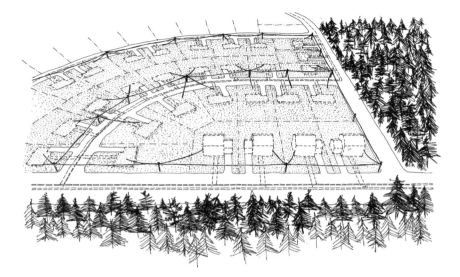

4-5. Erecting a group of new houses requires the installation of extensive above- and below-ground utilities as well as the construction of streets and buildings. Because it is most economical in the short term, builders usually raze the entire site, despite the environmental consequences.

true for sewers, electrical and phone lines, and cable television connections.

The areas covered by pavement stay visible and permanently change drainage patterns, but the rest of this destruction and intervention on the land itself quickly becomes hard to see. Even without human assistance, a new plant cover grows on bulldozed earth in all but the driest climates. Walking through a neighborhood of thirty-year-old houses we may admire the flowering shrubs and the large shade trees with squirrels running along their branches and imagine the area, before human habitation, as having looked the same, minus the houses and streets, with some large animals prowling about. In the same way, many city dwellers view large parks as remnants of a preexisting natural landscape without realizing the extent to which they have been carefully designed and built.

To say that the clearing of land for neighborhoods of freestanding homes is an environmental disadvantage may seem unduly judgmental. Like constructed public open spaces such as Central

Park in New York or Golden Gate Park in San Francisco, much of the private land around freestanding houses is beautiful, or becomes so over time, as trees grow and residents cultivate a quilt of individual landscapes. Though most of the original plants and animals are killed or displaced, others, both foreign and indigenous, take hold and thrive. Furthermore, as often as not, new neighborhoods are created not from undeveloped land but from areas with a previous human use, such as farms. Even some areas that we now consider pristine wilderness were in fact manipulated by humans for thousands of years. Native American tribes along the northeast coast, for instance, habitually burned large sections of underbrush in the forests of tall trees in order to create an open, sunlit forest floor that favored the growth of berries and grasses, and hence the game animals, such as deer and elk, that fed on them.[7]

The issue in comparing different housing forms is not that all human intervention on existing land is necessarily evil or even avoidable. Rather, in the case of freestanding houses, it is that the scale of the intervention is larger than it later appears, and that its consequences are therefore hard to appreciate or fully understand. This is particularly true today, when the web of technological and transportation connections that sustains modern homes of all forms is so elaborate and far-reaching. Seeing our houses as discrete, independent objects erected against a backdrop of nature, we discount the extent to which the whole setting has been designed and altered to our human purposes.

EVOLUTION OF COLONIAL HOUSES

The Europeans who settled along the coast of North America in the 1600s and 1700s brought with them building skills and ideas about what their homes should look like. These were based on the traditional designs and construction practices of their native countries and had to be adapted to a new climate and to the materials locally available. In the first years of a new settlement, a variety of makeshift shelters was constructed. One account of Boston in 1630, two years after its founding, describes "wigwams, mud-walled huts and tents of dilapidated sails mingled on the

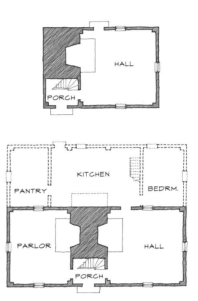

4-6. Early New England colonial houses often had only one ground floor room, the "hall," and a second-story bedroom above. Many were later enlarged with a formal parlor on the back side of the fireplace and rear additions like those shown by dotted lines. Larger houses retained the same basic floor plan and still little decoration beyond the typical cornices on the chimney and the wood pendants under the second floor overhang.

shore of the bay with gaunt frame houses still the raw color of new-cut lumber."[8]

During what must have been a difficult period of trial and error, settlers gradually became familiar and secure enough in their new environment to devise consistent regional house forms. They modified older European designs in ways appropriate to the varied climates up and down the eastern seaboard. Thus, typical houses developed differently in the cold New England colonies than they did in the warm and humid southern ones, though there were English settlers in both regions.

Early New England houses were compact. They had relatively small windows, low ceilings that retained heat in the harsh winters, and steeply pitched roofs to keep snow from accumulating. Even houses with only a single ground-floor room often had two stories, the upper one reached by a steeply winding stair and used for sleeping and storage. Larger houses had two first-floor rooms: the *hall*, used for day-to-day family activities, and a smaller, more formal *parlor*, where guests were entertained. Chimneys and fireplaces

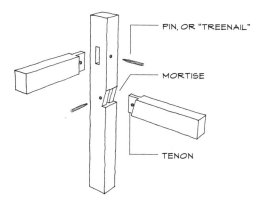

PIN, OR "TREENAIL"

MORTISE

TENON

4-7. Mortise and tenon joints were constructed entirely of hand-hewn wood. They were secured by wood "treenails" but did not depend on them for bearing or strength.

were in the center of the house where they could warm all rooms as efficiently as possible, given that fireplaces are never very efficient.

These houses were often expanded with a single-story rear addition that continued the steep roofline, giving them the characteristic asymmetrical shape that became known as a *saltbox*. The principal use of this addition was to create a separate kitchen, though it sometimes included a pantry or bedroom as well. For cooking and heat, a third fireplace was let in to the existing massive chimney.

The supporting structure of these houses was a heavy timber frame, the same system used at the time in much of England. Large tree trunks, generally oak, were hand-hewn to form the major posts and beams, as large as 10 or 12 inches on a side. In a time-consuming process they were notched and connected at their ends with carefully wrought mortise and tenon joints that did not depend on nails, still largely unavailable. This method created a durable structure but required both skilled carpenters and a large crew of men to handle the heavy individual components.

Other English building traditions did not work so well on this side of the Atlantic. The common practice of infilling between the timbers with a lattice of small sticks (*wattle*) covered with clay (*daub*), creating the English *half-timbered style*, quickly proved insufficiently weather-tight for the North American climate. Taking advantage of the abundance of wood in their new environment,

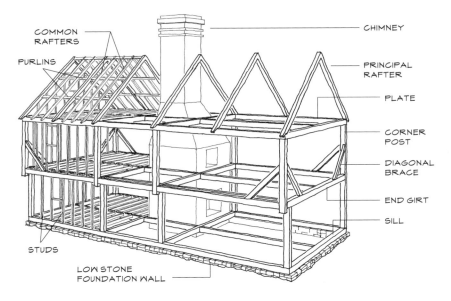

COMMON RAFTERS

PURLINS

STUDS

LOW STONE FOUNDATION WALL

CHIMNEY

PRINCIPAL RAFTER

PLATE

CORNER POST

DIAGONAL BRACE

END GIRT

SILL

4-8. Typical structural components of a timber-framed colonial house.

the settlers came to favor a more effective system for keeping out cold, snow, and rain. They used overlapping boards, or *siding*, to create a continuous skin that covered the previously exposed timber frame members as well as the spaces between them.

Southern homes were somewhat more spread out, allowing for better air circulation than those in New England. Fireplaces and chimneys were usually at one or both ends of the elongated plan, probably so that cooking could be done during warm weather without heating up the entire home. Without a central fireplace, the entry hall generally ran straight through the house and accommodated more activity. While many homes used the same basic timber frame and wood siding as those further north, more early houses in the South were made of brick, drawing on established British traditions of masonry building and reflecting the higher social status in England of some southern colonists. The Tidewater region in and around Virginia had a large supply of high-quality clay as well as deposits of lime for durable, watertight mortar; these were lacking in New England.

Though some large two-story homes were built, a greater number of houses in the South than in the North were single-story

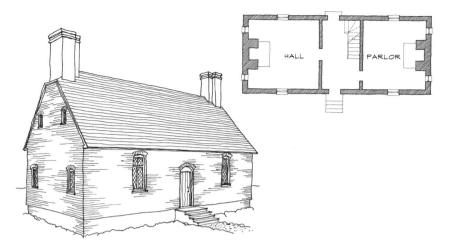

4-9. The small brick houses built by Southern colonists in the 1600s often resembled those of medieval England. Their double chimneys were sometimes set inside the end walls, as shown here; sometimes they protruded from the body of the house.

4-10. Simple hall-and-parlor houses, most commonly of wood, remained a widespread southern form through the 1800s. The continuous roofed porch helped to keep the interior cool and accommodated many family activities.

dwellings. One widespread southern innovation was a continuous roofed porch across the front facade, creating a shaded outdoor living area that was usable during rain and that protected the interior from direct sun. Those who could afford it also built their homes with high ceilings and large windows to improve ventilation.

4-11. Built around 1784, the Dyckman Farmhouse was the home of a prosperous Dutch family who owned extensive orchards in northern Manhattan. The characteristic gambrel roof extends over front and back porches. The house still sits on upper Broadway, now surrounded by apartment buildings and stores.

Below New England and above Virginia, along the mid-Atlantic coast, settlers came not just from England but from a number of other countries in northern Europe. The early city of New Amsterdam, founded in 1626 on Manhattan Island, was the geographic center of a region of Dutch settlements that extended north up the Hudson River valley, east onto Long Island, and west into New Jersey. Dutch building techniques, for both wood framing and brick, were similar to those used in England at the time, although masonry construction was predominant in Holland and the bricklaying more skillful.[9] Similar techniques, however, produced distinctive house forms and details; these persisted in America. While not the only form built by these settlers, the Dutch farmhouse, with stone or wood exterior walls and a broad, overhanging gambrel roof, its slope changing partway down, became well-known and has been much copied in the twentieth century.

A different method of construction was brought from regions of Europe that, unlike England and Holland, were still heavily

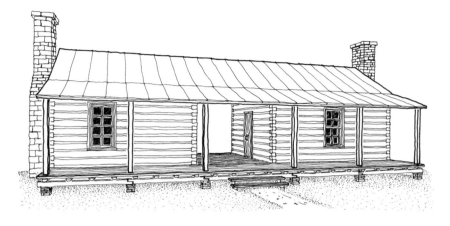

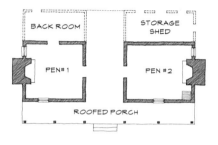

4-12. The dogtrot cabin, common in rural Arkansas and North Carolina, was a log house with two square "pens" separated by a roofed outdoor living area that also served as entry foyer. Rear additions were often added with less durable stud construction and with entry only from outside, unless the original log structures had rear doors. When previously rural areas grew more heavily settled, many dogtrot houses were enclosed to provide greater privacy.

forested. It may have been Swedish settlers in Delaware and Pennsylvania who originally introduced log-building techniques, but these were quickly adapted by the Germans and the Scotch-Irish as well.[10] This system utilized interlocking logs, stacked horizontally and notched and joined at the corners. Requiring a large volume of wood, it created massive, solid walls that eliminated the need for separate exterior and interior skins and went together more quickly than timber frames. In the new colonies, where trees were plentiful but tools and labor scarce, log houses were logical and durable. Their main disadvantage, as any modern child who plays with Lincoln Logs discovers, is that, once built, they are hard to alter or extend. Houses constructed this way are generally made up of separate *pens* or square, one-room units.

Most permanent log houses in the early United States, like those in Europe, used logs that had been hewn with an ax to a rectangular shape, so that they stacked tightly. Sometimes, to create an extra layer of weather protection or simply to make them look more like frame houses, they were covered with an outer layer of overlapping siding boards. As new settlers pushed inland, these houses spread from mid-Atlantic coastal areas into the Appalachian regions of central Pennsylvania, West Virginia, and Tennessee, where many examples still survive because they are so solidly built.

Distinctive house forms developed early in other parts of North America as well. In the Southwest, for instance, with its dry climate and canyon terrain, Native American tribes already had a well-developed tradition of building with *adobe* (mud bricks). They used wood sparingly, mostly to support their roofs, as indigenous trees were both small and sparse. The Spaniards who first explored and established missions in the area adapted their own traditions of masonry building to this new environment. What evolved in the Spanish territories were mostly single-story houses with heavy masonry walls made either of adobe bricks or of stone covered with stucco. Roofs were of two kinds: flat, with tile or wood drains projecting through parapet walls, or gently sloped and usually covered with semi-circular clay tiles like those used in the Mediterranean countries.

The growth pattern of Spanish colonial houses was quite unlike that of those in the east. Rooms were added in a linear fashion, so that houses remained only one room deep. New wings built at right angles created L- or U-shaped structures enclosing open courtyards, shaded and protected from strong winds. Providing the main circulation between rooms was a covered exterior walkway that bordered the courtyard; this *corridor* became a much-used outdoor living space, more private than the front porches of the Southeast.

While these and other early American house types differed greatly from one another in their materials, structure, and adaptations to climate, their interiors varied less. Each had at most a few rooms of similar size and shape, sometimes with a small central hall that could include stairs. Many had no separate circulation spaces at all. Inside most of the earliest houses, all rooms were used for multiple purposes. This was partly because homes were small in relation to the number of people living there but

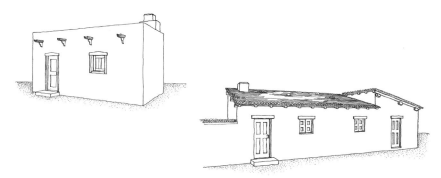

4-13. The earliest houses built in the southwestern Spanish territories had only small window openings, usually with wood shutters and no glass. The masonry walls absorbed heat during the day, keeping the interior cool, and released it to warm the inside space during cold desert nights. Flat-roofed houses predominated in the territories that would become Texas, New Mexico, and Arizona, while sloping tile roofs were typical of California.

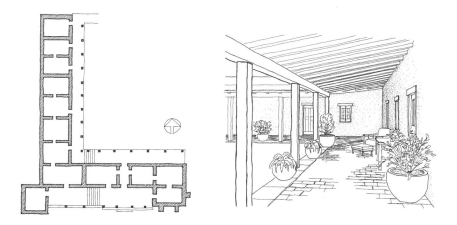

4-14. Left, a schematic floor plan showing walls and door openings in a large California house built in stages starting in 1839. Separate sections of the house were not connected internally but by a walkway bordering the southern and western sides of the courtyard. On the right is a view of a typical such *corredor.*

also because little special equipment was built into any space, despite the many separate tasks to be done. The fire for cooking was also the fire for heating, and water was carried in from outdoors, so nothing about the physical nature of a given room defined it as a kitchen. Daily household work, family cooking and meals, and sleeping for some family members commonly took place within a single room.

As some Americans accumulated wealth and expanded their homes or built new ones, rooms became more specialized. By the 1700s, throughout the thirteen colonies, freestanding houses constructed for well-to-do families were larger and had more exterior ornament as well. Instead of the earlier two-room hall-and-parlor plans, with assorted additions, the typical large house plan of the eighteenth and early nineteenth centuries had four rooms on a floor, two on either side of a central hall. In addition to separate kitchens and bedrooms, there were now such single-use spaces (at least nominally) as dining rooms, studies, libraries, and formal drawing rooms.

Even in these larger homes, however, rooms tended to be roughly the same size and shape, limited by the structural system and the need to be heated from a single point. As access to every room was from the same generous entrance hallway and each room had its own fireplace, they were often virtually interchangeable. This interior regularity was also reflected on the exterior. Americans who could afford to build elaborate homes generally adopted the same style popular in England at the time. Whether in brick or in wood, it included simple, classically inspired details, with building facades as symmetrical as possible and identically sized windows lined up horizontally and vertically. Hence, from the outside, even on an ornate house, there was little to distinguish a formal drawing room from a sleeping chamber; indeed, public spaces were sometimes placed on upper floors.

Because indoor plumbing was almost nonexistent and many daily household activities still took place outside, the outdoor spaces around these large houses were actually far more differentiated than their interior rooms. The site plan of the elegant Gibbes house, built in 1775 in Charleston, South Carolina, shows how a range of uses from outhouse and drying yard to formal rose garden were all carefully laid out within a large, walled city lot.

4-15. Like most eighteenth century town and city houses, the William Gibbes house in Charleston, S.C., faced the street directly. Large side and rear yards were beautifully landscaped and also served crucial outdoor functions. Public spaces and bedrooms were interspersed on both floors.

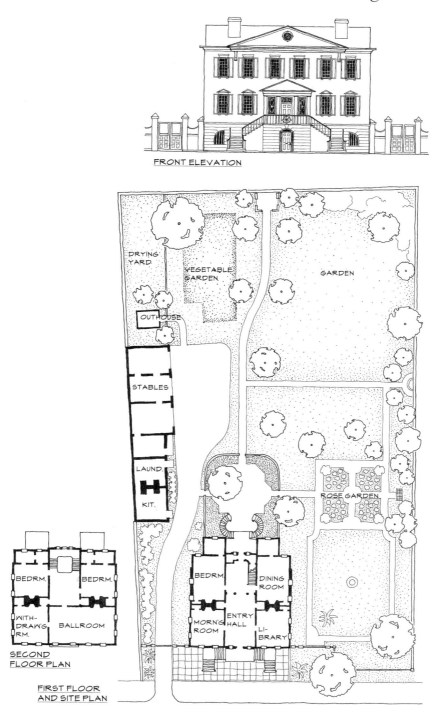

FRONT ELEVATION

DRYING YARD

VEGETABLE GARDEN

GARDEN

OUTHOUSE

STABLES

LAUND.

KIT.

ROSE GARDEN

BEDRM.

DINING ROOM

MORN'G ROOM

ENTRY HALL

LI-BRARY

BEDRM.

BEDRM.

WITH-DRAW'G RM.

BALLROOM

SECOND FLOOR PLAN

FIRST FLOOR AND SITE PLAN

Stud Wall Construction and the Balloon Frame

By the early 1800s, changes in the technology of building in the United States had begun to influence the form and construction of houses. Many commercial lumber mills were operating in forested regions, supplying identically sized sawn pieces of wood throughout much of the new nation. The ready availability of this milled wood for small framing members as well as siding, shingles, and trim undoubtedly made house-building easier. Even modest houses now became more style conscious, including new ornamental details around doors and windows. However, the large oak timbers used for the posts and beams of most house frames were still cut by hand on site, probably because they were too heavy and awkward to transport to and from a mill.[11]

What revolutionized wood construction in this country was the combination of milled lumber with inexpensive, machine-made nails, which became available in the 1830s. By eliminating the handwrought, mortised joints that had held wood buildings together for centuries, nails allowed the invention of a new and far more rapid system of building. Stud walls, assembled from thin, closely spaced pieces of milled lumber, were nailed together to form a rigid frame. Corner posts were built up from multiple studs, and all parts of a house above the foundation—exterior walls, interior walls, floors, and roof—worked together to give the structure stability and strength.

Probably because of its lightness relative to earlier timber frames, the system of stud wall construction commonly used in nineteenth-century houses was dubbed the *balloon frame*. Supporting walls were made up of vertical studs that extended from the top of the foundation to the roof rafters, with intermediate floors hung from this framework. During the twentieth century, this system would be modified to a more rigid one known as *platform framing*, in which multistory houses were built one floor at a time, with upper floors sitting directly on single-story stud walls below.

Used first in Chicago in 1839, the balloon frame had distinct advantages over older framing systems. Stud walls can be erected quickly and do not require skilled carpenters; with a little practice,

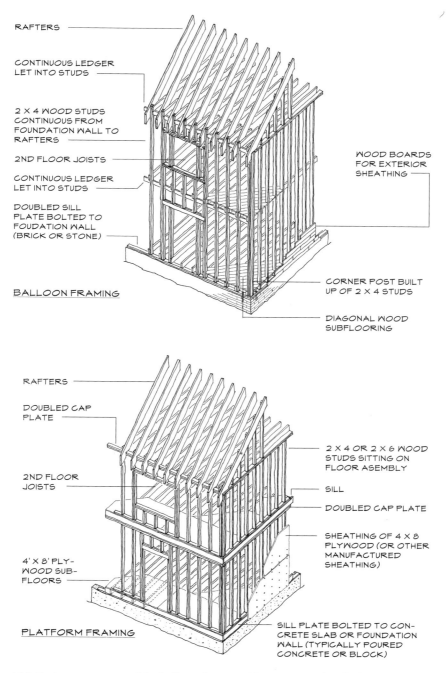

RAFTERS

CONTINUOUS LEDGER
LET INTO STUDS

2 X 4 WOOD STUDS
CONTINUOUS FROM
FOUNDATION WALL TO
RAFTERS

2ND FLOOR JOISTS

CONTINUOUS LEDGER
LET INTO STUDS

DOUBLED SILL
PLATE BOLTED TO
FOUDATION WALL
(BRICK OR STONE)

BALLOON FRAMING

WOOD BOARDS
FOR EXTERIOR
SHEATHING

CORNER POST BUILT
UP OF 2 X 4 STUDS

DIAGONAL WOOD
SUBFLOORING

RAFTERS

DOUBLED CAP
PLATE

2ND FLOOR
JOISTS

4' X 8' PLY-
WOOD SUB-
FLOORS

PLATFORM FRAMING

2 X 4 OR 2 X 6 WOOD
STUDS SITTING ON
FLOOR ASEMBLY

SILL

DOUBLED CAP PLATE

SHEATHING OF 4 X 8
PLYWOOD (OR OTHER
MANUFACTURED
SHEATHING)

SILL PLATE BOLTED TO CON-
CRETE SLAB OR FOUNDATION
WALL (TYPICALLY POURED
CONCRETE OR BLOCK)

4-16. Basic components of the balloon frame and its successor, the platform (or western) frame. Wood stud framing has evolved with changes in available materials, especially new metal connectors and laminated wood products such as plywood.

almost anyone can learn to drive in a nail. Because mortise and tenon joints required such craftsmanship, most earlier houses had been built as simple rectangles to minimize the number of connections. Now that framing inside and outside corners was easier and less time-consuming, more irregular and complicated house plans became possible.

An important quality of all stud wall houses was that they could be made to look like almost anything. The structural system supporting them was an open skeleton, which had to be covered outside and in with some kind of skin, or *cladding* material. One example of this was the overlapping clapboard siding already in wide use on older Colonial houses; others gave the illusion of a completely different structural system. Thin pieces of stone or cement stucco over rough boards applied to the studs, for example, could make a wood house look like one built of masonry. (In the twentieth century *brick veneer* is a widespread example of this illusion.) On a single framed house, different cladding materials could also be combined, permitting great variety in exterior design.

The development of the balloon frame allowed for considerable inventive thinking. It came along in an era of continuous change, the same period when growing industrial neighborhoods began to transform the landscapes of American cities. With high rates of immigration, the nation's population more than tripled between 1820 and 1860, from 9.6 to 31.4 million people. Finding the streets and buildings around them becoming congested and chaotic, many established middle- and upper-class city dwellers responded by moving. In areas farther from commercial downtowns, they built new homes that they hoped would prove more enduring. With all this uncertainty, the proper design of houses and their purported role in creating stable, moral American families became the focus of intense popular interest. Building designers, political thinkers, and social reformers all got involved in advocating new home designs and new types of neighborhoods.

Blessed with a seemingly infinite supply of land and lumber as well as a novel method of rapid construction, middle-class and wealthy Americans quickly got used to spacious homes in these freshly built neighborhoods. The standards and expectations for a modest house in the United States became and have remained far higher than those of the rest of the world, even of comparably wealthy countries. However, the obverse of the stud wall's ease and speed of assembly is its quick deterioration. Without vigilant exterior maintenance to keep them dry, thin studs rot quickly and nailed joints rust and lose strength. Stud wall houses burn in a flash. The hand-hewn joints and heavy timbers of older frame construction were far more durable. In neighborhoods that continued to change quickly, however, the relatively short lifespan of many houses was not widely noticed.

Notwithstanding a high rate of construction, home-building remained a small-scale and fragmented industry throughout most of the nineteenth century. While real estate investment and speculation were rampant, new homes were built only one or two at a time. Professional architects were few, and for those who did use the title there was no required training or licensing. Builders were self-taught or learned their trade through local apprenticeships. For both design inspiration and technical guidance, builders, developers, and homeowners often relied on published sets of house designs, or *patternbooks*, containing scaled drawings, rendered illustrations, and decorative details for a range of model houses. In keeping with the country's democratic ideals, and to appeal to as large an audience as possible, these usually included homes of differing sizes, some theoretically affordable by "families of modest means" as well as wealthier ones. (Often, however, the actual construction cost of a patternbook house proved to be much higher than the published estimate.[12]) Freestanding wood houses predominated in these manuals, but many also showed attached houses with exterior masonry walls, for construction on narrow lots.

In the 1700s and early 1800s, the popular styles for buildings with any formal pretentions, including houses, had been based on changing interpretations of older Greek and Roman forms. From about 1840 on, these gave way to a rapid succession of new fashions, most based very loosely on other periods of history. The flexibility and economy of balloon frame construction, together with the proliferation of precut, off-the-shelf ornamental elements, made it possible for American houses to become increasingly varied and ornate. Widely circulating patternbooks and the continual development of new ones helped to spread awareness around the country of the latest styles.

Among the earliest such collections of house plans sold in the United States were the works of Andrew Jackson Downing, popularizer of the open front lawn. Wordier than later patternbooks, they contained lengthy moral justifications for the schemes presented:

> in America, not only is the distinct family the best social form, but those elementary forces which give rise to the highest genius and the finest character may, for the most part, be traced back to the farmhouse and the rural cottage. It is the solitude and freedom of the family home in the country which constantly preserves the purity of the nation, and invigorates its intellectual powers.[13]

While such rationales for new house designs were no doubt reassuring to mobile middle-class families, even when they were actually displacing the agricultural countryside rather than building truly rural homes, it was largely the visual appeal of the homes that accounted for Downing's wide audience. In 1850, when he published *The Architecture of Country Houses,* even his simplest and smallest "workingman's cottage" skillfully made use of the potential of the stud wall system for more irregular and picturesque plans, representing a real departure from earlier rectangular house forms.

Other nineteenth-century technological advances also accelerated the spread of balloon-framed houses. By the 1850s a growing network of long-distance railroads was transporting both people and goods. Over the next half-century, as it expanded across the continent, milled lumber, nails, and other construction materials became newly available in regions where they were not produced. In regions with dry climates or grasslands, such as Texas, Kansas, and southern California, lumber yards were set up near the new train stations to sell wood from distant forests, precut to standard framing sizes or into stock sections of moldings and trim. People could now build more quickly than they had previously, and more easily imitate fashionable homes about which they had read or which they had seen. Stud wall construction was often used for additions to earlier regional forms such as the adobe houses of the Southwest, resulting in homes that became a kind of history of local building in themselves.

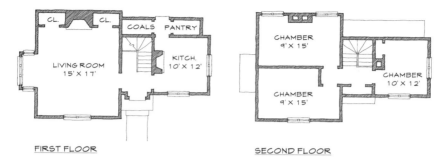

FIRST FLOOR   SECOND FLOOR

4-17. Floor plans of A. J. Downing's "small Bracketed Cottage" (shown on p. 115). Before balloon framing, a modest house with a deliberately irregular plan or features like the single-story window bay off the living room would have been rare.

Because of the increasing availability of framing lumber, regional differences in home-building became much less pronounced through the second half of the nineteenth century, though they never totally disappeared. While patternbooks with the latest styles were circulated nationally, every house went up on a specific site. A home in the deep south still needed more cross-ventilation and got more use out of a covered porch than one in New England, which in turn needed to be able to stay warm in the long winter. Gradual improvements in heating technology, however—first cast-iron wood-burning stoves and then central heating systems—did allow houses in cold climates to become more spread out and irregular in plan. (Not until the middle of this century would the technology of air-conditioning reduce the need for ample natural ventilation in southern homes.)

Domestic Havens: The Victorian Era

It was not just new building technologies and more free-ranging popular tastes in architecture that led to changes in American homes during the nineteenth century. The Industrial Revolution, by altering the nature of many workplaces, also had a profound effect on family lives. As nonagricultural jobs were concentrated in factories, mills, and other large businesses rather than in small establishments interspersed with dwellings, work and home life became more disconnected, especially for middle-class families in new neighborhoods now removed from burgeoning downtowns and congested factory districts. In reaction to this growing split, contemporary books and magazines promoted the idea that a properly designed house should be a desirable retreat from the increasingly commercial and chaotic life of American towns and cities. Such a home, they editorialized, would beckon men back from work, discouraging them from their tendency to rough and violent behavior, and provide a protected and healthy environment for raising the children who would grow into good American citizens.

Women, increasingly on their own during the day as their husbands worked away from home, were crucial to holding this setup together. Relentless emphasis was now placed on their separate roles and duties within the family, which had always existed but perhaps were blurred by the pragmatic realities of American life. Though women still had few legal rights, the popular press and prominent religious speakers encouraged the notion that they should be not just limited to but also dominant in the "home sphere," where their inborn talents lay. Acceptance of Darwin's recent theories of evolution and natural selection only strengthened this view. Thus the editor of *Popular Science Monthly* wrote in 1874:

> Birds often plunge into the watery deep and fishes sometimes rise into the air, but one is nevertheless formed for swimming and the other for flight. So women may make transient diversions from the sphere of activity for which they are constituted, but they are nevertheless formed and designed for maternity, the care of children, and the affairs of domestic life. They are the mothers of human kind, the natural educators of childhood, the guardians of the household.[14]

What historians now term the "cult of domesticity," which purported to elevate women by giving greater importance to their role, also contained inherent tensions. Middle-class wives, increasingly affluent and freed from some of the daily household production that had occupied their mothers and grandmothers, were now supposed to fulfill themselves and strengthen society by creating cultivated and individualized home environments. At the same time they were expected to devote greater personal attention to children, who a century earlier had been more apt simply to work alongside their parents. (While women always had primary responsibility for babies and toddlers, a twelve-year-old boy in the 1700s probably spent much of his time with his father, in a nearby blacksmith shop, for instance, or in the barn.) But as the size of homes increased, along with expectations for elaborate and artistic furnishings, so did housework. The magazines that showed parlors adorned with whatnot shelves and carefully placed easels displaying family portraits did not dwell on the details of maintaining them. Even in households with servants, nineteenth-century housewives had many simultaneous obligations, including a good deal of sick care and laborious food preparation. They dealt with these in growing isolation from their husbands and from a larger civic community.

Not surprisingly, some middle-class women were among the most avid social reformers of the second half of the century, throwing themselves into activities that conformed with their prescribed roles as educators and nurturers and also got them out of the house. While many reform organizations concentrated on problems of the urban poor, including their congested dwellings, a few female reformers also tried to improve the lot of their fellow middle-class homemakers, by advocating more scientifically designed and efficient houses.

One early and widely read advocate of changes in house design was Catharine Beecher, daughter of the well-known New England clergyman, Lyman Beecher. In 1869 she and her sister Harriet published *The American Woman's Home: Principles of Domestic Science*.[15] A manual of wide-ranging practical advice on home design, furnishing, housework, and family life, it included plans for an "economical, healthful, beautiful and Christian home." The dwelling illustrated was architecturally unsophisticated and out of scale; what looked like a small cottage was actually an awkwardly proportioned house of over 2,000 square feet. No match for more skillful patternbook schemes, its exterior imagery was explicitly linked to the residents' religious lives and incorporated rooftop crosses. But the technology and furnishings were thought through in far more detail than those in the patternbook houses of male designers and were designed to minimize a homemaker's labor

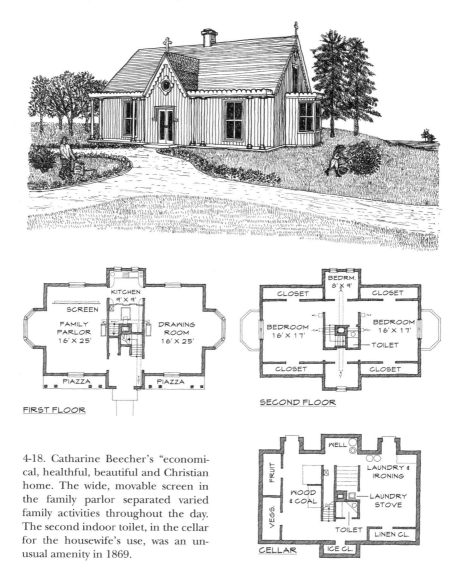

4-18. Catharine Beecher's "economical, healthful, beautiful and Christian home. The wide, movable screen in the family parlor separated varied family activities throughout the day. The second indoor toilet, in the cellar for the housewife's use, was an unusual amenity in 1869.

and protect her family's health. Large common living areas were intended for maximum flexibility, thereby eliminating needless specialized spaces. The heating and ventilating systems reflected contemporary concerns about the provision of fresh air, and the kitchen and basement included efficient built-in cabinetry and storage. Like other idealized houses of the time it was to be sited in the countryside, but, unlike Andrew Jackson Downing, the

Beechers specifically advocated a "working landscape" and showed the family out laboring in the front yard.

From a late-twentieth-century point of view, many of the claims made for the power of houses to transform and determine their occupants' lives are naive and unrealistic. As Clifford Clark points out in *The American Family Home 1800–1960,* there was an inherent contradiction between the idea that well-designed houses would cause rootless Americans to stay put in stable, virtuous lives and the relentless promotion of new and better houses, which encouraged families who could afford it to move frequently. Yet these houses were real attempts to make sense out of brand-new possibilities. Building materials, land, and fuel were available in the nineteenth-century United States in unprecedented quantity, and the changes wrought by mechanization and improvements in transportation allowed increasing numbers of families to enjoy the benefits of this abundance. At the same time, Americans unsure of themselves because of the rapid pace of change took very seriously the design and social advice available.

During the Victorian era, from about 1860 to 1900, the homes built for wealthy and upper-middle-class Americans grew increasingly large, complex, and ornate. This was true for all forms of housing, including the rowhouses going up along the blocks of many new city neighborhoods and the luxury apartments beginning to appear as well. But with continuing population growth and new forms of public transportation allowing people to live farther from work, ever more neighborhoods of freestanding houses were created. Builders, patternbook designers, and a growing number of professional architects competed with each other for shares of this active market.

Whatever their exact historic or ornamental styles, large Victorian houses generally had irregular and highly articulated forms. Important indoor spaces were expressed on the exterior with special windows, bays, cupolas, and ornamental balconies. On the first floor might be, at a minimum, a covered front porch, a formal entry hall, two parlors (one for guests and one for family), a dining room, a kitchen, and a serving pantry. Many houses also included one first-floor bedroom for use as a sickroom or by an elderly family member. Other bedrooms, ideally one for each member of the family, were upstairs, as well as what was typically a

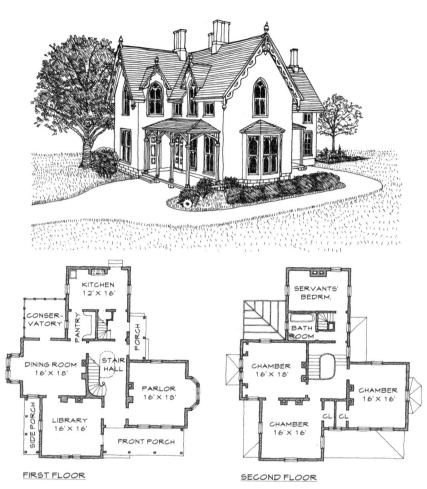

FIRST FLOOR   SECOND FLOOR

4-19. This four-bedroom, 2,000-square-foot "cottage" was prominently featured in *Village Builder*, a popular pattern book published in 1878 by A. J. Bicknell and Co. The illustration showed a brick exterior, but the model specifications described a frame house with wood siding; pattern books left many specifics to be worked out by owners and builders. The pinwheel arrangement of rooms allowed relatively efficient circulation and good ventilation. The rear wing housing the kitchen and servants' quarters was less ornate outside and in, with plain rectangular windows and lower ceilings.

single bathroom, which toward the end of the century might have had all the fixtures we now consider standard. A very elaborate house might also include a library, a sewing room, a children's playroom, and a screened summer *sleeping porch*. The sizes and shapes of these spaces were distinct from one another and they

4-20. A typical Victorian neighborhood in Waterbury, Conn., with large houses on modest lots.

were finished with varied materials and degrees of ornamentation. Entrance halls, front stairs, parlors, and dining rooms featured elaborate wood moldings, paneling, and ornate light fixtures, while bedrooms were more simply finished. Areas intended for use by servants, including separate back stairs and smaller bedrooms, were plain and often poorly heated.

Houses for middle-class families without live-in servants were naturally smaller and less elaborate, but they were designed to resemble grander ones as much as possible, and in them also more specialized spaces developed. The mother of the family might do the cooking herself, but she still carried dinner from the kitchen through the pantry to a formal dining room. In a modest house the desire for two parlors sometimes resulted in uncomfortably small sitting areas. Even when space was limited, however, the idea of clearly separate public and private regions within the home, built to look different, was entrenched.

Despite the images of family homes in idyllic settings and the rhetoric about country life, most new houses actually went up in areas just outside of existing towns and cities. They were built along streets newly laid out by land developers, who then sold off lots to builders or individual owners. By today's suburban standards these lots, in general, were small. Even in moderate-sized cities with plenty of undeveloped land, a large upper-middle-class house with over 2,000 square feet might sit on a property only 40 to 50 feet wide; lots for modest houses were narrower still. In many cases what determined this pattern was not just the cost of land but rather the need for access to trolley or train lines within walking distance. As most houses were built individually or in small groups, the result was often varied blocks of disparate styles standing cheek by jowl. While front yards were formally planted, those in the back surely were crowded and busy, full of clotheslines, small vegetable gardens, and other household adjuncts.

As the homes of wealthy and middle-class Americans grew larger and more complex, the gap between them and those of the working class grew wider. Especially in rural areas, some poorer families continued to build their own small houses in earlier regional styles, though they now more often used lightweight commercial lumber. Other families in rapidly changing communities rented rooms or subdivided apartments within houses left behind by those going to newer, more fashionable areas. But the numbers of people coming both from abroad and from the American countryside to work in the new factories were such that older housing alone could not satisfy the demand. During the Victorian era, in virtually every city or large town there were neighborhoods of new homes, erected for profit by commercial builders, that did not follow the standards of the patternbooks but provided basic shelter. The forms of these dwellings tended to be similar within a given area, not because of regional materials or climate but because of local development patterns and land costs. In many cities land was so expensive that freestanding houses at affordable rents were not feasible; any new homes built were tiny attached houses or tenement flats.

Throughout many towns and cities of the South and Southwest, however, where land values were still relatively low, small freestanding homes called *shotgun houses* were built in large numbers. These and the lots on which they were built were long rectangles in plan; the short end faced the street to allow as many as possible to fit on a given block. A string of two or three rooms, each

4-21. A closely spaced row of shotgun houses.

the full width of the house, opened directly one into the next, with no separate circulation space. Their name probably came from the observation that someone could shoot straight through the entry door and out the back. Though their front rooms may typically have been more formally furnished than those in the back, implying a separation between public and private space, shotgun houses gave family members little real opportunity for privacy from one another or from their neighbors on either side. On the other hand, they did incorporate cross-ventilation, usually included a comfortable front porch, and often featured some stock wood ornamentation that differentiated them from older basic homes and made them recognizably related to other new houses of the era.

Even as popular standards for middle-class homes grew more elaborate, many newly built freestanding houses provided only this kind of basic living space. The spatial organization of shotgun houses resembles that of tenement apartments built at the same time in New York City, and evolved for similar reasons of economy. But while new building laws made the most constricted forms of tenements illegal in New York after 1901, shotgun houses, with minimal indoor plumbing and backyard privies, continued to be built until the Depression.

COMPLEX TECHNOLOGY AND SIMPLIFIED PLANS

Early nineteenth-century improvements in building, heating, and transportation technologies made Victorian houses possible and widely available for many American families, but continuing technological advances also contributed to their disappearance. As both indoor plumbing and electrical wiring became standard and expected features of middle-class homes, the price of construction rose substantially. By some estimates, the incorporation of these two types of infrastructure, which involved new skilled labor as well as new materials, increased building costs per square foot from 25 to 40 percent.[16] In order to keep houses affordable for middle-class families while providing these new amenities, builders at the end of the nineteenth century had to look for ways to make them smaller and simpler.

It was, of course, in the building industry's interests to promote these scaled-back houses as an improvement over their larger, more visually elaborate predecessors. But there was also truth in many of their assertions. A family moving into a newly built Victorian house in the 1870s or '80s would have discovered, eight or ten years later, when the paint was peeling and the children kept pulling the balusters loose from the stair railings, what an enormous job it was to maintain the elaborate woodwork. The standard coal-burning furnaces and gaslights of the time left sooty dust on everything indoors, necessitating frequent cleaning and explaining the Victorian preference for dark interior color schemes.

Independent of the building industry, voices from several newly emerging professions at the turn of the century also advocated simplified houses. By this time, the concerns raised by reformers like Catharine Beecher had developed into a new field of study for women. Home economics was being taught at universities around the country, and its experts were arguing for more streamlined, hygienic kitchens and bathrooms as well as the incorporation of modern technology throughout the rest of the home. As housing and sanitation laws were enacted to prevent disease transmission in the poorest neighborhoods, middle-class houses came under greater scrutiny as well. Public health advocates criticized dust-catching interior moldings and paint colors that masked dirt. And, finally, architects, now becoming organized as a profession, advocated less ornate and complex house design for aesthetic reasons. Though they did not necessarily agree on what should come next, most felt that the eclectic historical styles of the last few decades had run their course and were growing gaudy and exaggerated.

Over the course of the century, social changes also began to make large houses less necessary. Between 1800 and 1900 the average number of live births for white women dropped by half, from 7.04 to 3.5. This was not quite as dramatic as it sounds, because mortality rates were also declining. Nonetheless, the trend was toward smaller households, with children spaced over a shorter span of years. Toward the end of this period, the part-time or live-in servants who had helped to maintain the large houses of the mid- to late 1800s became less available and more expensive, thanks to better-paying opportunities for women in factories and department stores. Between 1870 and 1920, the proportion of American families that employed domestic help declined steadily, from 12.5 percent of the population to 3.9 percent.[17] By the turn of the century, therefore, married women who did not work outside the home were increasingly on their own within it, without the daily company of servants or other adults. For them the allure of a simplified house, especially one with new laborsaving electrical appliances, was great.

With all these factors in play, there was a major shift after 1900 in the size and layouts of middle- and upper-class American houses. New ones had fewer bedrooms, and common family areas were simplified into fewer separate spaces. The gracious entry hall became a modest foyer or was omitted completely, so that the front door opened directly into the newly renamed *living room,* a single space that replaced earlier double parlors and sometimes the dining room as well. The large but often awkward Victorian kitchen and pantry were combined into a more efficient room with built-in counters and appliances. Back stairs for servants were eliminated from all but the most costly houses. Taken together, these changes reduced floor area significantly; they also helped to keep house prices stable. By one historian's estimate, a generous middle-class house in the 1880s might have had 2000 to 2500 square feet, while a comparably priced home by 1905 had between 1000 and 1500.[18]

Most houses were still built with stud wall construction like their Victorian predecessors, but their overall forms and exterior details were simplified. Some were designed to evoke more regular and compact forms from the past, such as American houses of the Colonial period or earlier English and Dutch buildings. Others were part of a national "bungalow craze," which started in California, for rectangular single- or one-and-a-half-story houses with a wide overhanging roof and often a deep porch spanning the front facade. Outside and in, *bungalows* featured earth tones and self-consciously rustic materials. Stone, textured brick, and stucco veneers as well as wood siding covered the exterior studs.

In their relative simplicity, both neo-Colonial houses and bungalows were quite democratic styles, available in a wide price range. By the early 1900s the standardization of wood house construction had gone beyond stock lumber sizes, moldings, and designs modeled on nationally circulated patternbooks. An extensive mail-order industry of precut houses now shipped, by rail, complete packages of framing members, siding, roofing, windows, doors, hardware, and even paint, for assembly on a custom-built foundation. These were available around the country from Sears, Roebuck and Montgomery Ward as well as numerous smaller companies. Thus, while large custom bungalows for the wealthy were being designed by well-known architects on both coasts, the basic shingled "Roseland," with three bedrooms, about 850 square feet, and a comfortable broad porch, could be purchased from the Aladdin Built-in-a-Day company for only $687.80.[19]

Around the Southwest, and especially in fast-growing Los Angeles, *bungalow courts* were widely built as an affordable form of rental housing. These were groups of small houses placed on a single large lot and oriented around a common landscaped entrance walk. Though the units were freestanding, the overall effect of their close grouping was not unlike that of the small garden apartment complexes being built around the same time. In a hot

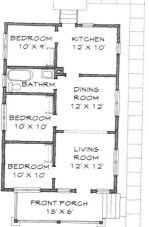

4-22. Both the "Roseland" on the right and the slightly larger "Boulevard" on the left were precut three-bedroom bungalows available by mail from the Michigan-based Aladdin Company through their 1917 catalog. The Roseland floor plan shows how corridors and entry halls were eliminated and the overall shape of the house simplified in comparison with earlier Victorian layouts.

climate they provided a shaded green entry space, and their utility connections were more efficient than if they had been built conventionally on individual lots.

While the popularity of bungalows was in part simply a matter of fashion, their rustic detailing also reflected a growing public interest in outdoor recreation and wilderness appreciation. In a shift of emphasis from earlier decades, advertisements and magazines now promoted the notion that healthy families did not need large and elaborate interior spaces. They were supposed to be outside enjoying themselves, boating or riding bicycles on a Sunday afternoon rather than sitting in the parlor playing charades or listening to their daughters play the piano. Though many bungalows were built as vacation homes, even those in cities and suburbs were promoted as having a relaxed and casual atmosphere.

The national interest in wilderness was part of a substantive change in American attitudes. It occurred at a point when undeveloped land, because it no longer seemed endless, came to be valued in a new way, and it culminated politically in the creation of a system of sizable national parks. But there was nothing inherent in the design of the compact freestanding houses built after the turn of the century that necessarily supported a more outdoor lifestyle. New neighborhoods of bungalows, neo-Colonial, or Tudor houses were laid out very much like earlier sections of modest Victorian homes, set back from streets and sidewalks with open front lawns and picturesque foundation plantings. Up through the mid-1920s, most continued to go up close together on narrow lots, within walking distance of the streetcar or train lines that connected them to workplaces. While blocks of homes were often exclusively residential, stores were not far away, near the station or trolley stop. Growing networks of door-to-door businesses delivered necessities such as ice, dairy products, and fresh produce. They also provided convenient services, sharpening knives and buying old clothing.

Rather than any real move toward a house form that was "closer to nature," what actually happened early in the twentieth century was a growing convergence between modest freestanding houses and other dwelling forms as they were built around the United States. Because of rising building costs, higher technological expectations, and changing social conditions, both attached and freestanding houses became more compact. At the same time new building laws required more natural light and air, as well as plumbing and electrical wiring, in apartments.

During the early decades of the century, and especially after World War I, there was a nationwide shortage of homes and con-

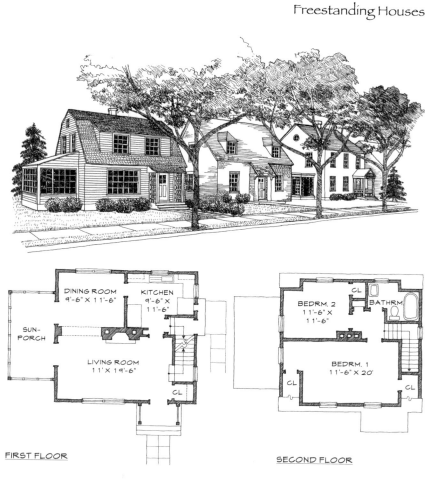

FIRST FLOOR   SECOND FLOOR

4-23. Three examples from a book of houses published by the Architects' Small House Bureau, set up in 1919 to provide well-designed and affordable houses for the middle class. Compact in floor plan, they were designed to fit on lots from 30' to 50' wide. The "Dutch Colonial," shown in plan and on the left in the perspective view, is a typical five-room house, with about 1,000 square feet. The front door opens directly into the living room, essentially making the right side of the room into a corridor. The kitchen includes a back door for ice delivery.

sequently a lot of experimentation in the design and production of affordable dwellings. Commercial builders as well as philanthropic housing groups undertook a wide variety of innovative developments. While freestanding houses did not predominate in these experimental projects, they were intermingled with other

4-24. Forest Hills Gardens, Queens, New York, about 1918, showing a freestanding house next to an elevator apartment building of the same era.

housing forms in ways that would become much less common after the enactment of zoning laws. One striking example was Forest Hills Gardens, a planned neighborhood begun in 1908 by the Russell Sage Foundation. It was sited in Queens County, Long Island, only recently made part of New York City through the 1898 five-borough consolidation. From its inception, the site plan included innovative elevator apartment buildings, rows of attached and semiattached houses, and individual freestanding houses, all built along a network of gently curving streets, with small parks and a train station at its edge. Though some lots were sold off to independent builders, there was a stylistic conformity along English Tudor lines among all the homes, from apartments to freestanding houses. The neighborhood was so successful that its original middle-income orientation was revised upwards, and it has remained fashionable to this day.

HOUSES AND THE AUTOMOBILE

Even as freestanding houses were being used in new ways and coexisting gracefully with other forms, technological changes were moving in another direction. Though very clumsy types of so-called horseless carriages had been built in Europe as early as the 1860s, the earliest automobiles did not work reliably and were regarded largely as novelties until the twentieth century. After the machines themselves became somewhat more dependable, related changes were still required before they could meet people's real needs for transportation. Cars had to be widely available at an affordable price and there had to be extensive networks of paved roads and convenient refueling stations.

The changes needed to make automobiles viable as a mode of daily transportation took place gradually between 1905 and 1950. Because the earliest cars did not have solid roofs, they had to be parked within covered structures. Initially some literally replaced horses in preexisting stables, but by the 1920s many new free-standing homes came with driveways and garages. Like stables, these first garages were usually separate buildings in a back- or side yard, unconnected to the house. As cars themselves grew more reliable and waterproof, roofed but open *carports* on the side of the house became popular as a less expensive alternative.

While accommodations for cars were becoming more standard, it was still impossible to appreciate the magnitude of the transformation that they would generate in the country's built environment. Eventually the automobile would affect virtually every type of building and human use of land. In the case of freestanding houses, it altered both their internal organization and the uses of the surrounding land. Driveways and garages took up a great deal of land, requiring either the enlargement of building lots or the elimination of other uses of residential yards. Local land values largely determined which of these approaches was taken. Bringing cars onto individual properties meant cutting curbs and crossing sidewalks, so that outdoor areas that had been exclusively for pedestrian use became less safe. Streets themselves, always hazardous, became potentially fatal. Finally, as people increasingly came and went from their houses by car, the back door often turned into the main entrance, affecting the use of other rooms as well. Because of the essentially conservative nature of home design, however, this internal change in the use of the house was seldom reflected on the exterior. The rarely used but still embellished front door remained facing the street, though often the paved entrace walk now led from the driveway.

In addition to the direct influence of the automobile on houses and the land around them, the use and the innovative assembly-line production of cars had far-reaching effects on our thinking about homes. Right from the start the car inspired new forms of temporary dwellings that were hard to categorize as either vehicle or building. Although the bungalow craze of the early 1900s did not really bring Americans closer to nature, what did paradoxically help to achieve that goal was the rapid growth of automobile ownership. Affordable cars made possible widespread access to previously remote wilderness areas without the physical rigors of hiking and backpacking.

In the years just before 1920, *auto-camping* became a popular national pastime. Initially it spawned a wide variety of custom-manufactured and homemade trailers, which were pulled behind the car. Trailer camps opened along rural highways, providing a grid of closely spaced berths as well as bathrooms, showers, and recreation facilities. The imagery used to advertise these early trailers ranged wildly from gypsy caravans and covered wagons to high-style Pullman cars and airplanes. Eventually, of course, modern technology won out. By the 1930s, sleek, hard-bodied *house trailers*, with neatly packed living and sleeping quarters, were widely available; the classic silver Airstream was first produced in 1935.[20]

Inevitably, some of the new vehicular trailers, designed for vacation use, became year-round homes. They were a convenient solution for those whose jobs involved travel or frequent relocation, such as salesmen and some specialized construction workers. In addition, during the Depression, many families who lost their homes or left them to seek work elsewhere turned to house trailers as homes of last resort. Across the country, towns that had previously welcomed vacationing auto-campers for the business that they brought now became alarmed at the sight of trailers grouped on vacant lots. Because trailer dwellers paid no property taxes, it was feared that they would overburden schools and other municipal resources. Ordinances were passed to ban them completely or

4-25. This sketch based on a photo taken in Detroit in the early 1930s shows an impromptu urban trailer park on a vacant lot.

to limit their length of stay. The vehicles themselves, which previously had a positive public image connected with middle-class, egalitarian recreation (unlike yachts, for instance), now acquired a double-edged reputation. It was okay to *vacation* on the road, but solid American citizens were supposed to *live* in permanent houses, attached to the earth.

However, as the country emerged from the Depression and defense production accelerated in support of World War II, there was a tremendous need for temporary housing around war-related industrial sites. Trailer manufacturers, whose sales had dropped in the late 1930s, suddenly had a new market. Starting in 1940 they began producing and selling thousands of units as theoretically temporary but nonetheless year-round homes. Some were purchased in large batches and set up in government-run camps outside new defense plants and shipyards. Others were individually owned by workers who rented space in private camps, where conditions were chaotic, but they were free to modify their units, adding on mudrooms, porches, and fences. Because of the speed with which these wartime units were produced, many were shoddily built, which did not help to improve their reputation. During the war there was little stigma attached to trailer living because it was part of the national defense effort, which required many sacrifices. Afterward, however, the same attitude did not apply.

The national shortage of housing after the war was acute. Relatively few new homes of any kind were built during the long, difficult decade of the 1930s, so that by 1945, when the war ended, there had been a fifteen-year lull in residential construction. Veterans returned home as heroes and found jobs in good supply but had to double up in crowded houses and apartments with family and friends. The house trailers that had served as temporary wartime dwellings remained in use. Although the trailer industry began to advertise again to a vacationers' market, in fact the majority of units produced in the late 1940s were bought or rented as year-round homes. Three years after the war, in 1948, approximately 7 percent of the national population was living in house trailers.[21] By this time most new units included full bathrooms, though the plumbing hookups in some camps were not adequate to support them.

Thanks both to rising prosperity and the impetus of new government programs, conventional site-built home construction was in full gear by the early 1950s, and record numbers of freestanding houses were added to the American landscape. Even as the overall shortage of dwellings gradually eased, however, demand for house trailers as permanent homes continued to grow. In response to this market, trailer manufacturers modified their products to make them more generous and houselike. In 1952 one Wisconsin-based start-up manufacturer, Marshfield Homes, built a 10-foot-wide unit, exceeding the standard 8-foot width allowed for trucks and trailers. This overt evidence that trailers were actually being produced for use as permanent buildings caused problems at first, as Marshfield's president, Elmer Frey, later recalled:

> It was not really the size of the object that highway officials objected to, it was the matter of what it was called. I could see clearly it was discrimination against the Gypsy ring of the, as they called it, house trailer industry. . . . We took the order for the LAKESIDE COTTAGE with a chassis attached under it and wrote the order up as a "construction shack." . . . It was after that when I decided that some day I will take on a fight with those discriminating highway officials and show them how to use the overwidth permit when the unit is called a MOBILE HOME.[22]

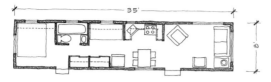

HOUSE TRAILER — 1940S AND EARLY 1950S
(280 SF MAXIMUM)

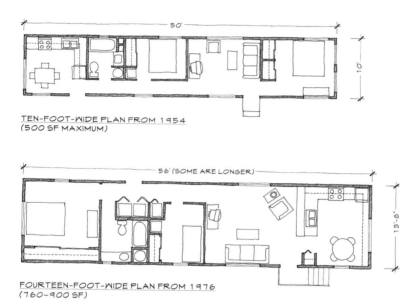

TEN-FOOT-WIDE PLAN FROM 1954
(500 SF MAXIMUM)

FOURTEEN-FOOT-WIDE PLAN FROM 1976
(760–900 SF)

4-26. The evolution of the mobile home. Early house trailers were designed like rail-road or boat accommodations, with overhead storage wherever possible and a walk-through second bedroom. As permissible dimensions increased, rooms grew larger and furnishings no longer had to be undersized. By the 1970s designers could offer floor plans in which all rooms were no longer strung out along a single, straight cor-ridor. Placing the two exterior doors on opposite sides of the unit created diagonal circulation through the living room and the feeling of a more conventional house.

After a few years regulators were persuaded to modify their requirements, and 10-foot-wide units became the industry stan-dard. Now the industry began to split, manufacturing two separate products. *Recreational vehicles*, meeting the requirements for vans and trucks, were designed to travel regularly from one spot to another. *Mobile homes*, increasingly large and unwieldy on the high-way, were small permanent homes fabricated in a central plant

4-27. A row of "single-wide" mobile homes in a contemporary California park. Typically the units are perpendicular to the street and set back only a few feet from the curb line. Projecting shed roofs on both sides form covered entranceways and carports.

and moved, usually only once, to a site where they were placed on concrete blocks and connected to utility and plumbing lines. Sometimes these sites were individually owned, but more typically they were rented spaces within *mobile home parks*, postwar descendants of the earlier trailer camps.

Why was there an ongoing and even growing demand for mobile homes when the national housing shortage was no longer severe? After the war, both codes and expectations had been raised so that all homes were supposed to have modern electrical wiring, plumbing, and sanitary drainage. With these improvements it was no longer possible to construct dwellings like the little shotgun houses of prewar decades at a price affordable to lower-income families. In areas without an existing stock of solid older homes to be recycled and where the government was not building subsidized public housing, mobile homes became the new basic dwelling. Though they had often been characterized as temporary or throwaway structures, in fact they were rarely totally discarded. A large resale and rental market made them available in a wide range of prices at the lower end of the market.

Because mobile homes were not classified as houses or subject to the same codes as conventionally built dwellings, their design and construction were largely unregulated for several decades. The situation had certain advantages. The industry remained one of small, independent, and sometimes innovative manufacturers, and prices were low enough to provide a real alternative to other homes. At the same time, however, many units were shoddily built and installed, presenting real hazards. Without proper anchoring to a foundation, they were vulnerable to windstorms and tornadoes, and once exposed to fire they burned very quickly.

Most American municipalities, even those that had relaxed restrictions on house trailers during the war years, quickly amended their zoning laws to ban mobile homes; it was forbidden to place one on a vacant lot within a neighborhood of freestanding houses. Throughout the 1950s and '60s, however, mobile home parks opened just outside the boundaries of many towns and cities, often on land zoned for industry. In rural areas with fewer restrictions, mobile homes began to appear next to older houses, in some cases replacing them and in others adding living space which the owners could not afford to build any other way. As mobile homes proliferated around the edges and along the back roads of most communities, many people, including architects and planners, failed to appreciate the major role they were playing in meeting Americans' needs for homes.

By the early 1970s, however, the number of mobile homes had grown to the point where they could no longer be ignored, and federal officials now acknowledged their importance as a form of low-cost housing. This legal recognition brought with it demands for regulation, but because units were made in one place and installed in many others, conflicting local building laws presented problems for manufacturers. In 1974 Congress enacted the Mobile Home Construction and Safety Standards Act, authorizing the development of a federal code. Like building laws around the turn of the century, this improved the safety of new homes but also increased their cost.

The most affluent group of mobile home residents was retired senior citizens, who valued them not only for their relative economy but also for their compactness and ease of maintenance. In 1955 a young and farsighted lawyer named Syd Adler, in partnership with Franklyn Macdonald, a mobile-home dealer, opened a 160-acre subdivision in Florida called Trailer Estates.[23] They sold off individual lots, the most expensive of which backed onto canals leading to Sarasota Bay, and built common recreation facilities as well as a community center with a full weekly schedule of activities. The development catered to middle-class retirees who owned homes up north but wintered in Florida. Highly successful, it inspired other service-oriented mobile home developments, many of them year-round. These were forerunners of modern condominium communities, often clustering individual lots around a golf course. During the 1950s and '60s, when conventional high-maintenance freestanding houses were being touted as the best form for all middle-class homes, such mobile home parks represented a real alternative, chosen freely by some older people despite the ongoing negative connotations of trailer living.

Because of their vehicular origins and their image as makeshift rather than permanent housing, mobile homes evolved largely outside the notice of those in the home-building industry. Within the design and construction fields, however, there was great interest in new building methods that might create homes more quickly and inexpensively. Inspired by the technological advances of the preceding century, and particularly by Henry Ford's assembly-line production of automobiles, visionary designers in Europe and America had sketched and talked for several decades about mass-producing high-quality affordable dwellings. Europeans, like the French architect Le Corbusier, tended to envision large apartment structures with plug-in interchangeable units, resembling wine bottles in a rack. Americans, like the designer R. Buckminster Fuller, conceived more often of freestanding houses made of factory-produced components that could be easily erected, attached to utilities, and demounted when they became technologically obsolete. In both cases, designers assumed that prefabricated homes would look totally unlike those built by earlier methods.

After World War II, on both sides of the Atlantic, there were new opportunities for bringing such visions into being. Based on the experiences of other industries, the notion that homes could be produced more inexpensively within factories than on their final sites was logical and compelling. In the United States, the federal government provided loans and even space in surplus defense factories to new prefabricated housing plants. These companies used a number of structural systems, from wood frames with stressed plywood panels to metal frames with, in one case, interior and exterior sheet-metal skins. (Pictures could be hung using magnets!) Though viable houses were produced, the start-up

4-28. A larger "double-wide" mobile home, transported in two sections and joined on site. In exterior design and floor plan such units resemble many conventionally built ranch houses, but in mobile home parks they typically sit on smaller plots of land and are oriented perpendicular to the street.

4-29. A 1940s prefabricated all-metal two-bedroom house manufactured by the Lustron Company with substantial backing from the federal government. Its components were designed to be packaged and transported on a single trailer truck.

times were longer than anticipated and the costs, not surprisingly, somewhat higher. In addition, not enough thought was given to the problems of getting these new units from the factory to a permanent location on the ground. Local building departments were suspicious and raised many obstacles. Public reaction to the houses actually erected was lukewarm, especially because prices were not substantially lower than those of conventional houses. Given all these problems, federal support for prefabrication weakened, and most companies were not strong enough to keep going on their own.[24]

POSTWAR HOUSES BY THE THOUSANDS

What proved much more successful than factory prefabrication was a large-scale system of streamlined, on-site construction. Starting in 1946 a family of experienced builders, Arthur Levitt and his sons William and Alfred, began to acquire 4,000 acres of inexpensive land on Long Island, about ten miles from the edge of New York City. Most recently used as potato fields, the property was some distance from existing commuter train lines, but thanks to new limited-access parkways it was now easily accessible by car. Here, between 1947 and 1950, the Levitts built 17,400 new homes, a development of unprecedented size in the United States. All were single-story freestanding houses with unfinished attics for future expansion. They had between 750 and 800 square feet of interior floor space, less than most mail-order bungalows of the early 1900s. The 60-by-100-foot lots on which they were erected, however, were almost double the size of modest house lots earlier in the century. This increased width allowed the longer side of the house to face the street while still comfortably accommodating an automobile alongside.

To keep the final cost of their houses as low as possible, the Levitts pioneered a newly efficient building process. As urban historian Kenneth T. Jackson described it in his 1985 book *Crabgrass Frontier:*

> After bulldozing the land and removing the trees, trucks carefully dropped off building materials at precise 60-foot intervals. . . . Plywood replaced ¾-inch strip lap, ¾-inch double lap was changed to ⅜-inch for roofing, and the horse and scoop were replaced by the bulldozer. . . . The construction process itself was divided into twenty-seven distinct steps. . . . Crews were trained to do one job— one day the white-paint men, then the red-paint men, then the tile layers. . . . Vertical integration also meant that the firm made its own concrete, grew its own timber, and cut its own lumber.[25]

Rather than producing homes on a distant assembly line and moving them to a final location, this system, in effect, created a factory on the site itself. It took advantage of the new industrial logic of trucking, which needed open horizontal space to deliver materials efficiently. Because the homes produced this way, though spare, were built out of standard wood studs and looked basically conventional, they again, like mobile homes, escaped or fell beneath the notice of most architectural theorists and planners seeking a new system of mass production.

The original Long Island Levittown was almost instantly successful, with waiting lists of prospective buyers. While the Levitts went on to construct similar projects with the same name in New Jersey and Pennsylvania, other developers quickly assembled large sites outside of major cities around the nation. Near Los Angeles, for instance, in the new town of Lakewood, 17,500 houses of about 1100 square feet each, larger than those in Levittown, were built in three years starting in 1950—a rate of almost sixteen houses per day.[26] By the early 1950s, such large-scale suburban developments accounted for a sizable majority of all new homes being constructed.[27]

In the second half of the nineteenth century balloon framing and a seemingly limitless supply of milled lumber made possible a surge in the size and complexity of middle-class houses, which eventually subsided as other costs increased. In the second half of the twentieth century the commodity that suddenly surged in availability was land. After World War II, the expanding highway system combined with growing car ownership to open up vast and inexpensive acres for new home lots all over the country. For at least a few decades, the typical ratio of house size to property size dropped dramatically. While the floor plans of homes in the original Levittown and subsequent developments included a few new features, the houses themselves were not substantially different from many that had come before. It was rather their density across the landscape and their distance from workplaces and shopping areas that were altered.

The so-called merchant builders who dominated postwar suburban construction benefited enormously from the new government-financed loan guarantee programs run by the Federal Housing Administration (FHA) and the Veteran's Administration (VA),

BEDROOM
12' X 12'

BEDROOM
8' X 12'

LIVINGROOM
12' X 16'

KITCHEN
10' X 10'

30'

25'

4-30. Plan and perspective view of the 750-square-foot Levittown Cape Cod house, built starting in 1947. Though minimal in size, it included a full set of modern appliances and the stairs led to an unfinished attic, which was easily converted to more bedroom space. The front entry path was deliberately curved to create a casual, non-urban atmosphere.

which insured the individual home mortgages made by private banks. Without directly building anything, these programs caused a major shift in where Americans lived and in how many of them owned their homes. As late as 1940, fewer than half of all dwelling units in the United States, or 41 percent, were owner occupied, and that percentage had changed little over the fifty years since 1890, when it was 37 percent. The terms on which local banks lent money were erratic and typically short-term, so that it was not uncommon for upper-middle-class families living in spacious houses to rent from a landlord. FHA/VA mortgage insurance allowed loans to be repaid slowly and at lower rates, greatly reducing monthly payments and making it possible for far more Americans to purchase their homes. In the twenty years before 1960 the percentage of

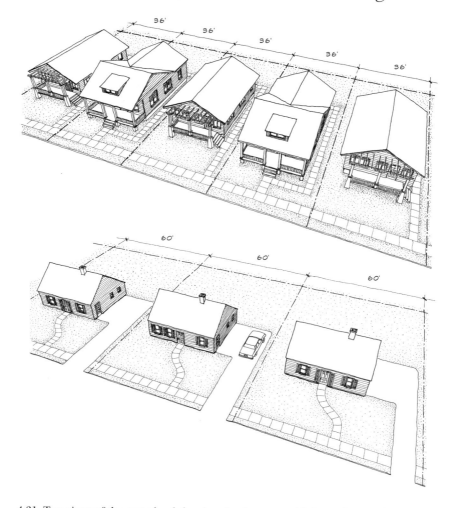

4-31. Two views of the same land showing development with bungalows as they might have been built in the early 1900s, above, and the Levittown Cape Cod houses below. Houses on larger lots were turned so the long side faced the street; front porches disappeared and facades were simplified. Driveways now interrupted the sidewalk at regular intervals.

homes that were owner occupied increased by almost half, to 61 percent, and has remained at about that level ever since.[28]

Levittown and other new developments of small houses were aimed initially at young veterans starting their work careers with few accumulated savings. Before the war they would not have been able to own homes; now they were able to buy them for monthly costs that were often less than what they had been paying as rent in their old neighborhoods. While the homes they purchased may not have been larger than those left behind, they were certainly less crowded with relatives. Moreover, they were new, and as basic houses on substantial lots they came with possibilities for additions. Their minimal, stripped-down quality, in fact, virtually invited change. In the Long Island Levittown it is now hard to find an original, unaltered house. Though these large-scale, low-cost suburbs were initially criticized for their sterility and cookie-cutter dwellings, no community remains static over fifty years, and they have grown more physically and socially varied with age.

The use of government funds for mortgage insurance was a creative and effective way to stimulate new home construction in the United States. Unfortunately and probably needlessly, however, the FHA set rigid eligibility standards for these loans, adopting a rating system not just for the structural soundness and design of individual houses but also for the neighborhoods around them. They gave lower scores to homes in areas with diverse building types or with populations that were mixed by race or income, on the grounds that such neighborhoods were inherently unstable. Homes would not retain their value, it was reasoned, and loans would more likely have to be foreclosed. Thus, freestanding or attached houses in some neighborhoods where they were intermingled with apartment buildings and businesses were denied FHA loans, as were houses in good condition that happened to stand next to others that were more run-down. Many new developments of homes built to qualify for government-insured loans were explicitly discriminatory, almost always excluding black residents and often Jews as well. Even after such overt practices were made illegal, the widespread perception that homes in "mixed" neighborhoods were bad investments contributed to continuing discrimination in actual practice.

Across the country private banks adopted FHA standards even for their non-government-insured lending, effectively denying financing to many urban neighborhoods. This practice later became known as *redlining*. What made the blanket application of these standards especially perverse was that an earlier federal loan program of the 1930s had actually shown a default rate somewhat higher in wealthy suburban areas than in more modest inner-city

4-32. One of the original Levittown Cape Cod houses today. It has been extended to the right, into what was the original parking area, and the steeply sloped attic has been converted to a full second story.

ones; it is thus not clear that the FHA standards really protected taxpayers' dollars.[29]

The social consequences of redlining in intensifying racial discrimination and segregation were severe and have been written about extensively. The irrationality of the FHA standards from an environmental point of view has been less widely noted. By cutting off the possibilities for continuing upkeep and growth, the denial of credit to low-rated neighborhoods became a self-fulfilling prophecy. Many communities only thirty or forty years old, with sound homes and modern infrastructure, quickly deteriorated, an incredible waste of human and natural resources. Had FHA and bank standards been more inclusive, the growth of automobile use would still have affected these neighborhoods, and newly accessible outlying areas would still have grown in popularity. Changes , however, would have been more gradual and, in a sense, evolutionary. Both new construction and alterations, including creative adaptations for accommodating cars, would have continued to take place within existing communities.

As it was, FHA guidelines and large-scale development patterns after the war restricted the popular image of what a good neighborhood looked like to a vision that included only one form of home. The concept of land use separation that was embedded in new zoning ordinances reinforced and codified this image. Between 1900 and 1930, apartments, attached houses, and freestanding houses were all built in a variety of sizes for both middle- and working-class people. From the 1950s through the early 1970s, outside of a few large cities where land was extremely expensive, new privately built neighborhoods consisted almost solely of freestanding houses.

Not all the homes built during this era were as minimal as the small houses of Levittown or Lakewood. The general level of prosperity in the 1950s and '60s meant that many families could afford larger houses, and the wide reach of the automobile allowed lot sizes for these upper-middle-class homes to grow as well. Now that cars were both safer and more universally used for coming and going throughout the day, the garage became an integral part of a larger house, and the door leading to it, usually from the kitchen, became the main functional entrance. Though this might have been expected to fundamentally alter the appearance of houses, some were still designed much as they had been in the 1910s and '20s, with a garage simply added as an extra wing.

Many other new houses were now lower and more spread out, a change made possible by larger lot sizes. During this period both the *ranch* and the *split-level* became common forms. Like the bungalows of a half-century earlier, ranch houses are said to have their American origin in California and were promoted as nurturing a healthy, informal, outdoor-oriented family life. The new ranches were single-story homes, usually rectangular or L-shaped, with the wide side of the house facing the street. They generally featured a shallow sloped roof but, unlike bungalows, had no front porch. Their main orientation was toward the backyard, and they had picture windows or sliding glass doors between family living spaces and a rear patio.

Though originally linked with the wide-open spaces of the Southwest, the term *ranch house* came to mean almost any contemporary one-story house, with stylistic details that ranged from stark and modern to vaguely Spanish or Colonial. Their popular-

4-33. A single-story ranch house became the most common form for new American homes after World War II. This 1,600-square-foot three-bedroom layout was typical; the now-standard two-car garage added another 30 percent to its floor area.

ity was associated with a new ease of living; climbing stairs was now an unnecessary and outdated form of work. In 1970 these low, spreading structures made up 74 percent of all new houses constructed.[30]

Split-level houses, also built nationwide but most popular in the East and Midwest, were more clearly defined as to size and layout. They were asymmetrical, with staggered two-story and one-story sections, which made them well suited to sloping sites. The garage was in the lower level of the two-story section, facing the street.

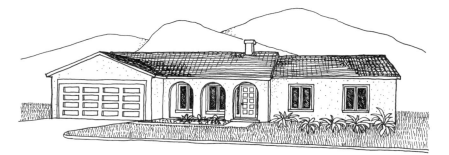

4-34. With a slight change in the roof line, stucco veneer, and a front porch, the three-bedroom ranch house shown in figure 4-33 might be built in a contemporary "Mission" style.

Behind it, with windows on the backyard, was generally an informal common area known as the rec room, or family room. A half-level up, in the one-story wing, were the now traditional common areas: living room, dining room or area, and kitchen. Another half-level up, over the garage, were the bedrooms. In larger houses of all styles, bathrooms now multiplied; a master bedroom "suite" with a private bathroom and sometimes a separate dressing area became standard.

The addition of the rec room to the split-level house was an example of the trend in larger postwar houses to more separate and specialized living areas. Essentially it was a return to the Victorian tradition of two parlors, one informal, for family and especially children, and a second one decorated and kept presentable for guests. Cooking and eating areas were also more differentiated; a large house might have a breakfast room adjacent to the kitchen as well as a formal dining room. In comparison with Victorian houses, these newer spaces were not always clearly separated by doors or hallways. Americans had now grown used to the feel of an open plan, and builders favored it because eliminating doors and separate circulation spaces saved money while giving a sense of spaciousness that appealed to prospective buyers. (It takes time in a new home to realize that the living room isn't really as furnishable as it should be for its size because it also functions as a corridor.)

Whatever their size, the freestanding houses of the 1950s and '60s were the focus of intense expectations. After the poverty,

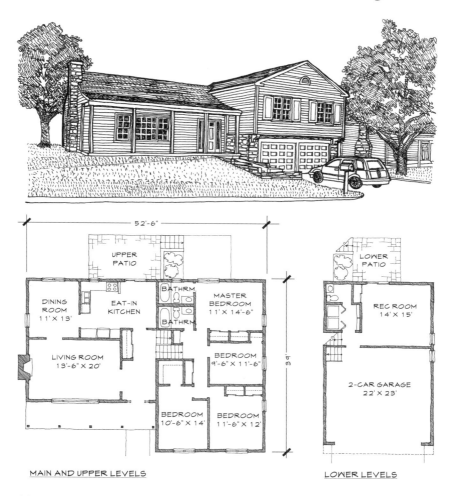

4-35. A 1,900-square-foot split-level house with Dutch Colonial detailing and a combination of stone veneer and wood siding. With a smaller footprint than ranch houses, large split levels fit comfortably on somewhat smaller lots.

insecurity, and social radicalism of the Depression and the international trauma of World War II, American popular culture now focused inward to promote stable family lives in comfortable private houses. Though the activities were different, the emphasis on total personal fulfillment at home for all family members was again similar to that of the Victorian era.

The birthrate rose sharply after the war, so that new houses bought by young couples were soon full. In suburbs that were now purely residential, children did not have independent access to much besides their own and neighbors' houses and yards. Some developments included public playgrounds or pools, and while new neighborhoods were still under construction, vacant lots provided the odd opportunity for another hangout. But overall, in-home entertainment, including television and an ever-growing volume of games and toys, burgeoned. Mothers were supposed to engineer a wholesome and stimulating environment where children could express themselves and make a mess when they needed to while also creating a cozy retreat that was tranquil and inviting for their husbands and guests. The pivotal role of the housewife was again emphasized by the popular press and the real estate industry, as it had been in the late 1800s. For example, though the decision to place kitchens on the street side of the Levittown houses had a lot to do with shortening sewer connections, advertisements stressed that it would improve women's lives: "We've put the kitchen on the front where it belongs, where it's just a step for your wife to answer the door, and where she can see who's there and what's going on."[31]

Although parallels can be drawn between the Victorian cult of domesticity and popular culture of the 1950s and early 1960s, differences in the actual design and building of houses are notable. After World War II the advice and expectations regarding family life were directed at a larger percentage of the population than they had been seventy years earlier. The middle class was smaller during the late 1800s, and working-class jobs were not expected to leave enough time or extra income for personal fulfillment. In an attempt to achieve the twin goals of home ownership and a free-standing house for the vast majority of Americans, the federal government became deeply involved in creating homes not just for the poor but for almost everybody. Virtually all builders now followed the design standards used to determine eligibility for FHA mortgage insurance. Government-employed architects assisted them, developing layouts of the smallest possible ranch houses to show how they might provide privacy and personal recreation space for everyone, even in a family of modest income.

Whether or not families used their new houses according to the rhetoric of the day, they certainly adapted to them and were often able to make extensive modifications over time. But given the vast scale on which almost identical houses were constructed, it is hard to say that many aspects of either house or neighborhood design during this period were freely chosen from an array of real alternatives. In earlier eras the smaller scale of private construction and more diffuse nature of design inspiration had offered more variety.

One major problem with the new neighborhoods was that, while a lot of thought and government support went into making them available to families with a wide range of incomes, little attention was paid, apparently, to how they would accommodate Americans throughout their lifespans. Victorian houses had been roomy and complex partly because they often sheltered several generations at once. While their floor plans were sometimes awkward and inefficient, they did allow for a lot of separate and simultaneous activities. Large entry halls, dual parlors, separate dining rooms and walled-off kitchens, all with doors, helped to accommodate extended family households with a combination of individual privacy and communal support for the infirm or elderly.

The young couples who bought new houses and started families after the war by and large left their own parents behind in older, more urban homes. Twenty-five or thirty years later, when these young couples themselves had aged, their suburban homes did not always continue to meet their needs. The wood-framed houses, not to mention the front- and backyards, required ongoing physical maintenance that was either strenuous or expensive. Heating costs and taxes for large houses with multiple living spaces and bedrooms were high, and taking in boarders was no longer legal. The death of a spouse, or any problem that precluded driving, could leave older residents isolated, sometimes dangerously so. But because their communities contained only houses of a similar type, moving to a more physically suitable home also meant breaking many personal ties and, in a sense, starting over.

By the 1960s the pattern of moving in retirement to a warm and scenic part of the country was firmly established. Some early forms of special neighborhoods for senior citizens, like the leisure-oriented trailer parks, had already appeared. But not everyone could afford to move far away, or wanted to. Responding to a growing market, developments exclusively for older people began to be built all over the United States in the 1970s. Often including low-rise apartments or attached cottages, along with common recreation facilities, they added variety to the dwelling forms available in many suburban towns but almost never were built directly within neighborhoods of freestanding houses. In the language of zoning ordinances, they now constituted a "different use," though they were homes for the same people who had recently lived in suburban houses.

At the other end of the life cycle, many of the children who grew up in the freestanding houses of the 1950s and '60s found themselves, on reaching adulthood, unable to buy a home in their neighborhood; again, there were no other options within their communities. Home prices and mortgage interest rates had risen drastically over the course of their childhood so that even if they now had better-paying jobs than those of their parents starting out, they still could not afford to live where they had grown up.

In many American neighborhoods the lack of affordable housing for people already very much part of the community is an ongoing problem. Some towns have permitted the construction of new types of homes, apartment and townhouse complexes, to meet this need. Usually close to commercial areas, these are sited along busy local streets or near highways—land thought of as less desirable for the preferred freestanding house developments. Major local battles are fought over these new forms because they are not seen as complementary to existing freestanding houses, or as a kind of community enrichment, but rather as a potentially destabilizing force in a homogeneous built environment. The subdividing of single-family homes into two or more apartments has become commonplace in many neighborhoods (including Levittown) but is almost never legal. Thus, although many communities built on the premise that all homes should be freestanding houses are becoming more physically diverse, largely in response to the needs of their own residents, the changes are not usually seen as positive. The freestanding home remains the "highest and best" use of land.

Today, freestanding houses still constitute the majority of new homes constructed in this country. However, they are less predominant and no longer built in as great a range of sizes as they were forty or fifty years ago. Because well-located land has become less available and more expensive, lot sizes have shrunk, while new houses have grown. The average new house in the early 1970s contained about 1,500 square feet, while today it has over 2,000. To create more interior space on smaller properties, houses are once again getting taller; while thirty years ago only 17 percent had two or more stories, the proportion now is almost half.[32] Other standards have changed as well: Houses built today have more electrical outlets, more bathrooms, and larger garages, as the ratio of cars to people has risen steadily. Thanks to a sharp increase in energy prices during the 1970s they are now better insulated and their appliances more energy-efficient. But the basic package remains a wood-framed house in the middle of a plot of land, connected by a driveway to a network of streets and similar homes that extends beyond walking distance.

The problem, an increasingly grave one, is that this package is affordable to far fewer people than it was forty years ago, but our thinking has not adjusted to include other forms. While Americans have diversified their family and living patterns—more people live alone, more families have two parents working outside the home, more parents are single, and more people work in home offices—the range of home types being built has not expanded as quickly. Our image of what constitutes a real house is deeply embedded.

5

ATTACHED HOUSES

Glancing down the interminable Brooklyn street you thought of those joined brownstones as one house reflected through a train of mirrors, with no walls between the houses but only vast rooms yawning endlessly one into the other. Yet, looking close, you saw that under the thick ivy each house had something distinctively its own. Some touch that was Gothic, Romanesque, Baroque, or Greek triumphed amid the Victorian clutter. . . .

Paule Marshall, *Brown Girl, Brownstones*

Over the last two hundred years, American homes of all forms have become steadily more connected to services provided by society. Virtually every dwelling is now attached to at least some strands of a complex web of physical infrastructure: electrical, telephone, and television cables, sewers, water supply pipes, gas lines, and an ever-expanding network of roads. These services have affected both the interior layout of our homes and the ways in which we use the outdoors immediately surrounding them. But the connections themselves are either concealed underground or, when that is too expensive, made as inconspicuous as possible. We do not decorate or call attention to our telephone poles and electrical transformers. Roads, certainly, are visible and occupy increasing acres of land, but in most cases houses are set as far away from them as possible. Our tradition of freestanding house design continues to treat each home as a self-contained object sitting in the "natural world."

When the exterior walls of two buildings touch along a property line, or when they actually share a wall, then they can no longer be clearly seen as distinct objects. A street lined with *attached houses* looks very different from one of freestanding structures. While houses can connect to one another in a number of geometric patterns or in a random assemblage, the form of attached house most common in this country is generally known as a *rowhouse* or *townhouse.* Certain cities and regions have specific local names for them, such as the narrow, one-room-wide *trinities* of Philadelphia or the *brownstones* of New York.

Throughout the eighteenth and nineteenth centuries and into the early twentieth, rowhouses were built in cities and towns across the United States. They were and still are a common form in northern Europe, and the first ones constructed by colonists in North America looked much like those of England and Holland at the time. Many American cities were laid out with repetitive and open-ended street grids that lent themselves to rowhouse development, with rectangular or square blocks easily subdivided into identically sized lots. Even when the scale of commercial building was small and houses constructed only a few at a time, they lined up with one another to form rows of consistent, though not identical, facades.

After World War II, when automobiles and a growing highway system opened up new acres of inexpensive land for homebuilding, the construction of all attached houses was cut back dramatically. Between 1950 and 1970 their total number actually fell by 29 percent; far more were demolished than built. (Over this same period the total number of all homes increased by 47 percent.)[1] Within the last thirty years, however, attached houses have reappeared, often in settings nothing like the towns and cities where they were once a standard form. Isolated clusters of townhouses may suddenly come into view along interstate highways going through open countryside, or in flourishing scenic resorts. They also now go up around the fringes or near the commercial areas of neighborhoods that previously contained only detached houses.

FORMAL AND ENVIRONMENTAL QUALITIES

Most rowhouses are straightforward and solid structures, built to create the greatest possible amount of living space on a small, individual piece of property. At their most basic they are simple rectangles in plan, with common or contiguous walls on two opposite sides. The lots on which they sit are long and rectangular, usually from 15 to 25 feet wide, though properties as narrow as 11 or

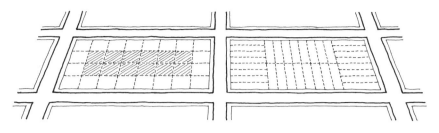

5-1. The left-hand block is divided into square lots of 2,500 square feet each (50' x 50'); shaded lots have no access to the street. The right-hand block has an equal number of long, narrow lots (25' x 100'), all with street frontage.

12 feet can be used. In order to fit as many houses as possible on a given block, the short ends of these lots face the street.

Houses on these narrow lots have been built for rich and working-class families, with rooms ranging from spacious to tiny. Regardless of their level of elegance, the vast majority have a structural system different from that of most American freestanding houses. In order to prevent the spread of fire from one home to another, the long side walls between most existing rowhouses are built of masonry, either brick or concrete block. When groups of houses are constructed at one time, such *party walls* are built with the property line running down their center.

Wood joists supporting each floor are placed at right angles to the party walls, supported by them and bracing them on either side. These joists are typically heavier and deeper than those used in framing for freestanding houses and run from wall to wall, except where openings are left for stairs. Wood decking nailed on top creates a continuous floor and ties the joists together structurally, so that the weight of individual loads, furniture, people, and interior walls is distributed across a wide area.

Masonry bearing walls and heavy wood joists are strong and long-lasting, but they go together more slowly than stud wall construction. Setting joists into individual pockets in the party walls requires time and planning, though perhaps less skill than that needed for the mortise and tenon joints of heavy timber framing. After the balloon frame was available for detached houses, fireproof rowhouse construction was generally more expensive per square foot, a fact that had to be weighed against its economical use of land.

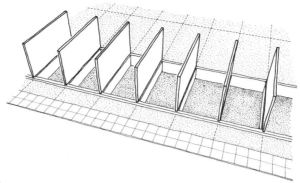

5-2. Rowhouse party walls sitting on four-sided cellar foundations.

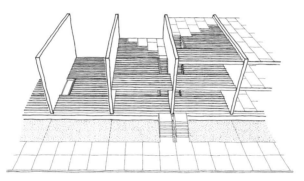

5-3. Wood joists span between party walls at each floor level. Joists are typically doubled around stair openings. The decking, or subflooring, used to be made of individual boards laid perpendicular to the joists but now is usually sheets of plywood.

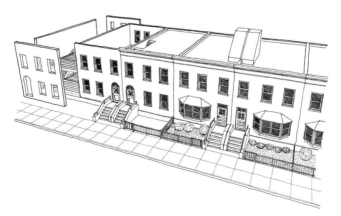

5-4. The front and back walls of most rowhouses sit on the foundation but do not actually support the floor joists. A covered bulkhead over the top stair allows residents to walk up to a flat roof.

5-5. A curved bay window across the entire front of this New York City rowhouse was added long after the initial construction.

One of the beauties of houses built this way is that neither their fronts nor their backs are actually necessary to hold them up. All the work is done by the solid side walls and the framing that runs between them. This leaves a lot of freedom in designing (and later altering) openings for windows and doors, and in the materials used for the parts of the house seen from outside.

When heavy floor joists span from party wall to party wall, as they do in most rowhouses, the interior layout is also flexible. Inside each house, the walls between rooms, technically called *partitions*, may be moved around or taken out completely without affecting the structure. Essentially, each floor of the house is no more than a clear rectangular space with an opening for stairs. Because of this fundamental simplicity, many older rowhouses have had long lives and adapted to repeated changes. Those built in the Victorian era, for example, with separate parlors, pantries, kitchens, and dining rooms, are often transformed today into a more open plan, with fewer rooms and visible, fully modernized kitchens.

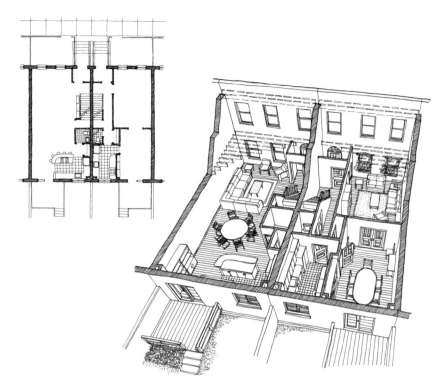

5-6. These neighboring mirror-image houses have identical structures and exteriors, but in the left-hand house the original partitions have been removed to create an open floor plan. The view down into the first floor from the back shows that in an open plan furniture is more important as a means of dividing space into areas for separate uses.

Others are transformed not for aesthetic reasons but to accommodate shifting social needs. Rowhouses are frequently changed back and forth from single-family dwellings to small apartment buildings. While this also happens in detached houses, the layout of a typical rowhouse adapts particularly well to such alterations. With the stairwell and corridor running along one party wall, it is easy to separate floors into discrete units. Plumbing almost always extends through the building in a single vertical stack, making it possible on each floor to add and subtract bathrooms and small kitchens as needed. In many rowhouse neighborhoods these modifications are made continually, not just as the entire community goes up or down economically but as the spatial requirements and budgets of individual owners vary over the course of their lives. A young couple or individual, for example, might buy a large house and live only on one floor, renting out the rest to pay the mortgage. With greater prosperity or the arrival of children they can use the whole building as a single dwelling for several decades, and subdivide it again as their family shrinks or it becomes harder to climb stairs. To be legal, of course, such changes require flexible zoning laws as well as flexible architecture. In recently built neighborhoods of freestanding houses, changes in income or family size more often lead to moving.

Rowhouses have a number of environmental advantages over freestanding houses. Surrounded on two sides by similar enclosed buildings, they neither lose heat nor gain it as fast as detached dwellings of comparable size and therefore require less space-heating and air-conditioning to keep them comfortable. Because they are closer to one another and usually to the street as well, electrical and plumbing connections involve less wire and pipe, as well as less excavation. In general, the staging area of land cleared or disturbed during construction is smaller for each house. Furthermore, because its long side walls are not exposed to weather, a rowhouse has only two facades, front and back, to maintain. This usually means that it needs a lot less upkeep—painting, caulking, and patching—than a detached house, especially one built of wood.

Rowhouses also, however, have clear environmental limitations. Sunlight and fresh air can enter only along the two opposite short ends or from the top. There are no corner rooms in the most straightforward rows, except of course in the end houses. Within a typical house, the only spaces that get light from two sides are those extending for its full length. For this reason the plan of houses longer than about 40 feet is often more complex than a simple rectangle. Tiny courtyards, called *light wells*, may be let into the middle of the house; partial rear extensions may allow windows, though rarely much direct sunlight, in center rooms. In a multistory house an operable skylight over the stairwell can also brighten the central circulation area and create an upward draft out of all connecting rooms. Design features such as bay windows and offset corners help to admit both sunlight and wind from multiple directions, as well as increasing views outward. In all rowhouses, effective cross-ventilation requires a sequence of rooms

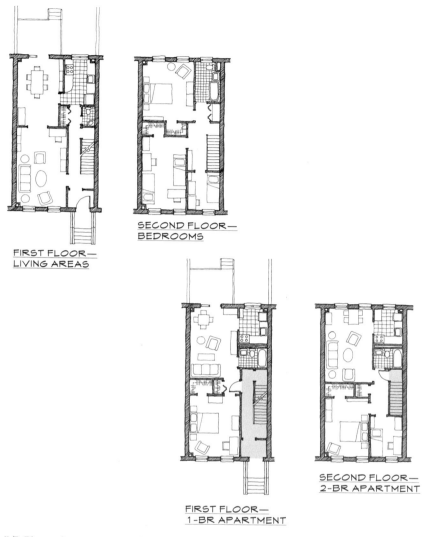

FIRST FLOOR—
LIVING AREAS

SECOND FLOOR—
BEDROOMS

FIRST FLOOR—
1-BR APARTMENT

SECOND FLOOR—
2-BR APARTMENT

5-7. Plans of a two-story rowhouse used as a single dwelling (top) and as two separate floor-through apartments (bottom). When the structure is divided into apartments some floor space around the entry and stair becomes semipublic circulation space (shaded gray), not part of either home.

and door openings that allows air to flow through the length of the house.

The restrictions on light and air that are inherent in the rowhouse form mean that the compass orientation of the street is far more critical than it is for freestanding houses. On a street that

5-8. Rowhouses with bowed fronts from the early 1900s, Queens, New York.

runs east-west, for example, houses will get only north and south light, and half of them—those with south-facing street entrances —will have private backyards that are always at least partly in shadow. Thus, while the two exposed faces of a rowhouse can be easily altered, fundamental environmental adaptations are more difficult to make on a house-by-house basis. In a moderate climate, rowhouses with east and west exposures are preferable because they get light on both ends over the course of the day.

The outdoor spaces of rowhouses are limited by the narrowness of the plot. Whether in the front or the rear, yards can only be as wide as the house itself. When it is long enough, a backyard 12 to 25 feet wide can be used in many ways, accommodating a spacious porch and garden, a child's climber and swings, a toolshed with useful work area around it, or even a small swimming pool. But fences, walls, or tall evergreen hedges are always necessary to maintain privacy from immediate neighbors. The American tradition of substituting horizontal stretches of lawn for clearer vertical divisions between adjoining spaces is simply not possible. The narrow width also precludes certain uses such as even the most

5-9. Private and individualized backyards.

makeshift baseball game, because the ball will always end up on someone else's inaccessible property. Where there is both vehicular access and sufficient parking space either in the front or the rear, the car and driveway will occupy virtually the entire yard, leaving scant area for planting or recreation.

Rowhouses and freestanding houses have profoundly different effects on the overall form of a neighborhood. Whether they are built one at a time on neighboring lots or designed and built in groups, rows of attached houses, taken together, make thick walls. These may be bumpy, with bays and porches that form protrusions and recesses. They may step up and down over hills or define a straight cornice line toward the horizon. The rhythm of entrances, windows, and ornament may be carefully planned and uniform or looser and more varied.

No matter what they look like, however, these walls have certain similar effects on their immediate environment. First, they clearly divide the outdoor space into private areas behind the houses and public areas on the street side. Around a freestanding house, side yards connect the land in front and behind; each corner of the house is visible, and glimpses of the back can often be seen from the street. When houses are attached in rows, the front and the

5-10. On this block most houses are set back from the street; the end units are brought forward, creating a somewhat enclosed space around the street itself and giving a feeling of separation from other blocks.

rear are never seen together. (The exposed end of a row presents a special condition that occasionally affords a glimpse into private yards but is often resolved with a solid freestanding wall or extra-long end building.)

This clear separation between public and private domains frequently translates into different materials and levels of design on the front and back of a house. The street facade of a rowhouse may have elegant arched windows and carved stone ornament while the back is common brick with plain rectangular openings. The various owners of a row designed and built many years ago often maintain carefully preserved and matching fronts while altering the private gardens one by one with protruding extensions, decks, and sliding glass doors. Because the back areas are not on display, this is usually an informality that everyone can live with.

A second important effect of rowhouses or attached buildings of any kind is to shape the open space around them. Essentially, they create outdoor rooms with varying degrees of enclosure. Like rooms within a house, outdoor rooms vary in microclimate according to their orientation and design. The courtyard formed by a four-sided block of rowhouses may be a calm oasis in a windy setting, while the corridors along the street remain far more gusty. Such street corridors are most often long and narrow, but, as with interior spaces, subtle differences in proportions are important.

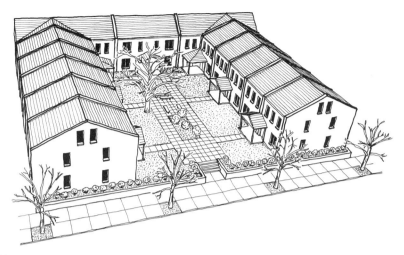

5-11. A U-shaped group of houses defines a courtyard opening off the street.

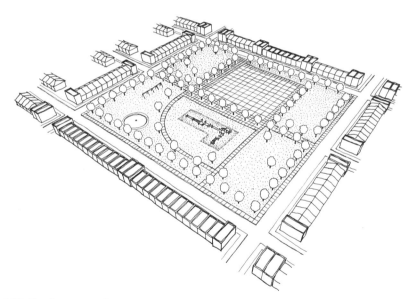

5-12. Rowhouses enclose a two-block neighborhood park.

Depending on the height of the buildings and the width of the street and front yards, a rowhouse block may feel oppressively closed in, comfortably scaled, or grand and formal. Rowhouses can also be grouped to create outdoor spaces both smaller and larger than individual blocks.

EVOLUTION OF ROWHOUSES

In North America rowhouses go back to the days of the earliest European colonies. By the 1630s English settlers in Jamestown, Virginia, and probably elsewhere, were putting up small groups of attached houses closely modeled on familiar English forms that had been built since medieval times.[2] Like many other early colonial houses, these had two roughly equal ground-floor rooms and a steep, winding staircase to sleeping areas above. The long hall-way along one party wall, however, was different in plan from any freestanding house of the era.

Throughout the eighteenth century, as towns and cities along the Atlantic coast grew and prospered, the value of land close to their bustling centers rose steadily. To make the most of narrow strips of property, rowhouses became a standard home form for urban families. Many of the earliest, for reasons of economy, were built entirely of wood. But periodic devastating fires in increasingly dense communities gradually led to the enactment of building laws, and often the creation of fire districts, within which exterior wood walls on or close to property lines were prohibited.

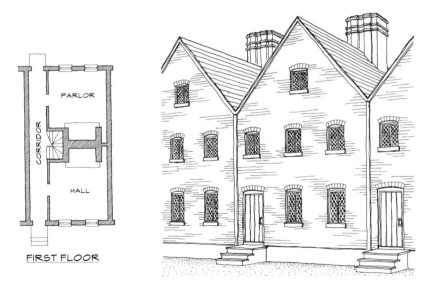

5-13. The early colonial settlement of Jamestown, Virginia, included a group of three rowhouses with floor plans like that on the left. Historians think that they looked something like the sketch on the right, with roof gables facing the street.

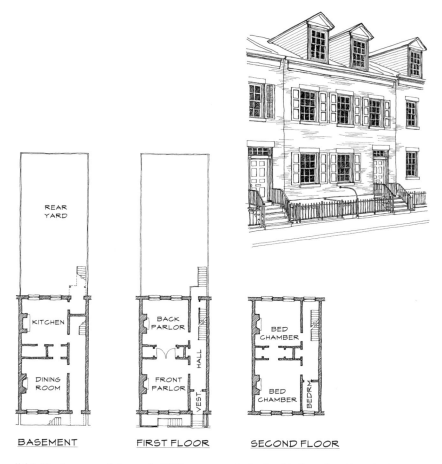

REAR
YARD

KITCHEN

DINING
ROOM

BACK
PARLOR

FRONT
PARLOR

HALL

VEST

BED
CHAMBER

BED
CHAMBER

BEDRM

<u>BASEMENT</u>   <u>FIRST FLOOR</u>   <u>SECOND FLOOR</u>

5-14. Rowhouses of the early 1800s commonly had gabled roofs with attic dormers. The floor plans show a layout typical of a large and prosperous home. Double doors between the parlors on the first floor allowed the two spaces to be opened up for entertaining and permitted breezes to flow through in hot weather. Even large houses usually occupied less than half their lots, leaving deep back yards.

By about 1800 most rowhouses were being built in the dominant Federal style, with simple details derived from Greek antiquity. Despite the fact that such classical details were being used to adorn a wide range of building types, from commercial structures to southern plantation houses, many Americans associated them with early Greek democracy and therefore felt that they expressed the egalitarian nature of the young republic. In *Building the Dream: A Social History of Housing in America*, architectural historian

Gwendolyn Wright describes how, immediately following the Revolution, "the pressure for restraint dominated appeals for the adornment of private property, at least through the 1830s. In theory, in classless America, all dwellings would embody the same principles and would therefore look alike."[3]

The rowhouse blocks of early-nineteenth-century American cities were indeed neat and homogeneous in their public appearance. Behind their repetitive facades, however, both the social uses of interior space and the physical development of private backyards were more varied. Wealthy families distributed their activities among the vertically organized rooms of an entire three-story townhouse in much the same way that they might have used a large detached house of the time. Kitchens were either in the basement or a rear single-story extension, especially when there was a back service alley. Other rooms were differentiated by use but tended to be similar to one another in size, shape, and interior finish, like those in freestanding homes of the same era. Rowhouses typically were built on or close to the front property line and were only 30 or 40 feet deep, leaving at least half the lot for backyards. The yards served a number of crucial functions, housing cisterns for fresh water as well as privies, which were set directly above a cesspool and frequently were connected to the house by a covered walkway. Deep yards also included vegetable gardens and often livestock, perhaps chickens or a pig.

Similar houses of the same size or smaller were used much more intensively by the households of less affluent artisans or laborers. The basic rowhouse layout, with its long side corridors, made it easy to rent individual rooms to boarders, and when neighborhoods grew crowded, basements were also commonly leased out. In cities where blocks were laid out with rear access, separate houses were sometimes built behind the privies, facing the alleys and creating almost invisible low rent districts. Sanitary conditions were poor in these areas of overuse but, aside from fire laws, few regulations pertained to dwelling design.

In this era, long before zoning laws separated homes from commercial or industrial building uses, all neighborhoods included an assortment of small workshops and stores. Many of these were housed on the first story of typical rowhouses, most often the homes of their proprietors. Thus, at the street level, signs and

5-15. The corner storefront remains in a house from the first half of the 1800s in Brooklyn, New York.

display windows enlivened long blocks of similar houses. Because the exterior front walls did not carry structural loads, they were relatively easy to alter, so shopwindows as well as separate entrance doors could be installed or removed as necessary.

As technological change and rapid immigration transformed cities over the first half of the nineteenth century, the homes of urban families became less consistent, reflecting growing social stratification. While conditions for the poor worsened with growing congestion, many increasingly affluent and established Americans focused on building new, more elaborate homes, in keeping with changing social and design standards. Most of the popular attention and the moralizing in patternbooks and magazines was devoted to freestanding houses; thanks to the invention of stud wall framing, these were now being constructed in a great variety of shapes and sizes. But while the idea of country houses in pastoral settings was very appealing, much of the growing wealth in the nation actually depended on urban commerce and industry, and the most practical form of daily transportation was still walking. Many prosperous couples must have pored over Andrew Jackson Downing's *Cottage Residences*, for instance, but they bought or leased a larger, more fashionable rowhouse just a little closer to the edge of town.

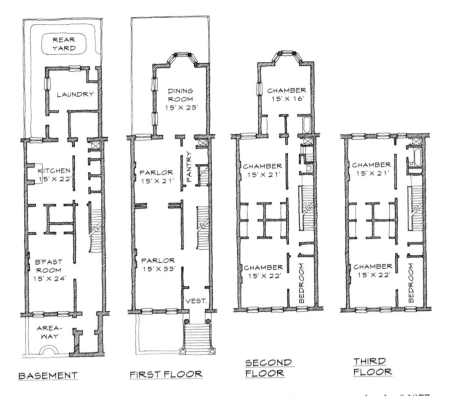

5-16. Plans for a "city house" in *Woodward's National Architect,* a patternbook of 1877. In addition to the four floors shown, the house was to have a subbasement for the furnace and coal storage, and a fifth floor of servant's rooms. A dumbwaiter linked the basement kitchen to a first-floor dining room. Designed for the same 25- by 100-foot lot as the Federal rowhouse shown in figure 5-14, the house had a rear yard only 16 feet deep.

Throughout the nineteenth century rows of attached middle- and upper-class houses continued to be built in large numbers. Their front facades and interior detailing followed a succession of changing fashions related to those of freestanding houses. In most cases, however, the brick, carved stone, or terra-cotta ornament would survive far longer than decoration executed in wood. Many patternbooks included, usually toward the end of the volume, schemes for so-called city houses. During the last third of the century, commercial builders as well as wealthy individuals also hired architects for the custom design of elegant rowhouses.

By the 1860s the spatial expectations for all middle-class and expensive homes in the United States had grown substantially. In

5-17. The difference in scale between a large Victorian rowhouse and its older neighbors to the left is still evident today on a block in Brooklyn, New York. The original front stairs have been removed; the basement door now serves as the main entrance.

addition to requiring twin parlors, formal dining rooms, and spacious entrance halls, Victorian morality and notions of family life now dictated that each child, ideally, have a separate bedroom, not a common practice fifty years earlier. As building lot sizes were generally restricted by street layouts and rising land values, rowhouses built for the upper end of the market had to grow both longer and taller to accommodate these new standards. Some went as high as five stories, the top floor usually containing servants' rooms. With the new emphasis on individuality and creative expression in the design of homes, front facades became much less uniform. Carefully designed and ornate rows of incredible beauty were built during this era, but there were also awkward juxtapositions where houses of wildly different styles adjoined one another without any coordination.

As Victorian rowhouses got deeper, their footprints were no longer simple rectangles but included light wells or side yards along rear extensions to brighten and ventilate dark central rooms. The backyards of these houses, in consequence, became smaller and more irregular, frequently in shadow for most of the day. Many cities now had reliable water supply systems with underground piping, and new middle-class homes began to include interior plumbing, making rear yards less necessary for cisterns and privies. Unfortunately, once private outdoor space was no longer needed for mundane sanitary purposes, the pressure of ever-rising city land values caused it to erode rapidly. The interior courts of new rowhouse blocks in the 1880s no longer provided as much light or as extensive a private outdoor realm, distinct from public city streets and parks.

Around the same time, however, a new form of home for well-to-do urban residents appeared. In the final decades of the nineteenth century, spacious elevator apartments began to offer an alternative to individual private houses in the city. By utilizing height to their advantage, and setting back farther from other buildings, these new dwellings were often brighter and airier than large rowhouses overbuilt on small lots. As it became both technologically feasible and profitable to build twenty or thirty luxury apartment homes on a 100-by-100-foot lot that would have accommodated only four or five townhouses, the value of land in fashionable downtown locations rose even further. By the early 1900s, in cities from Los Angeles to Boston, there were areas where property was simply too valuable to permit the building of individual houses, except for the occasional urban mansion. Within New York City, 1,300 permits were issued for new single-family houses in 1886; most of these were rowhouses. By 1904 the form no longer made economic sense in such a built-up environment, and the number of permits for individual houses had dropped to 40.[4]

After about 1900, though many rowhouses continued to rise, they were more likely to be in outlying sections of a city. This was the same point at which builders, because of the rising cost and complexity of construction, were starting to reduce the overall size and simplify the layouts of freestanding houses for middle-class families; the design of rowhouses followed much the same

5-18. A row of "modern porch houses," as described in the 1909 advertisement of a Philadelphia developer. Houses were marketed through a sales office set up in the new trolley terminal serving the rapidly expanding western reaches of the city.

pattern. A single living room replaced double parlors, kitchens became smaller but more efficient, and entry foyers shrank or disappeared completely.

During the first decades of the twentieth century, new rowhouses continued to reflect many of the same popular concerns that underlay the design and marketing of their detached counterparts. At the same time that the bungalow craze was sweeping the country, for example, rows of small homes known as *porch houses* or *daylighters* were built along the trolley lines now extending outward into new sections of Philadelphia, Baltimore, and Washington.[5] Providing modern amenities for families often moving from older homes without electrical wiring or even indoor bathrooms, the rooms were finished simply in accordance with the current image of a modern, hygienic home. They were set farther back from the street than earlier rowhouses, so that narrow gardens or raised planting beds could separate the public sidewalk from a comfortable front porch spanning the facade. Like many bungalows on narrow lots, they emphasized "nature" while actually forming part of a broad expansion of the city.

A wide variety of moderately sized rowhouses were built between 1900 and the mid-1930s, a time when experimental efforts in neighborhood design were taking place all over the United States. As the typical scale of construction increased, the old pattern of lot-by-lot development was sometimes replaced by more comprehensive neighborhood planning. In a variety of new developments, attached houses formed the basic building blocks or were included in a range of home types. They were put up by private developers for individual sale or rent, by large industrial enterprises for employee housing, by the federal government for shipyard workers during World War I, and by socially motivated limited-dividend housing companies, whose aim was to provide high-quality homes for middle- or working-class Americans while realizing a modest profit. Like the porch houses popular in the mid-Atlantic region, most incorporated a small area of planted front yard. In addition to streets and individual yards, larger complexes now included a variety of public or semiprivate open spaces: small parks, squares, or common courtyards defined by building walls. Overall, the economies and land-conserving benefits of rowhouses were combined with suburban ideals of greenery and open space in newly sophisticated ways.

Perhaps the most conceptually ambitious of these planned neighborhoods were designed with ideas derived from the *garden city movement* initiated a few decades earlier in England. In response to the congestion, overbuilding, and unhealthy conditions of nineteenth-century European cities, Sir Ebenezer Howard and other British architects attempted to define a new form of city that would not extend existing urban areas but rather function as a self-contained community some distance away. The garden city was to include homes, industry, civic functions, agriculture, and stretches of naturalistic parkland in a rational arrangement that

5-19. A schematic partial site plan, typical house plan, and sketch of the planned neighborhood of Chatham Village, built in the early 1930s on a sloping site in Pittsburgh. Sponsored by a private foundation as a middle-income for-profit development, it was designed by Clarence Stein and Henry Wright. All homes were 2- or 3-bedroom houses between 900 and 1,100 square feet, comparable in size to contemporary freestanding houses designed by the Architect's Small House Bureau (see page 149) but less expensive to build. The complex included wooded walking trails and a recreation center.

Attached Houses

2nd FLOOR

BEDRM.

BEDRM.

BEDRM.

1st FLOOR

KIT.

DINING ROOM

LIVING ROOM

2- & 3-BEDROOM ROWHOUSES

GARAGES

STORES

COMMON PARK SPACE

LANDSCAPING AND PRIVATE YARDS

would ensure a high quality of life for all residents, especially the factory workers whose living conditions were then so miserable.

While no such truly self-sustaining new towns were built in the United States, a series of residential developments in the 1920s and 1930s did illustrate and explore some garden city principles. The American architects Clarence Stein and Henry Wright, working both individually and jointly, were involved in many of them. On open sites in outlying sections of New York City, Pittsburgh, and Los Angeles new complexes comprised rows of modest houses with small private yards that opened onto larger green commons. The arrangement allowed all residents to circulate between homes without using the streets, thus providing an unusual degree of safety and independence for children. Sometimes small apartment houses were also included. To keep housing costs affordable for families of moderate income, the buildings themselves were often quite plain and repetitive. The designers felt that a rich and thoughtful development of the surrounding landscape would, over time, prove more meaningful than elaborate detailing of the dwellings. By eliminating the often wasted areas between detached homes, rowhouses allowed everyone to benefit from larger and more continuous open space.

ROWHOUSES AND THE AUTOMOBILE

Through the first third of the century the designers of new rowhouse developments, like those planning new freestanding houses, had to figure out how to make room for the automobile. This was inherently a more difficult problem for attached homes built in rows. Most existing nineteenth-century rowhouses simply could not be adapted to accommodate cars; residents who acquired them either had to park on the street or find and pay for garage space.

Where older city blocks included rear service alleys, people were sometimes able to park behind their homes, but in so doing they lost their own outdoor living space and changed the feeling and surroundings of their neighbors' backyards. In new developments of rowhouses, some builders began to set houses far enough from the street to allow cars to park in front. This arrangement largely precluded real gardens, leaving at best a small planting box

5-20. Cars did not fit on many existing rowhouse lots.

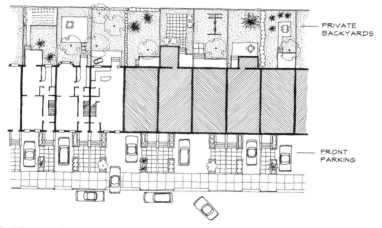

PRIVATE
BACKYARDS

FRONT
PARKING

5-21. When rowhouses were built to allow parking in front, streetscapes were drastically altered but small private backyards remained.

or symbolic patch of grass. It also required frequent curb cuts for driveways, so on-street parking was greatly reduced.

A more elegant and expensive version of this scheme brought the car into the house itself by raising the main floor and putting a garage underneath. Rowhouses were built this way several decades before garages were commonly made part of freestanding American houses.

5-22. These Tudor-style houses from the late 1920s included front porches and living room windows with views out over the cars. However, the foundations and garage structures were costly, and the arrangement left very little on-street parking.

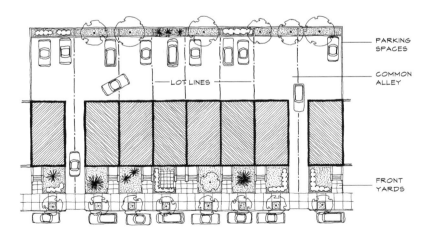

5-23. Arrangements for rear parking typically set houses far enough back from the street to allow small planted front yards but left no private outdoor space for family use.

An alternative development pattern kept houses somewhat closer to the street but reduced the number of continuously attached homes, allowing for common driveways leading to rear *parking alleys.* These alleys cut across individual building lots and had to be maintained jointly by all the homeowners in a row, but they permitted cars to be parked on each individual lot, either in an open air space, a separate rear garage, or under the house in the back.

All these arrangements gave a great deal of privately owned outdoor space over to cars. What might once have been play space or garden was now paved for parking areas and driveways. Though rear parking alleys created fewer curb cuts than schemes with individual front driveways, they nonetheless violated the strict division between sidewalks for pedestrians and streets for vehicles that had existed on early rowhouse blocks. Around new and existing freestanding houses, of course, the same changes occurred, but initially at least they were less visible in the architecture. Until after World War II, Americans kept building freestanding houses that appeared traditional, even while life was drastically changing inside and outside their homes. With rowhouses it was impossible to accommodate a car just by making the house a little narrower or the lot a little wider. The basic patterns of attachment and connection to the street had to change. Comparing successive rows of homes developed in the late nineteenth and early twentieth centuries reveals just how much automobiles came to dominate our outdoor areas and to push buildings apart from one another.

While the steady growth of private automobiles was impossible for builders to ignore, alternative ways of handling its invasive takeover of land did and still do exist. In a few well-planned complexes of the 1920s and early 1930s, such as Chatham Village, parking areas with garages were clustered away from the houses themselves, so that most residents had to walk a short distance between their parking space and their home. Group parking for private homes has many clear advantages. It is the most spatially efficient way to house automobiles, requiring the least paved land per car while still maintaining generous dimensions for backing and turning. Keeping cars away from home entrances and yards creates a much safer and more flexible outdoor environment, especially for children and the elderly. Particularly within the picturesque American tradition of houses surrounded by carefully arranged "nature," it also looks better, permitting richer and more continuous landscaping.

Two major drawbacks pertain to any shared parking arrangement for private houses. First, it requires joint ownership or control, which can always become contentious and complicates the traditional American division of residential land into discrete, privately owned lots. Second, even if homes are arranged so that residents can pull up right in front of them to unload groceries, shared parking arrangements nonetheless entail a moderate amount of walking. Hence, though examples of successful clustered parking schemes can be found, they have never become part of a standard pattern of private house development.

SEMIDETACHED HOUSES

While some designers manipulated rowhouse schemes to allow the incorporation of cars, other builders developing middle-class neighborhoods in the 1910s and '20s began to rely more frequently on an alternate form, the *semidetached house*. Also referred to as *twins, duplexes,* or *double houses,* these were mirror-image pairs of homes sharing only one long wall. They required street frontages of at least 20 to 25 feet, more than some narrow rowhouses but still a lot less than the 35 to 40 feet needed for a small freestanding house. Their great advantage was that driveways, often shared by neighbors, could be located to one side of the house. This arrangement preserved both front- and backyards and did not require continuous rear alleys.

Semidetached houses were frequently designed and built like masonry rowhouses simply pulled apart, creating gap-toothed but continuous blocks. In cities with established rowhouse traditions, such as Philadelphia, they often extended or filled in existing neighborhoods without any abrupt sense of change between one type and the other.

In less crowded situations where land is not as expensive, semidetached houses have a separate tradition as modest homes built to economize on construction costs rather than land. Because only two houses are connected, rather than a whole row, many

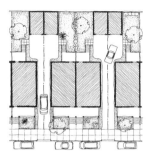

5-24. Semidetached houses were widely built in both wood and masonry, in a multitude of styles, during the first few decades of the 1900s. Since the 1950s their development has been limited by the restrictions of modern zoning ordinances.

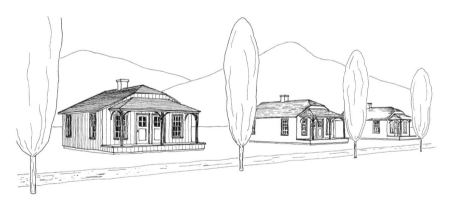

5-25. Small twin cabins built by a Colorado mining company around 1902 and publicized to demonstrate the good housing conditions provided for their workers.

local building codes do not require the heavy masonry party walls used in rowhouses to prevent the spread of fire; semidetached houses are thus often framed completely with wood and look more like symmetrical freestanding houses with two front doors. In the late nineteenth and early twentieth centuries they were often built as workers' housing by large companies in rural locations, or simply as moderately priced alternates to freestanding houses in middle- and working-class suburbs.

While they are not as energy-efficient as rowhouses because they share only one wall with another heated building, the additional exposed wall gives semidetached houses more flexibility in their layout and more possibilities for cross-ventilation.

OTHER WAYS TO ATTACH HOUSES

Though rows and pairs are not the only ways in which houses can be attached, in the United States they are by far the most common, thanks to their structural simplicity and efficient use of land. Along curved streets or distinctive natural boundaries, such as cliffs and lakes, rowhouses may be staggered, creating varied corners and entrances, but their side walls are almost always parallel and their lots long and narrow.

Another way of attaching houses is to *cluster* them so that they share adjoining rather than parallel walls. Semidetached houses are the simplest, binary version of this type, but an equally straightforward and more energy-efficient cluster comprises four houses that form either a rectangle or a pinwheel in plan, each house sitting in the corner of its lot. As with rowhouses, each house shares two walls, reducing heat loss and allowing for grouped utility connections. Unlike rowhouses, however, they can be built on lots of many different sizes and shapes, which gives them the potential to provide an atmosphere and a relationship to the outdoors more like that of freestanding homes.

Clustered homes have never become a standard form in the United States. One reason is undoubtedly the way that most

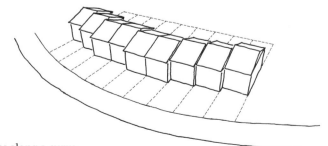

5-26. Rowhouses along a curve.

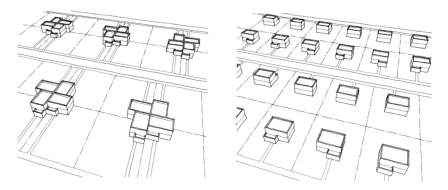

5-27. Two ways of arranging identically sized homes and lots. Clustering houses creates a single large yard for each house and leaves more uninterrupted open space, but also requires buildings to be set far back from the street.

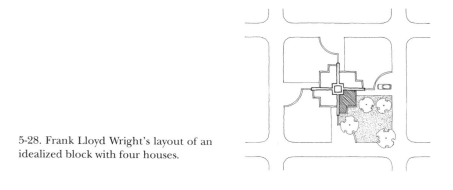

5-28. Frank Lloyd Wright's layout of an idealized block with four houses.

American zoning laws are now written, requiring that new homes be set back specific distances from the front, back, and side property lines. In zones where attached houses are permitted, they may be joined only along the lot lines perpendicular to the street, to form conventional rowhouses.

Frank Lloyd Wright is best known for the pioneering and beautiful individual houses he designed for wealthy clients, as well as for larger civic and industrial buildings. However, he also had a strong interest in the design of more affordable middle-class dwellings and suggested clustered houses as a new prototype for modest American homes. In his 1930s scheme for an ideal American city, called Broadacres, he proposed square blocks each with a single cluster of four houses arranged in a pinwheel.

Though the ratio of streets to houses in this layout was impractical, Wright later designed a small complex of four homes within a larger block that was built in 1939 in a suburb of Philadelphia. Its very modern style was not well received by neighbors, who petitioned to block construction of additional units.[6] Today it sits virtually concealed behind slatted-wood fences, on a street of traditional freestanding houses and open front lawns.

The possibilities for this system of attaching houses, however, endure. To conserve both land and energy, clustered houses might gain acceptance as a practical, easily buildable form compatible with American dwelling preferences.

MODERN ATTACHED HOUSES AND CONDOMINIUMS

During the Depression of the 1930s, a marked decline in the construction of all forms of housing brought an end to a century and a half of substantial rowhouse development. When the housing industry finally revived after World War II, the volume of construction was unprecedented but the range of homes built was much narrower than it had been in prior decades. As already discussed in chapter 4, the combination of rapidly increasing car ownership, newly available land for development, and explicit government policies now favored the exclusive construction of freestanding single-family houses for all but the poorest Americans. In new suburban towns and in outlying sections of existing cities, zoning ordinances were enacted or revised to forbid many previously common forms, such as two- and three-family houses on single lots and attached or semiattached houses on adjoining ones. Rowhousing was seen as old-fashioned and was associated with neighborhoods where homes were mixed with small business and stores in what city planners now regarded as an undesirable clutter. For people who could not afford modern freestanding houses or who remained in cities with prohibitive land costs, the best and healthiest form of home was now felt to be elevator apartment towers separated from other buildings.

Within twenty-five years, however, the limitations of neighborhoods made up exclusively of freestanding houses became apparent. As house prices escalated beyond the means of many middle-class and now suburban Americans, local governments began to come under pressure to amend their zoning laws and permit a wider range of home types. Battles over zoning changes were and still are intense, but gradually, starting in the early 1970s, isolated complexes of low-rise apartments and attached homes began to appear on the suburban landscape. Typically these were not mixed in among blocks of single-family houses but went up either close to existing commercial strips or on open land near highways. The notion that neighborhoods of freestanding homes had to be protected from the incursions of other forms remained strong.

In recent decades, significant numbers of so-called townhouse developments have been built all over the United States, sometimes in remote rural areas that are not part of any legal town at all. While in physical form these are rowhouses, most of them probably are not individually owned homes on separate strips of property. Like many new low-rise and high-rise apartments, they are part of larger complexes known as *condominiums,* a term that refers not to a particular physical form of housing but to an ownership arrangement. In a condominium, people own only the interior of their home, while a separate corporation keeps title to and maintains the supporting structure, land, and any common facilities. Residents pay monthly maintenance fees to this corporation for as long as they own their unit. In return, they get the grass outside their windows mowed, their roof leaks repaired, and their shrubs pruned and mulched without having to hire someone or do it themselves. Their choices regarding the uses of the immediate outdoor space, however, are limited and subject to approval by a governing board. They might be able, for example, to plant small flowerbeds and add a patio, but probably not erect a swing set or fence in a dog run.

Condominium units may be attached or detached houses or apartment buildings of any size. They embody a new kind of ownership, which has many implications for how homes can physically change and adapt over time. Will the separation between interior and exterior ownership mean that indoor spaces find new uses and get individually reconfigured while the outdoors remains uniform and continuous? Or will alterations and extensions occur despite regulations, gradually changing the exterior faces of individual units so that an entire complex becomes a more informal collage than that originally planned by the architect?

Wherever they are built and whatever their form of ownership, the new townhouses have some of the same basic formal characteristics as older urban rowhouses. Though concrete blocks replace bricks, and, sometimes, lightweight trusses replace solid wood joists, their structure still usually consists of parallel, fireproof party walls with perpendicular joists spanning between them. Combined, townhouses still make thick walls across the landscape, with separate public and private faces.

Even when they are built on the rectangular blocks of existing cities, however, rowhouse walls are rarely as long and continuous as those of a century ago. Shorter and often more irregular rows are now interspersed with parking lots and narrow strips of landscaping. The homes are designed to look as unlike older urban townhouses as possible, evoking instead the freestanding houses of nearby communities. The more expensive they are, the more likely they are to have individual garages built into or attached to them.

Compared with the planned communities of the early twentieth century, most recent townhouse developments have few communal or parklike open spaces. Cars tend to occupy the center of whatever outdoor "rooms" are defined by building walls. When new complexes are large and luxurious enough to include special shared facilities, they are likely to be amenities for individual use, such as tennis courts or a hiking trail, rather than a central green where residents might congregate.

In many popular vacation areas, condominiums or individual attached houses have largely replaced the old resort hotels to which well-to-do families journeyed by train with bulky trunks for a long stay. They would eat elegant meals served by waiters in a common dining hall, relax in the hotel's pool or hot springs, and mingle with other guests on a large common porch or terrace with a beautiful view. Now vacationers get no servants but their own kitchens with sleek modern appliances, whirlpool tubs for relaxation, and individual decks, perhaps with the same spectacular view.

Attached houses now exist in a wide variety of settings in the United States. Many older neighborhoods of nineteenth- and early-twentieth-century rowhouses have proven remarkably resilient, both physically and socially. Masonry party walls remain

5-29. Suburban townhouses north of New York City, 1980s.

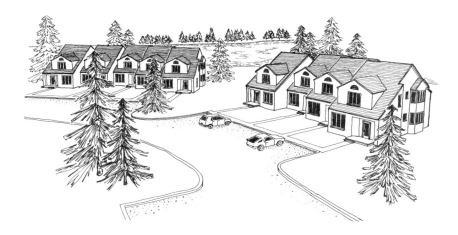

5-30. Rowhouse condominiums on the lakeside site of a former resort hotel in the Adirondack mountains.

standing even when roofs leak and joists crack or rot, so the buildings don't fall down and even the most decrepit are often successfully renovated. Because individual houses have been easily transformed over the years, sometimes back and forth, into apartments, rooming houses, small offices, and stores, entire blocks have been more likely to remain intact than blocks of freestanding houses from the same eras. Where rowhouse neighborhoods have disappeared, it has not been because of fire or the gradual forces of natural decay but rather because of human decisions, economic, political, and social.

Most older rowhouses, like the newer ones in townhouse complexes outside the city, were built as pragmatic structures that made the most of scarce and costly land. Their collective ability to shape space and their inherent environmental efficiency were not deeply considered as part of their design. Neither were they freighted with the emotional and behavioral expectations that are attached to freestanding houses in the United States. The notion that children would be happiest or would develop most fully and morally growing up in a rowhouse was not generally part of the strategy used to market them. (Such a case could easily be made for rowhouse living on the basis of neighborly behavior patterns, urban access to culture and education, and the possibilities for extended families to stay close to one another while still maintaining some independence. These, however, are qualities of low-rise city neighborhoods that have been observed or rued after their demolition, rather than used as rationale for their construction.)

In America, our homes are supposed to be our castles. Compared with the freestanding house that most of us associate with this vision, even the grandest attached house has a kind of natural modesty. The attached house is hard to picture as a castle because it is always part of a larger assemblage of buildings; a castle is supposed to stand out against and dominate its landscape (even if the landscape is only a 40-by-100-foot lot). But well-designed attached houses have the environmental and economic potential to provide truly satisfactory American homes. They deserve to be given stronger popular philosophical underpinnings as well as a wider range of considered use.

APARTMENTS

One man's ceiling is another man's floor.
Paul Simon

Both freestanding and attached houses were built by early colonists in North America starting almost four hundred years ago. Only within the last century and a half, however, have we formally recognized *apartment houses* in this country as a separate type of home. During this relatively short period we have built a wide variety of apartment structures, ranging in size from the double-decker house, barely distinguishable from its single-family neighbors, to the high-rise elevator tower. The sequence of their development is closely tied both to advancing technology and to an ever-growing set of legal requirements, or minimum standards, for all American dwellings.

Though apartments may be relatively new in the United States, spatial arrangements that include individual homes within larger structures have been built around the world and go back as far as our knowledge of architectural history. On this continent, a number of Native American cultures developed forms that we might today call apartment buildings: the rectilinear longhouses of the Iroquois and the more irregular multistory complexes of southwestern Pueblo tribes are two well-known examples. Both had social as well as environmental advantages, providing security against enemies in addition to interior comfort in harsh climates. Both featured clearly defined personal spaces with some degree of privacy for each family and an open-ended structure that allowed the addition of more homes as communities grew.

For many settlers coming from densely populated European countries where property ownership was often concentrated in the hands of the wealthy, a principal attraction of the New World was the opportunity to live and build on their own private land. But while this goal was indeed easier to realize here than elsewhere, it was never affordable or practical for all Americans. Partly as a consequence, the individual houses that were built were occupied by a much wider variety of households than the nuclear family for which most houses are designed today. Many included long- and short-term paying boarders, servants, and apprentices; particularly in commercial cities, groups of rooms or entire floors were also rented out to separate families who cooked and kept house independently. Over the first several hundred years of our history, however, none of these arrangements constituted a distinct building form. They simply represented a range of ways in which people used their houses. Beyond sheltered space and some minimal means for cooking and keeping warm, there were no physical requirements to define homes in any case.

Through the mid-nineteenth century, the term *apartment* referred to any individual room within a dwelling. Thus Andrew Jackson Downing, describing one of the schemes presented in *The Architecture of Country Houses*, wrote in 1850, "The parlor here is quite a handsome apartment for a cottage, being sixteen by twenty-two feet, with a bay window."[1]

By 1880, however, at least in American cities, the word acquired a new meaning: a modern, multiroom dwelling within one of the new high-rise elevator buildings that were just beginning to be constructed for the wealthy. The use of the new term *apartment house* set these homes apart, in the public mind, from the groups of rooms rented by much poorer families within large walk-up buildings, usually without bathrooms and running water. Such structures were common in England long before they began to appear in the United States, and were known on both sides of the Atlantic as *tenement houses*. Over the next forty years, because of rising prosperity, advances in technology, and new building codes, these two types of homes grew more similar, and the term apartment developed its current and more universal meaning. To be

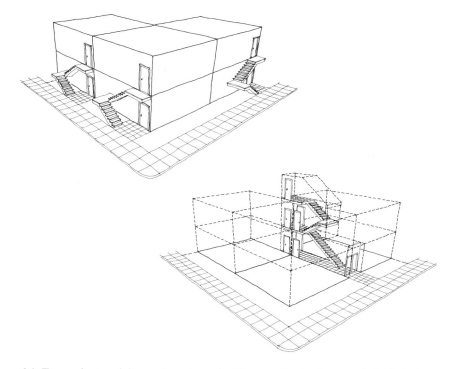

6-1. Top, a cluster of six apartments, each with separate street access. A single indoor circulation system, below, frees up exterior walls for windows, requires fewer stairs, and conserves heat by creating, in effect, one vestibule for all entry doors.

legal today in the United States, an *apartment* must have all the same basic spaces and connections as an attached or freestanding house: a full bathroom and kitchen, hot and cold running water, living spaces of certain minimum dimensions, electrical wiring, operable windows, and, not least important, a registered, discrete address.

Apartment buildings also generally include a type of space not found in private homes. Theoretically, dwellings stacked or placed adjacent to one another above the first floor can be individually connected to the ground and street, but only the smallest apartment structures, usually called *two-* and *three-family houses*, are built this way. Grouping dwellings within a single building usually requires the creation of semipublic spaces for entry and circulation. These may be spacious and elegant, adding a measure of grandeur to the homes themselves. In other cases they are absolutely minimal, providing only the space necessary for people and furniture to get safely in and out of the building. Whatever their configuration, such areas serve apartment dwellers as a transition zone between home and the public spaces of their neighborhood.

Potentially, these semipublic spaces can include an array of amenities that residents might not be able to afford or maintain individually. Swimming pools, health clubs, dining facilities, libraries, rooftop and ground-level gardens, playgrounds, child-care centers, and meeting rooms have all been included in American apartment buildings or complexes. The most frequent common facility, however, is the mundane laundry room, and the second is probably the semiprivate parking lot. Certain human services, such as those of doormen and building custodians, may be shared as well, adding safety and convenience to all the homes in the building. Of course, in the same way that so many free-standing houses don't make the most of their potential for fine-tuning to their climate and site, many apartment buildings offer few common services. Sometimes it is harder to get the landlord or managing agent to plaster and paint over that old leak in the bathroom ceiling than it is to do it oneself. But the possibility for sharing desirable features among many homes is built into the form of an apartment building in a way that it is not in a single-family house.

For many Americans, the advantages of these shared amenities may be offset by the lack of individual control over services and spatial arrangements. Early apartment buildings in this country typically involved rental arrangements for tenants, though owners often lived in their own buildings. While individual houses were frequently rented as well, they were nonetheless associated with national ideals of self-determination and independence. Today, condominium and cooperative forms of ownership give apartment residents more legal control and, in some communities, higher social standing.

Apartments are also created in buildings with separate, nonresidential uses. One of the earliest and most universal building forms is a single structure containing a shop as well as the shopkeeper's or craftsman's home. This was once common in the United States, but zoning laws and changing neighborhood patterns now make it rare. In older communities there are still a few commercial establishments where the owner lives directly above or behind the business. Many apartment buildings, however, do include stores and offices that are unrelated to the dwellings, usually with separate entrances from the street. Growing numbers of apartments also are being created in buildings originally built for other purposes, such as factories and schools. Some of these are totally converted to residences, but others remain mixed-use structures.

FORMAL AND ENVIRONMENTAL QUALITIES

Apartments are inherently the most energy-efficient form of human dwelling. Sharing the greatest surface area with neighboring indoor spaces, they neither lose heat nor gain it as fast as free-standing or even attached houses. What they do need can often be more efficiently supplied by a single central heating system than by many individual ones. The same principle also applies to other services such as hot water and air-conditioning. In addition, the initial resources and energy needed to connect new dwellings to existing streets and mechanical services are much less for an apartment building than for an equal number of houses, and the area of land disrupted or permanently altered by the connections is far smaller.

What is an environmental advantage in one way, however, can be disadvantageous in another. The geometric characteristics that make apartments efficient to heat also severely limit the range of options for providing natural light and ventilation, especially as buildings grow horizontally, with many units on a single floor.

Architects often refer to the vertical connections between the floors of a multistory building as the *core;* like the core of an apple it runs from the bottom to the top, usually, though not always, straight. The core of a small apartment building may consist of a single set of stairs, with apartment entrances off the landings. Unless residents can get to the ground safely from their windows, however, this is not an ideal layout, because they can be trapped by a fire in the stairwell. As buildings get larger and higher, codes require that every apartment have two alternate ways out. Exterior fire escapes, reached by climbing through apartment windows, used to meet the requirement for a second means of egress and still do in many older buildings. But over the last thirty years or so,

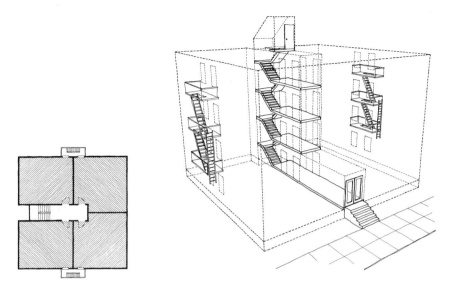

6-2. Perspective view and typical floor plan of a simple walk-up building with four apartments per floor. Fire escapes connect to one window in each unit to provide a second means of egress.

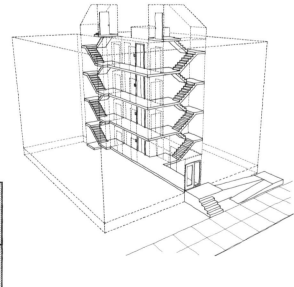

6-3. A core in a small modern elevator building, also with four units per floor. There are two separate internal stairs, each enclosed, and ramped access to the front door for the handicapped.

most codes have been revised and no longer permit fire escapes in newly constructed buildings. The stairs now required for egress usually must be enclosed within fireproof shafts, to protect people who are inside and descending and to prevent the spread of flames and smoke from one floor to another.

Even when they are used most of the time to get from one floor to another, elevators are not considered means of egress because they can't function if the electricity is cut off. Thus, the core of a tall building becomes a complex assembly of enclosed stairs, elevators, and connecting corridors. Generally, as more apartments are grouped around each core on a single floor, there is less exterior wall for the apartments and less opportunity for them to have windows facing in more than one direction.

In modern apartment buildings, the most common layout of core elements and dwelling units is known as the *double-loaded corridor*. Most apartments are hemmed in on opposite sides by adjacent homes and on a third by a common hallway, leaving only one side exposed to the exterior. This arrangement, repeated on every floor, is an efficient way to provide elevator access and two alternate means of egress for a large number of units with relatively few elevators and stairs. From an environmental point of view, however, homes built this way have several drawbacks. No matter how many rooms there are, all have basically the same view and quality of light throughout the day. If the exposed wall faces east, for example, then the dining room as well as the bedrooms and living room will be sunny during breakfast but in shade by lunchtime and thereafter. Overall, such apartments do not offer the variety of natural environments and visual access to the outdoors that exist within a home with more exposures.

This lack of complexity is not a critical issue for everyone. Some people prefer indoor light and keep curtains drawn most of the time. Others lucky enough to have a special view, such as the ocean, distant mountains, or a spectacular cityscape, may not miss less interesting vistas in other directions. But air quality and comfort are also compromised, because cross-ventilation is minimal in apartments with a single exposure. The relative energy efficiency of the building in terms of heating may therefore be offset by an inevitably greater reliance on mechanical air-conditioning, even in moderate climates.

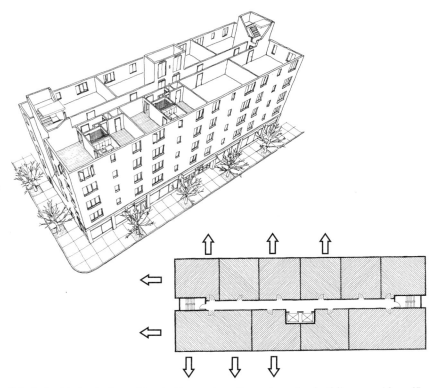

6-4. A double-loaded corridor in the center of a rectangular building provides efficient elevator access to many apartments at once, but only the corner units have more than one exposure. The plan and perspective alternative stair arrangements.

Fortunately, even as the number of apartments in a building increases, there are alternatives to rectangular plans with double-loaded corridors. One way to create apartments with a greater variety of views and more cross-ventilation is to build separate cores for different sections of the building, reducing the number of units around each core. This strategy improves apartment floor plans and reduces the amount of public corridor, but obviously increases the number of stairways and, in taller buildings, elevators. Because stairs are less expensive to build than elevators and cost nothing to operate, many low-rise apartment buildings but far fewer high-rise ones are designed with multiple cores. Sometimes two or more cores connect at ground level in a common lobby; in other cases each core has a separate entrance from the street or a courtyard.

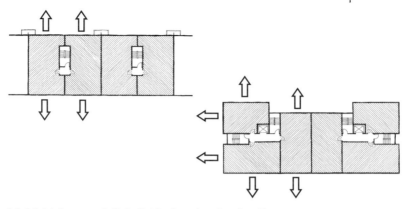

6-5. Multiple cores: left, individual enclosed stairwells serve two apartments on each floor; fire balconies at the rear allow residents to enter adjacent apartments in an emergency and exit via an alternate stair. Right, modern elevator cores that serve three units per floor.

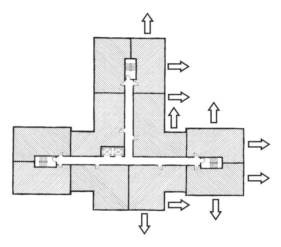

6-6. Projecting wings in a variety of formations make possible many inside and outside corner units, all reasonably close to the elevators. Because building codes limit the length of "dead end" corridors, additional fire stairs are often necessary.

Recesses and projections that add surface area to the building provide another way to increase the number of exposures and improve the light and air in each apartment. Angled bays, deeply recessed balconies, and projecting wings all can help to create a more three-dimensional relationship between the interior of an apartment and the outdoors. In general, these elements result in a more articulated and complex building exterior and can greatly improve apartments laid out along a double-loaded corridor.

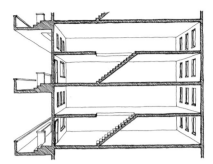

6-7. An open corridor on every other floor means walking outside after getting off the elevator, but allows the creation of apartments that are essentially two-story rowhouses lifted off the ground

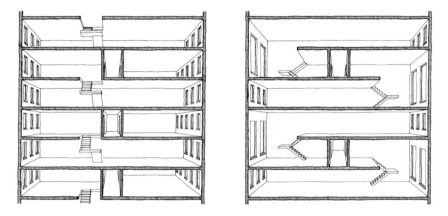

6-8. A variety of cross-sections can be created using skip-stop elevators. In the left-hand drawing, corridors on every other floor lead to single-story, handicapped-accessible apartments (on the right) and to the upper level of duplex apartments (on the left). In the drawing at right, corridors every third floor lead to duplex apartments with double-height living areas.

A third strategy for creating better ventilated and more house-like apartments without additional core elements is to alter the building cross section. If the public corridor is pulled to one side of the building and left unenclosed, then apartments can extend through the building like rowhouses. These open corridors are sometimes referred to as *streets in the air*.

Floor-through units, with exposures at opposite ends, are also created by building central public corridors only on every second or third floor; apartments then extend across the whole building on the floors without corridors. Such layoutst reduce the area of corridor as a percentage of a building's square footage and allow for *skip-stop elevators*, with fewer doors and controls.

Overall, apartment houses come in a wider range of forms and sizes than do single-family dwellings, and consequently their environmental qualities vary more as well. They may be freestanding or attached to other buildings. In the latter case their spatial effects on a neighborhood are similar to those of rowhouses, creating continuous walls and defining outdoor spaces.

Many apartments have no door opening directly outdoors, and this can be unsettling for people used to a simple, individual connection between the interior of their home and the ground around it. A lack of even the most mundane private exterior space complicates some everyday tasks—stepping outside in the morning to test the weather, or shaking sand out of children's shoes. Apartment dwellers, of course, adapt to their homes as all humans do to a range of built settings or preexisting climates. They adjust their habitual behavior, perhaps listening more closely to the weather report or learning to plan what they need to do outside before getting on the elevator to their front door. The fact remains, however, that designing apartments whose interior spaces are effectively integrated with the outdoor environment around them is often neither easy nor intuitive. Balconies, for example, may symbolize a connection to the outdoors, but while some provide real open-air living space others are merely awkward, wind-blown appendages, more ornamental than useful. Enclosed courts or yards surrounding an apartment building sometimes appear simply left over, accurately reflecting that they exist only to meet legal requirements for light and ventilation within apartments. Within and around other buildings, however, they are positively developed, either with formal planting or amenities for residents' use.

In comparing apartment buildings with other forms of homes in the United States, it is important to remember that they are relatively new. All building types evolve gradually as their designers observe and learn from what already exists while incorporating new technology and social requirements. This is certainly true of what we now take for granted as a standard American suburban house; it developed from one or two rooms with a fireplace to a complex set of highly differentiated spaces with mandatory, built-in mechanical and plumbing connections.

Apartment buildings present a more involved design problem than do single-family houses. Their individual dwellings must provide all the same spaces and connections as houses but under greater spatial restrictions. Designers must simultaneously resolve the needs for semipublic space, safe egress, and a more complicated and fireproof structure. Because they are larger and must ensure the safety of greater numbers of people, apartment buildings today are almost always designed by licensed architects or engineers.

The history of apartment houses in the United States is hence linked both to the development of technology and to shifting aesthetic fashion within the architectural and engineering professions. These connections have led to sometimes abrupt changes in appearance. On their exterior, apartment buildings often have more in common with other professionally designed structures than with smaller houses. In the 1940s, for example, after the widespread adoption of the stripped-down modern style by architects, apartment houses—like office buildings, stores, schools, and city halls—lost most exterior ornamentation and references to earlier historic styles. A multistory building of modest, middle-class apartments from the 1910s or 1920s typically included some version of a classically proportioned facade, with decorative elements creating a three-part base, middle, and top. By the early 1950s, however, a new building aimed at a similar market had plain exterior walls, usually of brick or exposed concrete, with identical windows from bottom to top. To some degree this change was the result of shifting costs within the building industry, as skilled labor grew more expensive and building components more standardized, but it also reflected new training and changing criteria for highly regarded design in architecture schools.

Over the same period the transformation of freestanding houses was less radical. While the scale of their production increased dramatically and they also lost some decorative touches, most remained identifiable as Cape Cods or Colonials. Even the new ranches and split levels came with details linking them to earlier popular styles; those that were too austere were quickly modified by residents. Decorative shutters were added around bare window

6 - 9 (above) and 6-10 (below). Two street views of middle-class apartment buildings constructed less than fifty years apart in Queens, New York City. Though the newer building has only one more story, it sits on a much larger site, has many more units, and is set farther back from the street. The exteriors of all floors above the first are identical plain brick walls relieved only by fire escapes and air-conditioning sleeves.

openings, wrought-iron columns and projecting gabled roofs at front entrances. Popular culture and the pragmatic thinking of individual homeowners and commercial builders, who determined the design of most houses, were visually conservative even while incorporating technological change. Thus, to many Americans, new architect-designed apartment buildings during this period appeared ever less homelike and more institutional than individual houses, even when the latter were produced in identical models by the thousands and contained interior rooms finished and decorated just like the apartments.

In large numbers, freestanding houses create a low carpet effect that is known negatively as *sprawl*, obliterating earlier plant and animal life while still largely following the existing terrain. Tall apartment buildings, in contrast, become major new features of the landscape. Like office towers, they cast long shadows and alter local wind patterns in a way that you can feel, suddenly coming around a corner. They can also create dramatic vistas where none existed before. Scientists investigating the possibility of innate human preferences for certain natural settings and life forms speculate that we instinctively choose the type of sites where our early ancestors were safest: elevated plateaus with open views of their surroundings, rather than damp lowlands or dense mountain forests.[2] In this sense there may be something inherently satisfying about living in the high reaches of an apartment tower; certainly it can provide a secure and peaceful home setting within a densely built-up neighborhood.

One of the main drawbacks often attributed to apartment living is a lack of privacy. Indeed, an apartment within a multifamily building can never provide the total isolation of a freestanding house without visible or audible neighbors. When groups of homes are compared, however, the issues are more complex. The open front lawns, picture windows, and single-story, ground-level layout of many American houses do not inherently provide much privacy from neighbors, especially in neighborhoods where homes are closely spaced. Visual privacy within standard contemporary apartments is actually greater than in many common house forms. (To some degree this may contribute to the suspect nature of apartment living.) Because most units are above the first floor and are entered through a solid door in a solid wall, it is often impossible to see into an apartment, notwithstanding movies in which the hero observes the villain's deeds through a window across the courtyard.

When people watch their neighbors, what they actually see are largely the comings and goings from other homes. Even on an empty street of curtained houses people can be identified by their cars in the driveway (an element of life that is also important to movie plots). Someone entering the lobby of a large building, however, may be bound for any number of different homes and, once inside, becomes invisible.

Acoustic privacy is a different matter. Both the impact sounds of people walking or vacuuming on the next floor up and the airborne noise of voices and music from adjacent apartments can be nagging and perpetual annoyances. Of course, noise carries between and around individual houses as well. The sounds of cars, leaf blowers, and electronic alarms are often a negative side effect of modern technology rather than home form. The extent to which noise is transmitted within an apartment building depends on its structural and finish materials and on the care taken in designing both mechanical systems and partitions, or *demising walls*, between apartments. Over the last hundred years, the technology of high-rise apartment building construction has changed rapidly and, sadly, the systems in use early in the twentieth century were more inherently sound-reducing than those being applied today. While acoustic engineers and architects have sophisticated ways to virtually eliminate sound transmission between adjacent technical laboratories and studios, these design details are rarely applied to apartments, which tend to be built to the bottom line.

An increasingly important rationale for the construction of apartment buildings today is their accessibility. While people with a variety of disabilities can and do live independently in homes of all forms, apartment houses are inherently well suited to accommodating special needs. Elevator buildings make it possible for individuals who use wheelchairs or have difficulty climbing stairs to live above ground level, or the few feet up that may be attained with ramps. They have other advantages too. Compared with single- story houses, for instance, another inherently accessible form, apartment buildings are much more likely to be located in densely populated communities with a variety of other building types close by, so that people who do not drive can get easily on their own to stores, schools, or work. Whether apartments are owned or rented, arrangements for common maintenance relieve residents of responsibilities for shoveling snowy sidewalks and dealing with major building problems. In larger complexes, an on-site handyman or super who helps with minor tasks such as changing bulbs in ceiling fixtures and unclogging toilets is invaluable to residents with limited agility or vision.

More specialized apartment buildings can economically include shared services, semipublic spaces, and technology to facilitate, as much as possible, safe independence and comfort. Emergency call systems, for instance, installed in all apartments, can be wired to a central station so that if residents fall in their bathroom or feel ill in bed they can push an alarm button and get immediate help from staff on duty. Central dining rooms give people the choice not to shop for and cook all their meals while still having their own small kitchens to use when they prefer. Common recreation facilities oriented toward those with specific disabilities can be more fully developed than in private houses. An outdoor garden, for instance, might contain scented plants and a fountain to be enjoyed by residents who are blind.

Over the last thirty years, the average size of households in the United States has dropped steadily, with fewer people living in extended family groups. To meet the needs of retired and elderly people on their own, widely varied residential complexes made up partially or entirely of apartments have been built to meet new standards of accessibility. Hence, while we may still think of detached houses as the quintessential American dwellings, we are less and less likely to live out our lives in them.

Appearing in the United States around 1850, apartment houses have gone through a rich and complex development. Grappling with the issues of safety, health, and livability raised by their construction led to the enactment of laws that now apply to all our homes. Since the World War II, however, the formal range of new apartment houses has been far more limited than it was in the first half of this century. Many factors now operate against diversity in their design. High initial capital costs and rigid local zoning laws discourage risk and make small-scale experimentation difficult.

Low prices for purchased fuel and electricity give builders little incentive to construct apartments that are naturally well lit and ventilated. Thus, repetitive and predictable layouts along dark, double-loaded corridors predominate. Most new units are small, with few bedrooms, because of a widespread social assumption that "real" houses are preferable for families with children. The most interesting and often the largest apartments built within the last twenty-five years are those created within older, nonresidential buildings.

At the same time there are many reasons—economic, environmental, and social—why apartments will probably constitute a greater proportion of American homes in the future than they do at present. The rest of this chapter briefly examines some of the wide range of apartments actually built in this country, not just to rue the loss of an earlier diversity and formal richness but also to illustrate their potential for the future.

THE TENEMENT HOUSE

My father took us to Rutgers Street and East Broadway. He had an apartment for us—what an apartment! The toilet was in the yard. The sink was a black sink in the hall. Everybody was washing there. There was only cold water running. There were three rooms. If it wasn't enough, we slept on the roof. Why not?
Martha Dolinko, quoted in *You Must Remember This*

The rapid and seemingly uncontrollable growth of industrial cities in the mid-1800s spurred several diverging developments in the design of American homes. On one hand, it led to a national obsession with freestanding country houses as a source of order and stability, while on the other it required the creation of new forms in the cities themselves. Over the course of just a few years, established urban neighborhoods became noisier, dirtier, and more crowded, with new kinds of businesses and small factories. In response to these changes, respectable middle-class residents tended to leave and sell their houses, moving farther away from growing commercial centers. The earliest apartments in the United States were created by dividing up or adding to existing single-family houses, both freestanding and attached.

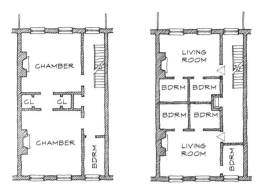

6-11. The upper floor of a typical large rowhouse from the early 1800s, on the left, transformed into two small "flats" with tiny interior bedrooms, on the right.

Though the practice of renting out rooms and even floors within individual dwellings was long-standing, surging populations and newly concentrated job opportunities made it ever more widespread. Extra stories and rear additions were added to existing houses, and separate, often more jerry-built structures filled in backyards. Depending on the city and its street layout, these were known as *alley dwellings, court houses,* or *backbuildings,* and were often the least expensive homes available.

As rents rose along with the demand for housing, the subdivision of new residential structures became more systematic. On Manhattan Island, where business was booming and space restricted by encircling rivers, builders and property owners figured out sooner than anywhere else how to design buildings for narrow city lots that would house more families, and therefore yield more profit, than converted single-family homes. By the 1860s such structures were being built as high as six stories, much higher than the older homes around them. In general, they were laid out in a way that divided up the building into many more small rooms than an earlier rowhouse built on the same size property. On a lot 25 feet wide, the stairs were moved into the center to create two long, narrow apartments on either side. The rooms in these apartments, like those in shotgun houses, opened directly into one another, with no separate corridors to allow for privacy. Because of their layout, like the cars on a train, they became known as *railroad flats.*

With four apartments on each of six floors, many of these New York tenements housed twenty-four families on the same amount

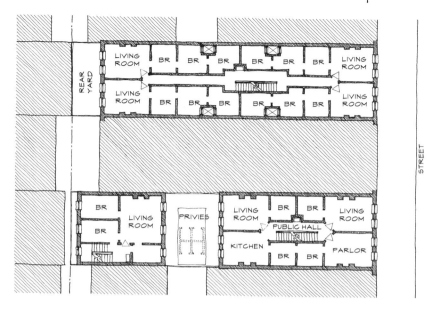

6-12. The bottom floor plans show an early tenement with a separate backbuilding in the rear and a shed housing privies between the two. Above is the plan of a larger tenement with four four-room railroad flats per floor; this plan was termed "improved" because of the light shafts, perhaps 4 by 6 feet each, in the center of the building. With few regulations enforced, block interiors were crowded, and windows sometimes faced onto exterior spaces of only 1 or 2 feet.

of land that had earlier housed just one. They covered even more of the lot than the deep Victorian rowhouses of the same era; many interior rooms had no windows. Because early tenements, like most houses of the time, lacked indoor plumbing, what remained as a rear yard was most often used for outdoor privies. In other cases these were put in the cellar. Indoors or out, they typically were not connected to a sewer system but sat over a festering and frequently overflowing cesspool.

Tenements were not simply the demonic invention of greedy New York landlords. They were built in many American cities as well as in Europe during the nineteenth century because of changes in the nature of work caused by the Industrial Revolution. In urban centers from San Francisco to Boston, factories increased both in size and number, clustering near water or rail lines. The population of industrial workers and their families grew astronomically and included a steady stream of recent immigrants from

6-13. A row of tenements still standing today on the Lower East Side of Manhattan, next to what was probably a factory loft building of the same era.

countries where job opportunities were not as plentiful. Without any means of daily transportation other than walking, people had to live within a short distance of work. Thus, even with high rents, tenements met a large and continuous demand.

Most tenements were built not more than two or three at a time by small investors and builders, some of whom lived in their own buildings. In New York, where fire laws required that they have exterior walls of masonry, their facades included bands of stone ornament and decorative cornices, similar to those on rowhouses of the same era. Elsewhere, in cities such as Chicago and Newark, tenements were more often only two to four stories high and sometimes built of wood, with roof details and window trim that resembled smaller freestanding houses. To justify the highest possible rents, owners frequently included a few stylish interior finishes: decorative tile floors and wainscots in the entrance lobbies or nice wallpaper in the public halls. In newer buildings tenants were often established and upwardly mobile immigrant families.

6-14. A Chicago streetscape with a mixture of brick tenements and smaller wood structures. The drawing is based on a photo taken in 1940, when close to 75 percent of the homes on the block still had no toilet or bath.

Recently constructed tenement apartments hence were not always the worst housing in the burgeoning factory neighborhoods. Perpetually damp cellars or more haphazardly built alley dwellings and backbuildings, hidden from public view, often contained the most squalid conditions. But inadequate ventilation within the new apartments, and the lack of sewer connections, meant that the atmosphere within and around the buildings was unpleasant and unhealthy. High occupancy rates exacerbated their inherent design flaws and accelerated their overall deterioration. With as many as eight or ten people, families as well as unrelated boarders, living and often working in small flats of perhaps 400 square feet apiece, the buildings were intensively used.

As they proliferated across the gridded blocks of America's fast-growing industrial cities, without parks or other planned open spaces to provide breathing room, the tightly packed tenements created neighborhoods with unprecedented population densities. In 1894 it was estimated that a section of Manhattan's Lower East Side had a residential density of over 800 people per acre, more than anywhere else in the world at the time, including the most crowded sections of Bombay.[3] Though Chicago never attained the overall density of New York, by one scholar's calculation there were 900 people per acre in its worst slums in 1900.[4]

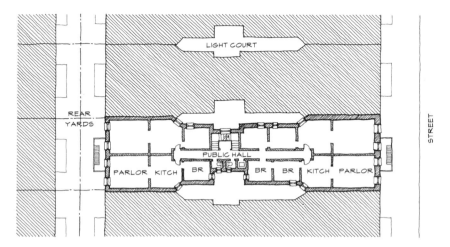

6-15. Laws that required a window in every room and shared toilets and sinks on each floor of a newly constructed tenement house were enforced in New York City by 1887. Fire escapes were also mandatory. The permissible dimensions of light courts and rear yards were still quite narrow, resulting in buildings with a characteristic "dumbbell" shape.

Changes in the design of new tenement buildings came slowly and piecemeal. In the attention focused on poor urban neighborhoods by reformers, politicians, and the popular press, many issues were intermingled. Leaving aside the social concerns and prejudices of the time, even basic public health problems were not related solely to tenement design. They also stemmed from lack of sanitary infrastructure, overcrowding in homes of all forms, factory pollution, poverty, and child labor. Hence the solutions proposed were many, and as specific local laws were enacted, the responsibility for their enforcement was not always clear. In New York, for instance, the growing city health department vied with the newer Department of Buildings for authority to inspect both new and existing buildings.[5] Throughout the country, enforcement of new laws was also hindered by corrupt or untrained officials and by the political pressure of building owners who fought any restriction on the right to use their private property for maximum profit.

The sudden and chaotic growth of urban slums and the difficulties of effecting meaningful change must have seemed overwhelming to American reformers in the late 1800s. Yet gradually, from about 1860 to 1930, most large towns and cities built new

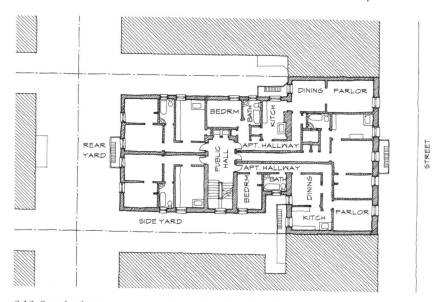

6-16. Standards were again raised significantly in New York in 1901 under the so-called New Law. Minimum court and yard dimensions were increased, and all new apartments had to have their own full bathrooms. Most now included hallway circulation space, giving individual rooms more privacy. Many different building configurations were constructed; to be economically feasible, all required wider lots than the "Old Law" tenements.

infrastructure and passed legislation to safeguard public health, outlawing the worst existing practices of private residential construction. Municipal sewer systems were installed, indoor plumbing became standard in new homes, cellar apartments completely below grade were forbidden, and backbuilding was restricted.

One effect of public emphasis on the problems of tenement neighborhoods was to interest some professional architects—who up until then had worked mostly on large institutional buildings or homes of the wealthy—in the design of more modest dwellings. Starting in 1878, a number of professional and philanthropic groups based in New York held a series of tenement house design competitions, for which architects, among others, submitted drawings. In many cities they were also employed to design a variety of "model tenements" actually constructed by socially motivated individuals and housing organizations. All these efforts, built and unbuilt, stimulated early thinking about apartment design that eventually affected buildings outside of tenement neighborhoods.

By 1901, New York City laws required toilets and sinks with running water within each apartment and operable windows in every room, including bathrooms and kitchens. A comprehensive ordinance regulating tenement design was passed in Chicago in 1902, and by 1913 Los Angeles enacted similar legislation. New laws specified both a minimum depth for rear yards and the dimensions of interior courts, so that most windows would actually get a little light and fresh air. In addition, most local ordinances limited to 70 percent the overall area of a lot that could be covered by a building. Such standards were locally enforced for all new tenement construction and substantially improved the livability of subsequent apartments.

The new laws enacted by local governments to improve homes in poor neighborhoods were roughly concurrent with a major shift in middle-class house design. As noted in chapter 4, the incorporation of advancing technologies, especially plumbing and electrical wiring, caused a significant rise in construction costs and forced builders around the turn of the century to reduce the size of new single-family houses in order to keep them affordable. By requiring additional exterior walls and windows around light courts, in addition to plumbing systems and reduced lot coverage, new housing ordinances increased the minimum square footage costs of homes for poor and working class families as well. But in the case of apartments that were minimal in size and typically overcrowded to begin with, it was infeasible to make them any smaller.

Instead, two other changes occurred in homes newly constructed for the lower end of the market. Their rents rose somewhat, and their location shifted. Apartments were now built on less expensive land made available by changing modes of transportation. The horse-drawn streetcars of the 1860s and 1870s had enabled some middle-class urban dwellers to live up to several miles from their workplaces, but they were relatively expensive, moved slowly, and in growing numbers caused great congestion. By the 1890s electric streetcars were faster and carried more people efficiently. Once established, they were also cheaper to run, so fares dropped to a level affordable to the working class. As trolley lines extended outward from existing downtowns, the range of areas from which people could commute, even to low-paying factory jobs, increased dramatically. Thus, apartment houses that complied with the new regulations were usually built farther out than the older neighborhoods. These newer homes became available as a next step up for more prosperous families living in tenements.

While the poorest tenants and most recent immigrants still occupied the older buildings, the need for extremely dense neighborhoods around large workplaces gradually eased in cities all over the country. In most places the term *tenement* fell out of use for new apartment buildings; it referred to relics of an earlier time.

EARLY WALK-UP APARTMENTS

In the mid-1800s, when many poor families were moving into subdivided houses and small tenement apartments in order to take advantage of new factory job opportunities, larger apartments for middle-class families were looked on with some suspicion. Popularly referred to as *French flats*, because so many had been built in Paris, they were considered slightly suspect and definitely un-American. Nonetheless, in cities where land values and building costs were rising rapidly, there was an inevitable logic to their construction, as even rowhouses on narrow lots became prohibitively expensive for many city dwellers. By the late 1860s in New York, attached apartment buildings, mostly four and five stories, began to appear side by side with the traditional single-family brownstone rowhouses. After the devastating fire of 1871, many blocks of Chicago that had contained only wood-framed houses were rebuilt with two- and three-story apartment structures, both attached and freestanding. And while they were never on the cover, numerous two-story "two-family houses" appeared in Victorian and early-twentieth-century patternbooks and precut house catalogs. Most had one apartment per floor and were designed to fit on the same lots as single-family houses of the period.

During the last decades of the nineteenth century and the first decades of the twentieth, local or regional forms of small walk-up apartment houses went up in large numbers around the fringes and in the growing suburbs of most American cities. Perhaps most numerous were the freestanding wood *triple-deckers*, which originated in the Boston area but proliferated throughout New England.[6] In Washington, D.C., many employees of the expanding

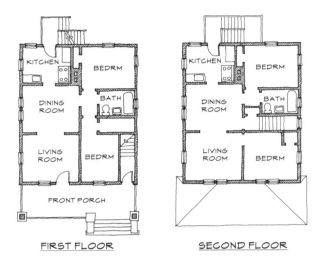

FIRST FLOOR   SECOND FLOOR

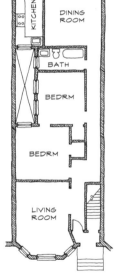

6-17. Plans for the two-family "Garfield" in the Sears Roebuck mail-order house catalog. Each apartment had about 850 square feet, a separate entrance, and a layout like a small bungalow.

6-18. The first-floor plan of a three-story building of "rowhouse flats" designed by architect Nicholas Grimm and erected in 1902 by the Washington developer Harry Wardman, who built large numbers of such units. Although the apartments were fairly generous, with about 1,100 square feet, the bedrooms and bathroom were lit and ventilated only by a narrow internal light court.

federal bureaucracy found homes within three-story attached brick buildings known locally as *rowhouse flats*. More picturesque apartment structures in Los Angeles provided an alternative to the growing number of bungalow courts.

These middle- and working-class apartments had larger rooms than those in the tenements, and each room had at least one window, though it often faced only a narrow court or alley. The build-

6-19. A middle-class Boston triple-decker.

ings were most frequently put up by commercial builders, with simple and standardized layouts, but purchased by individual owners who lived in one unit while renting out the others. Like rowhouses, they had an inherent flexibility: apartments could be easily combined and then redivided to meet changing needs. Their front and rear yards were small but often accommodated an owner's or ground-floor tenant's garden. Typical triple-deckers included unenclosed wooden stairwells at the rear, providing a second means of egress and also a usable balcony for upper-floor apartments.

More elaborate walk-up apartment houses for upper-middle-class families were built only where land values were highest. A few such early buildings in Manhattan had gracious common entry lobbies and two sets of interior stairs, one for residents and one for servants. Surrounded by four- and five-story buildings, however, the apartments themselves, like Victorian rowhouses, had many rooms without much view or sunlight. In wealthier Americans' minds even the best designed flat remained a compromise; it

6-20. Two-and-a-half-story houses with two or three apartments and double front porches are a common form in New Haven, Connecticut.

6-21. A walk-up apartment house from the 1920s in Los Angeles.

236

provided adequate living space at a price more affordable than a townhouse, but inconveniently required constant stair climbing and lacked a proper individual identity on the exterior.

ELEVATOR APARTMENTS

With a million neon rainbows burning below me,
And a million blazing taxis raising a roar,
Here I sit above the town, in my pet paillated gown,
Down in the depths, [on the ninetieth floor].

Cole Porter

Both the public image and the physical reality of apartment living in the United States changed radically with the introduction of the passenger elevator. Early types of mechanical lifts were used in a few five- and six-story buildings starting in the 1850s, but it was not until the 1870s that steam-powered elevators were reliable enough to service buildings above that height. Innovative builders quickly combined them with other new technological conveniences to create an ultramodern and distinctly American building type for the wealthy. By the 1880s, towers of up to ten stories with spacious individual apartments were built across the country. Like the office towers also made possible by the elevator, the earliest apartment buildings had a combination of masonry bearing walls and newly available steel beams for floor supports. Later structures used a complete steel frame of columns and beams, fireproofed and infilled with masonry.

In a reversal of traditional rental values, homes on the higher floors of these new apartment buildings, with sunlight and previously unavailable views, were more expensive than those close to the ground. Their elevators were hand-operated by employees in starched uniforms, and they were also provided with central heating, indoor plumbing, electrical wiring, central refrigeration, central vacuum systems, and telephone connections before such luxuries were common even in individual mansions.

While the rents were extremely high, these buildings offered many services that well-to-do families in those days otherwise paid large staffs of servants to perform. There were doormen to screen and announce visitors, valets to carry packages, maids who cleaned and did other housework, central laundry services, and sometimes even central kitchens and wine cellars that provided custom meals to individual apartments. Some buildings included separate banquet rooms for large private parties. All this was organized and run by the building management, so that tenants, especially women, spent less of their time overseeing household operations.

Ordinary Americans as well as the popular press were at once fascinated by and suspicious of these newfangled dwellings. Impressed by their advanced technology, many thought that they were the wave of the future. Others felt that women relieved of their domestic duties would become irresponsible and flighty. Though the individual dwellings often were as large as elegant houses, there was speculation that a physical arrangement of many households under one roof would tend to weaken or break up families. This idea was, of course, related to the concurrent fear that the physical surroundings of the tenements caused crime and immoral behavior. As one critic warned in 1917, "It is a shortcut from the apartment house to the divorce court."[7]

Despite their critics, elevator apartments rapidly became popular with wealthy Americans and remained so through the early 1930s. They had many real advantages over private city houses. In addition to their high-tech features, their interiors were lighter and airier than those of deep Victorian rowhouses. They offered tighter security against burglaries in an era when crime was widespread and the gap between rich and poor was tremendous. For wealthy people who traveled for long periods at a time, it was convenient to have a building management that took care of household details. And at a time when streets were still full of horse manure and often lacking sewers, being elevated above ground level was pleasant even without a view, especially when climbing stairs was unnecessary.

Between 1880 and 1930, architects grew increasingly skillful with this new dwelling form. In addition to organizing within a new framework all the specialized spaces expected in a Victorian upper-class home, they faced the problem of exterior image. What should these new dwellings look like? Walk-up apartment buildings, even the most constrained tenements, generally took their cue from surrounding houses. Thus, attached masonry flats had facades and entry stoops much like their rowhouse contemporaries (though fire escapes were usually a dead giveaway), and detached wood-framed double- and triple-deckers were designed to blend in as much as possible with single-family wooden urban houses. (The connecting porches and stairs typical of triple deckers were usually in the rear.) But because elevators were brand-new, there was no model for dwellings over five or six stories high.

The scale and detailing of two early buildings reveal some of the issues that designers had to resolve. The Portman Flats, opened in

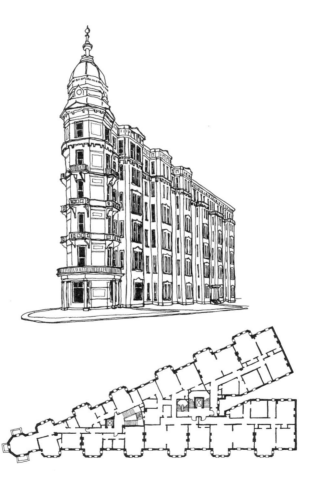

6-22. The Portman Flats in Washington D.C. had two separate cores, each serving three apartments per floor. The three smaller units on the left had no kitchens, so residents depended on a first-floor dining room. Larger units had kitchens and pantries as well as servants' quarters.

1880, were Washington, D.C.'s first elevator apartments. The architect, Adolph Cluss, was well known in the capital for his rowhouses and schools but had never designed an apartment building.[8] Built on a narrow triangular site, the new six-story structure resembled a series of tall rowhouses, culminating at the corner with an octagonal tower that housed a pharmacy at street level. Its odd proportions did not hinder its immediate success. Many of the first residents were elected officials who did not want to maintain a second house in Washington. The Portman Flats offered the combination of a private apartment with a luxurious ground-floor public dining room, preferable to a boarding house or hotel.

Four years later, the Dakota was completed in New York, quite far to the north of other luxury apartment towers built in the city over the previous decade. The Dakota stood by itself facing Central Park on Manhattan's Upper West Side, in a landscape of laid-out but only partially developed blocks, where a shantytown was gradually being displaced by ornate Victorian rowhouses. The eight-story structure was designed to look like an overscaled mansion, with a two-story-high roof made up of separate gables, perhaps to denote the individual homes below. Though its combination of massive size and traditional residential details didn't quite work, it was beloved by New Yorkers and remains home to celebrities even today.

Later apartment buildings were more often modeled on larger building types, either the somber Renaissance palaces of Italy or the spread-out and heavily ornamented resort hotels that were also popular in the late nineteenth century. In fact, because of their extensive staffs and services, many early apartment buildings were called *apartment hotels,* though they were used as permanent residences. Sometimes this designation enabled builders to circumvent laws regarding residential construction.

Though large and supplied with every available mechanical convenience, the earliest elevator apartments were awkwardly laid out. This shows clearly in the plan of a single corner unit at the Dakota that is well over 3,000 square feet. Formal living areas, private bedchambers, and spaces intended for servants were interspersed and strung out along long, twisting corridors. To some extent these problems also existed in the freestanding Victorian houses of the same era, but apartment planning presented new

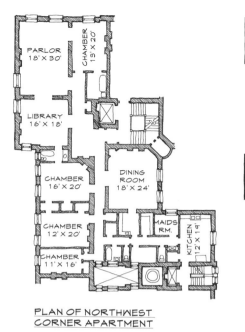

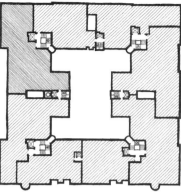

CORES AND APARTMENTS AT
7TH FL.

PLAN OF NORTHWEST
CORNER APARTMENT

6-23. The Dakota, designed by Henry Hardenbergh, had four double cores, with a passenger elevator, a service elevator, and two stairs for every two units. A central courtyard and three air shafts provided light and air for every room in the rambling apartments.

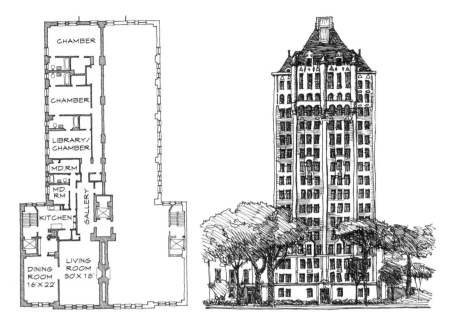

6-24. A tower on Chicago's Lake Shore Drive, designed by Huszagh & Hill and completed in 1928. With only two apartments per floor, it was typical of luxury buildings that made the most of small, prime sites and probably replaced an individual mansion or two with thirty-two homes all overlooking Lake Michigan. The rooms were as large as those at the Dakota, but the apartments were better organized around the generous entrance gallery. Even the maids' rooms were now more private and had their own full bath.

and inherent challenges. Getting from an apartment entrance near the elevator, usually in the dark center of the building, to the areas with views and corner exposures suitable for the main living spaces remains a tricky problem.

By the early twentieth century, however, architects had gained enough experience with unit layouts to make them both more gracious and more efficient. Many apartments were organized around a generous central foyer, from which radiated the various zones of the dwelling. Bedrooms, service functions, and common living areas were clearly separated. A few buildings included two-story apartments, or *duplexes*, with internal stairs, organized like a house with bedrooms above the living areas. These, however, were rare; it was simpler to omit extra stairs and build spacious single-story layouts that repeated from floor to floor.

As they grew more adept at creating large luxury buildings, architects also began to design and develop outdoor spaces for the enjoyment of residents. While tenement builders had to be forced by public regulation to allow light and air into their dwellings, the developers of the new elevator buildings, still profit oriented but catering to a much more demanding market, included side yards and open interior courts before they were required by law. Gradually they came to appreciate that the outdoor spaces on large sites could be landscaped and serve as amenities—and marketing features—for the homes within. When buildings faced a dramatic setting, such as those in Chicago along Lake Shore Drive, they were less likely to include their own landscaped areas, but for those on more humdrum city blocks the semiprivate open space truly enhanced the dwellings. Because land was expensive and architects were still inexperienced with high-rise design of all types, many early efforts were oddly proportioned. Outdoor areas that seemed generous in plan were dwarfed in three dimensions by the high surrounding building walls. One simple form first used successfully in luxury apartment buildings was the *perimeter block*, with a central courtyard serving as the entry space or anteroom to individual lobbies and vertical cores.

As apartment towers spread to many cities and the manufacture of elevators themselves became more standardized, it was natural for the form to be developed for and marketed to upper-middle-class as well as wealthy families. By the 1920s, builders were erecting new towers that resembled earlier luxury buildings on the exterior and still had ornate lobbies with doormen and elevator operators but contained many more and substantially smaller apartments. They grouped more units around each elevator core and often had projecting wings in varied configurations. In both size and spatial organization, the individual homes were similar to the simplified small houses of the 1910s and 1920s. They had a single living room, a well-organized, modern kitchen, and sometimes but not always a separate dining room.

These tall developments of upper-middle-class units had smaller staffs and fewer common spaces, such as banquet halls and rooftop sunrooms, than those included with grander apartments. Nonetheless they provided well-constructed and gracious urban homes. They remain intact to this day far more often than their

117th Street

Seventh Avenue

116th Street

6-25. Graham Court, designed by architects Clinton and Russell and opened in 1901, was the first and smallest in a series of New York apartment houses that developed the block interior as a gracious enclosed courtyard. The site was slightly narrower than the Dakota's but the building was more tightly organized, with a larger open space in the center. An arched entryway led from the street to an oval walkway and carriage drive. Compared with the leftover and awkward outdoor areas around the neighboring dumbbell apartment buildings, Graham Court showed what could be created through the careful design of a larger-scale complex.

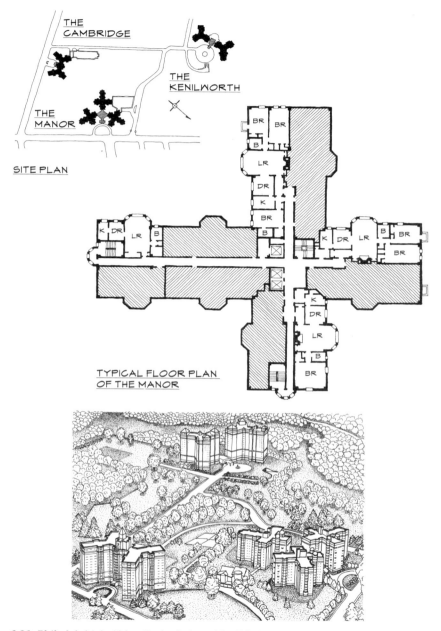

THE
CAMBRIDGE

THE
KENILWORTH

THE
MANOR

SITE PLAN

TYPICAL FLOOR PLAN
OF THE MANOR

6-26. Philadelphia's Alden Park, designed by Edwin Rorke, was begun in 1925 after similar projects had been completed by the same developer on the outskirts of Boston and Detroit. It included three distinct tower complexes on a wooded site close to the commuter train and overlooking the Wissahickon Valley section of Fairmount Park. Apartments in the least expensive complex, The Manor, ranged from studios to three-bedrooms, with small kitchens and no servants' rooms.

elaborate predecessors. The largest apartments often lost their services and were carved into smaller dwellings as fashionable neighborhoods shifted and economic realities changed. Even in the Dakota, still a well-located and expensive building, the original central kitchen, wine cellar, and dining hall were all converted to additional apartments.

By about 1920 the technology of electronic controls had improved so that self-service push-button elevators became available. Not requiring special employees to run them, these could therefore be used in lower-rent buildings. They were not totally reliable, however, and were initially installed in buildings of five to seven stories, where walking up was not too hard in the case of a breakdown. It wasn't until after World War II that push-button elevators were commonly used in taller buildings.

GARDEN APARTMENTS

Between 1870 and 1920, both the technology of building and architects' skills in apartment design made huge advances. By the beginning of the 1920s a remarkable variety of homes were being constructed around the United States. Streetcars and subways gave new areas access to the downtown regions where jobs were concentrated. Though building costs continued to rise and many urban families could not afford the purchase price or rent for a modern single-family house, more reasonably priced land was available for apartments.

In general, the scale of home building as a business venture had increased. Developers with greater capital now bought more property and constructed more units at one time, whether homes for factory workers or middle-class professionals. As apartments were built on larger plots of land for residents who also had a new range of choices about where they might live, builders and architects began to more fully incorporate and design the outdoor areas around modest apartment houses.

After World War I and continuing through the 1930s, a fashionable and widely used term for the homes in many new developments was *garden apartment*. The name was loosely applied to almost any configuration of apartment buildings with planted outdoor space, and its broad connotation was a combination of the

6-27. The Latham Apartments in Columbus, Ohio, designed by Miller and Reeves, Architects and built in the early 1920s, were a complex of three-story walk-up units set back from the street and surrounded by lawn and shrubs. Apartments ranged in size from studios with Murphy beds to small three-bedroom homes. A row of garages was located in the rear.

best of city and suburban life. Most garden apartments were six stories or less, reached via stairs or push-button elevators. They used far fewer service employees than earlier buildings with elevator operators and were associated with a more informal, middle-class lifestyle.

Quite a range of dwellings built all across the United States were described as garden apartments. The common name masked significant differences in form and historical precedents. Especially in suburban settings near train stations and stores, standard apartment houses were simply set back from the street to create an unused but formally landscaped front yard similar to those of surrounding freestanding houses. Other buildings or complexes were designed in a U-shape to create a planted entry courtyard facing the street, often with sitting areas. Many larger projects used a perimeter block layout with single or multiple interior courts. The most ambitious developments set buildings within a landscaped "campus" that included recreational facilities such as playgrounds and tennis courts.

The fashion for garden apartments stemmed at least in part from those national preoccupations that underlay the widespread popularity of bungalows and the more limited construction of attached porch houses starting a decade earlier. After the extreme contrasts and excesses of the Victorian era, simplified, well-lit homes looking out on planted outdoor surroundings were appealing in all forms. The same concerns for hygiene, fresh air, and new labor-saving technologies could be met by well-designed modern apartments integrated with greater open space than were earlier flats.

Among some architects, especially on the East Coast, the concept of garden apartments was more explicitly linked to the British Garden City movement (mentioned in chapter 5), and to other innovative apartment design taking place in Europe. The rapid development of New York City's outer boroughs in the 1920s inspired a particularly wide range of inventive garden apartment complexes; among them were early housing cooperatives owned and run by residents. Some of these were sponsored by labor organizations such as the powerful and progressive Amalgamated Clothing Workers Union and occupied by families moving out of older tenement neighborhoods. They included both practical and cultural amenities: cooperative stores, nursery schools, libraries, craft studios, and meeting rooms. Others were privately developed and marketed to the upper middle class as close-in but gracious suburbs, with recreational facilities such as tennis courts and golf courses.

In southwestern and western cities, particularly Los Angeles, a different tradition underlay the design of two- and three-story apartment complexes with common central courtyards. Both the indigenous architecture of Spain and its colonial adaptations featured a number of building types organized around a sheltered open center. Californians, New Mexicans, and Texans all were familiar with local historic mission compounds, made up of churches and outbuildings enclosing tranquil squares planted with fruit trees and herb gardens. In the early 1900s a number of architects practicing in southern California visited and studied historic Spanish forms of housing, both individual patio houses and grouped apartment dwellings known as *casas de vecinos* (neighbors' houses), which were two-story courtyard complexes, sometimes with an open gallery around the second floor.[9]

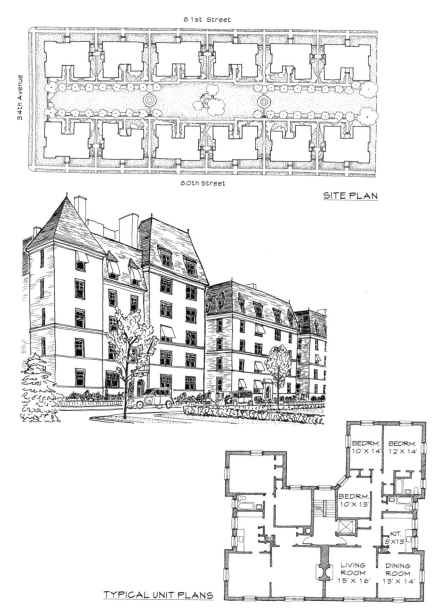

81st Street

34th Avenue

80th Street

SITE PLAN

BEDRM.
10' X 14'

BEDRM.
12' X 14'

BEDRM.
10' X 13'

KIT.
8' X 13'

LIVING
ROOM
15' X 16'

DINING
ROOM
13' X 14'

TYPICAL UNIT PLANS

6-28. The Chateau, designed by Andrew Thomas and completed in 1922, took up most of a city block in Jackson Heights, Queens. It was part of a community developed by a private corporation that pioneered the design of garden apartments as upper-middle-class homes. The complex was composed of twelve freestanding buildings, each with two units per floor, a push-button elevator, and a ground-level connection to the formally planted inner court. The sketch shows the front facades facing an open block across the street, before the neighborhood was fully built up.

249

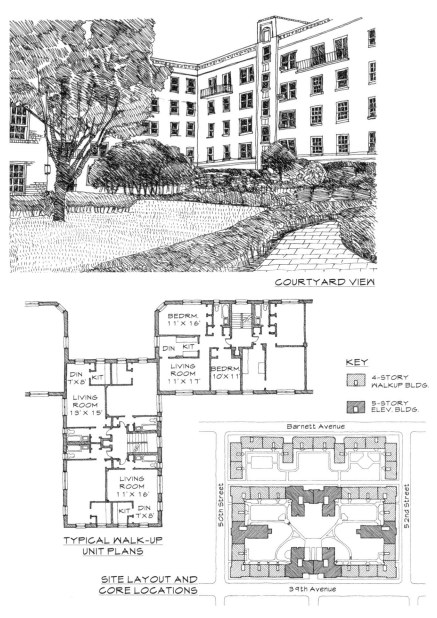

COURTYARD VIEW

TYPICAL WALK-UP
UNIT PLANS

SITE LAYOUT AND
CORE LOCATIONS

KEY

4-STORY
WALKUP BLDG.

5-STORY
ELEV. BLDG.

6-29. Not far from the Chateau, Phipps Garden Apartments, designed by Clarence Stein, was erected by a philanthropic housing group in 1929 (lower court) and 1935 (upper court). Intended for working- and middle-class tenants, it was a rental complex of attached walk-up and elevator buildings forming continuous street facades. The units were small but carefully planned; even the studios had multiple exposures and views of the spacious, naturalistically landscaped courtyards.

During the 1920s a series of luxurious and highly detailed garden apartment buildings in Los Angeles deliberately evoked these Spanish precedents. They were small in scale, usually containing between eight and twenty units. The apartments themselves were individualized, some with two stories and dramatic double-height spaces as well as picturesque balconies and private patios. Both historically evocative and technologically precocious, they managed to include off-street parking courtyards and garages more gracefully than most complexes of the time (or even today). While they had no socially motivated underpinnings, they were land-conserving and highly livable homes that made effective use of small common outdoor spaces.

More modest courtyard apartment complexes were also common in the Southwest. In many cases they developed as low-rise apartment versions of the earlier bungalow courts. The courtyard, or garden, was the main entry path to all dwellings, and in some cases was quite narrow—but a shaded courtyard is pleasant in a hot, arid climate. Small areas of planting in front of the units used limited resources to create an effective green oasis requiring far less water than broad front lawns.

The diverse garden apartments of the 1920s included types of outdoor space that were completely new in this country—neither public parks nor individual yards nor productive gardens. Designers had to experiment in developing semipublic areas that would appeal to a range of future residents without compromising the privacy of individual apartments. Successful designs increased the sense of community within an apartment complex by giving residents a comfortable place to socialize outdoors, but conflicts did sometimes develop. Often adults did not want to hear children's play right outside their windows. Hence some courtyards were restricted to "passive" recreation—that is, sitting and strolling—which limited their usefulness for families. Developments with extensive grounds were able to zone noisier recreation away from dwelling units. Garden apartments marketed to upper-middle-class families often included courtyards elaborately furnished with sculpture, fountains, and gazebos. Like the fancy wood scrollwork and railings on Victorian houses fifty years earlier, these were hard to maintain and did not always wear well.

<u>COURTYARD VIEW</u>

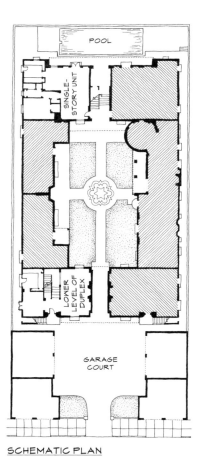

6-30. The Andalusia, built in 1926 in West Hollywood, had nine one- and two-story apartments organized around a beautifully scaled central court. It was one of a series of courtyard buildings designed and developed by the husband-and-wife team of Arthur and Nina Zwebell, neither of whom had formal architectural training. A corner of the entry court with garages is shown below. The central court had a symmetrical layout broken by a tower to one side that housed the dining room of the Zwebells' own apartment.

SCHEMATIC PLAN

Overall, however, the garden apartments built around the country provided some of the most livable and, especially from an environmental point of view, economical homes of the twentieth century. Typically they have modest, frequently spaced cores, either stairs alone or in combination with single, small self-service elevators, so that apartments have sunlight and cross-ventilation. And by combining and developing at a larger scale the outdoor space necessary to meet light and air standards, they create more continuous planted areas, with both climate-moderating and visually soothing qualities, than would a smaller number of closely spaced detached houses with yards. Almost always located within walking distance of public transportation, these garden apartments still permit a combination of easy access to jobs and stores with pleasant and usable outdoor space.

As with other home forms from early in the century, however, even as the most sophisticated examples of garden apartment design were being realized, the forces of further change were already in motion. The need to incorporate cars and parking, especially in neighborhoods far from downtown, was clear by the early 1920s. In middle-class apartment complexes parking gradually took precedence over common outdoor recreation space. A few such developments completed in the late 1930s and early 1940s continued to use the term *gardens*, but as the amount of parking relative to the number of apartments grew, the actual gardens atrophied. By the 1940s they were often reduced to narrow planted strips around paved lots or low banks of garages. Today the term "garden apartment" is not widely used; in some cities it denotes merely a ground-floor or basement unit, perhaps with access to a yard.

PUBLIC HOUSING BEFORE AND AFTER WORLD WAR II

> The conquest of height brings with it the solution to essential problems in the planning of modern cities, to wit: the possibility of reinstating *natural conditions* (sun, space, greenery); the separation of pedestrian from automobile; the creation of qualified arrangements we can call "extensions of the dwelling". . . .
>
> Charles Edouard Jeanneret-Gris (Le Corbusier)

Beginning in 1932 apartment construction dropped off dramatically, as did construction of other home forms. Residents of recently built complexes, especially those undertaken by labor unions and socially motivated housing groups, struggled to meet rents or common maintenance charges; some of the early cooperatives failed. As discusssed in chapter 2, it was during these grim Depression years that the federal government first became involved in non-war-related homebuilding. In 1933 a separate housing arm of the new Public Works Administration was established. It began by providing financial grants to existing private housing organizations but went on to build new complexes directly with federal funds.[10] Most of these initial *public housing* developments, built around the nation in the thirties, were low-rise complexes designed in the garden apartment tradition. The buildings were close to the street and arranged to define landscaped courtyards and playgrounds for tenants' use. Like other city apartment houses, those fronting on commercial streets often included ground-level stores. Some went up on vacant urban sites, usually adjacent to an existing poor neighborhood; others were erected on blocks cleared of earlier buildings.

Toward the end of the decade and in the early 1940s, however, a few federally funded developments were designed with a less traditional arrangement of apartment buildings on city blocks. Heavily influenced by emerging European theories of housing design, the buildings were no longer placed along the street, enclosing the open space within. Instead they were lined up or distributed more randomly throughout the block, sometimes at an odd angle to the street grid. In 1941 a publicly funded complex in New York City, the East River Houses, for the first time included ten- and eleven-story push-button elevator towers. Improved construction technology now made them slightly cheaper to build, on a square-foot basis, than the same number of homes in lower buildings that covered more ground and required more excavation.

During World War II, national priorities shifted away from the diverse building projects of the Depression toward support of the war effort. In strategic locations, recently constructed public housing was cleared of its original tenants and rented to workers involved in war-related industries. The federal government also commissioned the rapid construction of other groups of new homes near important defense plants. Private developers who undertook these contracts suddenly gained experience in build-

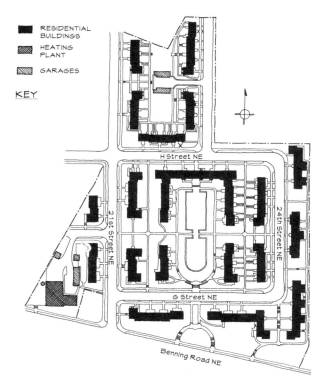

KEY

- RESIDENTIAL BUILDINGS
- HEATING PLANT
- GARAGES

H Street NE

21st Street NE

24th Street NE

G Street NE

Benning Road NE

6-31. The site plan of Langston Terrace, a federally financed, 273-unit complex of walk-up apartments and two-story rowhouses in Washington, D.C. Designed by architect Hilyard Robinson and completed in 1938, it was intended for black residents at a time when segregation was taken for granted by even the federal government. Though more spread out than many earlier garden apartment developments, it had a strong central axis around a common open court and provided homes with direct connections both to the street and to the landscaped block interiors.

ing at a new scale. House trailers, conventional houses, or apartments were now planned and constructed in much larger groups than any built before the war.

Though not devastated like countless communities in Europe or Asia, by 1945 many American neighborhoods were nonetheless physically run-down from lack of maintenance during the the Depression and war years. Overcrowding within homes grew worse as millions of soldiers returned from overseas. In an effort to stimulate the economy and relieve the social tensions caused by overcrowding, the national government remained involved in home construction, though it never had been previously in a healthy

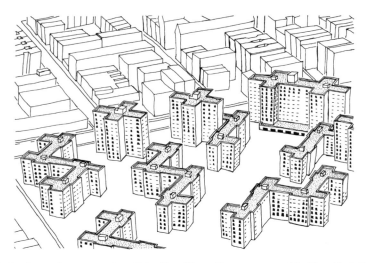

6-32. A schematic perspective of the East River Houses, opened in New York City in 1941, shows how they were turned at 45 degrees from the existing street grid. While an eleven-story tower defined the end of a central court flanked by lower buildings, this outdoor space was neither closed off from the public street nor directly open to it. Visually the complex had little to do with the surrounding neighborhood.

peacetime economy. In terms of tax dollars expended, its primary initiative was the Veterans Administration/Federal Housing Administration (VA/FHA) mortgage insurance program, which enabled middle-class families to purchase single-family houses on newly affordable terms. While it was more politically controversial, the Public Housing program, through which new rental apartments were built for poorer families, was also continued and enlarged, with some important changes and restrictions.

Comparing these two major federal efforts helps to reveal why, in combination, they had such a profound effect on so many American neighborhoods. Both programs, in practice, operated at an unprecedented scale of construction, made possible in part by the experience many industrialists had gained through wartime production. In theory, a small developer could erect just a few houses at a time and sell them with FHA insurance. However, it was the new merchant builders such as the Levitts, cutting costs through large-scale land acquisition and on-site assembly-line construction techniques, who made freestanding homes affordable to so many families. After the war, apartments were also constructed in increasingly large groups as public housing. Tall, repetitive buildings now went up on multiblock sites cleared of all earlier structures. The garden apartment and tower developments of the 1920s had contained a few hundred dwellings at most. Units in postwar public housing developments, like those in many new suburbs, numbered in the thousands.

Because of the large scale at which they were applied, both federal programs were extremely destructive to the environment. In the case of the new suburban communities, existing plant and animal life was cleared along with older homes and farm buildings. Water absorption and drainage patterns were also altered. On the city blocks condemned en masse for public housing, there was of course plant and nonhuman animal life, but mostly a wide variety of preexisting human constructions: infrastructure, streets, and buildings, including dwellings of all forms as well as stores and factories. Though existing residents were helped to some degree with relocation, many businesses never reopened elsewhere.

As younger, prosperous families began to leave for newly affordable suburbs and others, usually poor, were relocated away from sites slated for public housing, surrounding city neighborhoods also underwent rapid and unsettling changes. These were compounded by other nonresidential building projects taking place at the same time, particularly new highways that cut through built-up blocks to create access for the rapidly multiplying suburbs. All over the country, in the 1950s and 1960s, soundly built and stable communities that had successfully weathered the two previous difficult decades began to deteriorate.

After 1949 the homes built as public housing were limited by federal law to what were certified as *slum clearance sites*: they could not be erected on open land, outside of or even within existing cities.[11] Like the VA/FHA guidelines that determined which houses qualified for loans, this policy now specified at a national level what had previously been decided by local governments or individual banks and builders. Financing for middle-class homes, largely restricted in practice to white families, was given mostly in areas outside older cities. Rental homes, for those who couldn't afford or were excluded from the new financing, were constructed only within them.

The process involved in selecting an area for slum clearance was in theory a scientific one, but social and political decisions played a major role. Buildings were rated on the basis of overcrowding, inadequate plumbing and electricity, compliance with modern building codes, and overall condition, leading to a possible designation of *substandard*. This rating did not take into account the actual form and structure of the building or its potential for longer and more useful life. Moreover, as large sites were assembled, individual blocks required only a certain percentage of substandard structures to be condemned. Many fundamentally sound apartment buildings and houses were demolished, including some with historic importance and beauty. Thriving neighborhood businesses were also razed, or declined more gradually as they lost their customer base.

In size and interior layout, the new dwellings constructed under the two programs were quite similar, though of course their outdoor surroundings were not. Both programs incorporated modern minimum standards for an American home, now also for the first time promulgated at the federal level. While FHA guidelines were completely separate from the standards of the United States Housing Authority, which set policy for the new public housing, most of the assumptions about the sizes and relationships of various rooms and about the layouts and minimum fixturing of bathrooms and kitchens were similar. Both programs explicitly promoted what had become the widely accepted notion that homes should not be intermingled with other types of buildings. While many of the public housing complexes built during the Depression had included retail stores along existing streets, a decision at the national level eliminated all such uses from public housing built after World War II.[12]

If many of the same assumptions about what constituted a basic home underlay postwar public housing and large-scale suburban development, why did the homes built under the two programs look so different? Essentially, they were each the bare-bones, quickly built expressions of diametrically different design philosophies. The small ranches and Cape Cod houses underwritten by the FHA were the descendants of two long-standing American traditions, one social and the other visual. Widespread individual ownership of land and homes had been seen by American social theorists since Thomas Jefferson as important to creating a stable and democratic society. Property owners were thought to have a greater stake in society and therefore be more responsible citizens. This notion by itself, however, did not specify a particular home form. Rowhouse cities such as Baltimore and Philadelphia provided working- and middle-class families with opportunities for homeownership as effectively as many communities of detached houses. It was the idea of ownership combined with a picturesque vision of the freestanding country house, popularized in the mid-1800s by Andrew Jackson Downing, that inspired the new suburbs. In practice, these two traditions led to an open-ended extension of urban areas. Farms and undeveloped land were continually displaced by homes for those who wanted their own country houses, though their livelihoods depended on the city.

The apartment tower complexes built as public housing were the product of a more recent design approach, originating in Europe under social conditions different from those in this country. Living in an era of political upheaval and physical destruction, during and between two world wars, progressive European architects embraced new technologies and mass production techniques as a means to correct the ills of the past. In their view, the existing city fabric of low, continuous buildings and frequent narrow streets needed to be replaced rather than extended. Because home ownership had never been as widespread in Europe as in America, and population densities were too high to allow the displacement of needed farmland by freestanding houses, some new form of multifamily housing was a logical solution.

By the 1940s, the availability of self-service elevators in combination with modern building techniques made possible high-rise towers for everyone, not just the wealthy. These were now seen by some European architects as an optimal form of urban home, especially when spaced well apart from one another on large blocks, so that all apartments could be sunlit, well ventilated, and surrounded by greenery. Such an arrangement could release city dwellers from what was scathingly referred to as the "tyranny of the street."[13] While residents walked along footpaths, new streets would become wide, modern boulevards that handled automobile traffic efficiently and kept it away from human dwellings. Businesses and factories, also redesigned, would be located in separate zones. In what became a famous phrase, the French architect Le Corbusier named this vision "Towers in the Park";

homes would sit above a continuous green landscape, planted and maintained for everyone's enjoyment. He described this new urban layout as a "vertical garden city," presenting it as a healthier and more scientific embodiment of the earlier visions of British town planners.[14]

The sketches and theories of the European *modernists*, as they became known, were optimistic and compelling. They were also extremely influential among American architects, who still tended to look across the Atlantic for inspiration and cultural edification. The reality was, however, that their schemes remained largely untried and portions of them sketchy. Individual buildings were constructed in Europe, some of them visually striking and truly innovative, but nothing on the scale of an entire city.

Particularly abstract was the notion of neighborhood life in the park. While true business districts were to be elsewhere, the new apartment towers, in Le Corbusier's sketches, contained what he called "extensions of the dwelling" at roof and ground levels. These included indoor exercise areas, nursery care for children, small clinics, and a vague function named "food supply service," which had underground truck connections. That this group kitchen or commissary might substitute for the highly developed network of butchers, bakeries, cafés, and other small stores that existed along the old streets of European cities was dubious at best.

In the United States, unfortunately, these utopian visions for a radically different type of city became the basis for new apartment house designs that were dictated at the national level. By the late 1940s low-rise garden apartments, which constituted the first public housing complexes, were criticized for covering too much ground. They were also discouraged because they placed some dwelling windows close to the now reviled street and sidewalk. Moreover, as demonstrated first in New York's East River Houses, it had grown cheaper to build upward; a twelve-story tower was more economical than two at six stories apiece. Although the original guidelines for public housing stated that it was preferable to house families with children in low-rise buildings, this policy was altered to conform to the changing realities of construction. It was now said that an equal number of homes in taller buildings would leave more open space for recreational use. Wherever possible, smaller streets were eliminated and grounds for the new housing

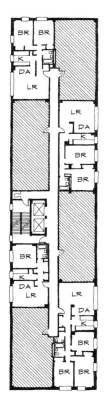

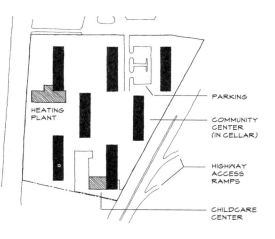

PARKING

COMMUNITY
CENTER
(IN CELLAR)

HIGHWAY
ACCESS
RAMPS

CHILDCARE
CENTER

HEATING
PLANT

6-33. Prototype plan of a plain, double-loaded "slab," up to twenty stories high, developed in 1950 by the architects Skidmore, Owings and Merrill for multiple public housing projects around New York City. The site plan above shows its application to one site in the Bronx; the sketch below is based on SOM's rendering of another site in Harlem. Both show the common placement of public housing on land close to new highway interchanges; in combination, federal highway projects and public housing had a devastating effect on many older neighborhoods.

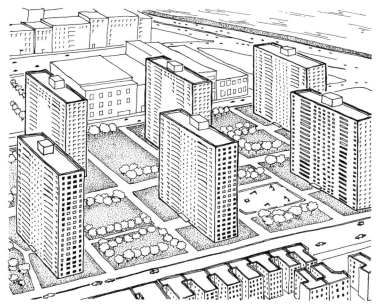

261

combined into large *superblocks*. The result was continuous, open sites with identical elevator apartment towers spaced more or less evenly across them.

The floor plans of these towers were carefully worked out to group as many well-ventilated apartments as possible around a single core. Initially this approach produced a variety of shapes with projecting wings, usually Zs or crosses. But gradually these complex shapes with many corners and a lot of exterior surface were abandoned in favor of simpler and less costly rectangular slabs. While the apartments themselves were decently sized and arranged, the semipublic circulation spaces, especially the common entry lobbies, were minimal and often poorly designed. This was a real change from earlier apartment houses built commercially for working-class families. In those, even when the apartments were small and lacking in basic services, the main lobbies and front facades were as grand and stylish as builders could manage. Even the earliest tenements had included a public face, with entrance details and ornament that mimicked their more gracious neighbors.

The austerity of public housing towers resulted both from public attitudes toward government buildings intended only for poor people and from a new design ideology. True beauty, it was now proclaimed, derived not from ornament but from honest use of materials and clarity of structure. In this case, design theory and economics led in the same direction; resulting designs were not tested through competition, because new for-profit homes in poor city neighborhoods simply were not being built.

Though stores were no longer included, the new complexes did contain other ground-level spaces intended to serve residents, like Le Corbusier's "extensions of the dwelling." Laundry rooms and some form of indoor community or youth recreation center were part of most developments, and every building had a perambulator storage room for the heavy baby carriages of the era. Outdoor areas included playgrounds for young children, athletic courts for older ones, sitting areas, and open parking lots for some tenants.

Overall, while outdoor space was plentiful enough, the proportions and spacing of the towers made it often seem left over and random rather than inviting. This problem was not so much the fault of individual designers as it was inherent to the concept of towers placed in, rather than around, a park. Most traditional city parks, both large and small, are defined spatially by the buildings around them. These perimeter buildings may be high, like those around Central Park in Manhattan or the much smaller Ritten-house Square in Philadelphia, or low, like those around Golden Gate Park in San Francisco. The park edges become desirable places to live as well as popular routes for strolling, and the land enclosed is clearly for public rather than private use. Any buildings within the parks themselves are of civic or historic importance— museums, zoos, or churches such as those on the original central green of New Haven.

The new public housing towers looked simple, clean, and orderly in comparison with the mixed and run-down streetscapes of the neighborhoods they replaced. Whether or not one admired their architecture, it was easy to feel, as many people did initially, that "bad" neighborhoods were being cleaned up and made healthier. But their large-scale, repetitive site plans lacked a rec-ognizable pattern of uses at ground level, and the theoretical parks, which sounded so inviting and humane, proved quite dif-ferent in practice.

All earlier forms of homes in American neighborhoods had entrances either directly off the street or through well-defined semipublic outdoor spaces. The masonry steps and wrought-iron railings of a rowhouse or small apartment building led right from the sidewalk's edge, while the paved path to a freestanding house went through an open yard to a porch or front door visually emphasized with special design features. Entry lobbies of garden apartments opened directly off the street or were reached through planted, semiprivate entry courtyards that were clearly defined by the arrangement of buildings.

Entry lobbies for the new apartment towers, spaced evenly throughout the site at varying distances from the street, were reached via walkways that crisscrossed the superblocks. Most com-plexes had multiple entrance points and lacked an overall enclosure, such as a high fence or hedge, with a single controlled opening. Outdoor recreation spaces such as playgrounds and basketball courts were reached via the same network of paths as the building entrances, with no perceivable hierarchy as to which areas were more or less public. So plain and uniform were the buildings them-

6-34. A typical building entrance in a six-story, early post-war public housing complex in Queens, New York, today. Overall these homes and their grounds are well maintained and entrances have been upgraded to provide handicapped access and security lighting. But they still face away from the street, tucked into rear building corners, quite unlike the front doors of the private homes surrounding them.

selves, moreover, that unlike most dwellings they lacked a clear front and back. This made the spaces around them hard to read.

Because their basic pattern was different from any previous common form of American home, these new structures were readily identifiable from city to city. They soon became popularly known as *housing projects*, or simply *projects*. Whatever the origin of the term, its implication of a design that was only for practice, and not quite real, matched the clumsiness of their presence.

Given both their economy and the optimism underlying their conception, it is not surprising or even necessarily regrettable that the futuristic schemes of the European modernists were used experimentally as the basis for new designs. What is troubling is how many homes based roughly on their principles were built over the next several decades without evaluation or refinement. Equally disturbing is how quickly both architects and government planners devalued the expertise in apartment house design that had already developed in the United States in the first third of the century.

Both FHA guidelines for home mortgages and the federal design standards for public housing towers led to the creation of new homes that were far less varied than those built earlier in the century. But the postwar suburban houses conformed to long-standing American patterns for both home and neighborhood design. The new public housing projects, in contrast, used what was virtually a brand-new building type—the high-rise apartment house with self-service elevators—and placed it in an unconventional and untested relationship to surrounding streets. Some of the weaknesses of the tract houses, their small size, unrealistically open layouts, and dull exteriors, were readily modified by residents, who could enlarge and alter them. Individual tenants in public housing, however, had no such control. They could not create custom facades for their own apartments, or fence them off from neighbors.

Within a decade of their construction, it was widely noted that many public housing complexes, rather than having a positive impact on the neighborhoods around them, were deteriorating and becoming centers of crime and social problems in their own right. As with nineteenth-century responses to conditions in tenement neighborhoods, there were many points of view about the causes. During the 1960s crime rates rose in neighborhoods with all forms of homes—hence, not everyone felt that physical design was a major factor. As middle-class whites moved to the new suburbs and inner-city communities were increasingly occupied by poor and minority families, racial attitudes and class prejudices clouded discussions on issues pertaining to the built environment.

Studies comparing public housing projects to one another and to older low-income neighborhoods, however, did reveal that the "towers in the park" complexes had a disproportionate share of problems.[15] In particular, entrance lobbies, untended self-service elevators, outdoor spaces in the middle of the superblocks, and isolated playgrounds and ball courts were all areas where tenants were at risk of being preyed on. Without stores or other uses to generate pedestrian traffic and provide an adult presence, these outdoor areas, now feared by tenants, became prime locations for youth gangs to dominate and vandalize.

Increasingly aware of these problems, architects and planners tried harder in new buildings to create secure public and semi-public areas. The easiest response was technological: by the late 1960s there were more locked gates and widespread use of new devices such as intercoms. But considerable thought was also given to the harder task of understanding how building design, at large and small scales, might create secure environments that did not resemble fortresses. In 1972 an influential book called *Defensible Space*, by the architect Oscar Newman, examined housing projects across the country in detail.[16] Newman recommended specific ways that apartment complexes could create "spheres of territorial influence" where residents would be able to observe and feel responsible for what went on outside their own apartments. Many of the successful examples it cited were prewar buildings, including some of the first garden apartment–style public housing.

Not all designers agreed with Newman's recommendations, and not all attempts to carry them out were successful. But at least there was a new level of questioning. And after a period when large stretches of the existing built environment were essentially deemed worthless, certain qualities of older city homes were once again seen as having value in creating livable neighborhoods.

Many architects now sought more sensitive solutions to the design of new public housing. The problem of improving the safety and livability of existing multitower projects, however, was never resolved. This was not for lack of interesting suggestions. As early as 1962, in *The Death and Life of Great American Cities*, an influential critique of modern city planning, Jane Jacobs proposed hiring elevator attendants from among residents to provide round-the-clock security within buildings, as in earlier elevator towers.[17] Human surveillance obviously would have increased operating costs, but it might well have been cost effective, preventing vandalism as well as crime and trauma.

In the late 1960s a number of architects also proposed schemes to insert more buildings, both homes and stores, around the edges of existing superblocks. Such a strategy, they reasoned, would reduce the amount of open land but add life along perimeter sidewalks and create safer outdoor areas, enclosed and clearly semiprivate, within the older projects. It would also have resulted in complexes that more closely resembled new middle-class developments that were designed with greater attention to security. Yet while local housing authorities spent considerable amounts of money to maintain and repair the public housing complexes, they never made serious attempts to alter them fundamentally or

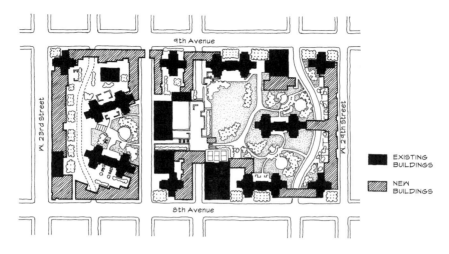

6-35. A 1968 proposal by Lawrence Halprin Associates to improve a ten-year-old project in New York City by adding new, lower buildings along the street, filling in space between existing freestanding towers. The remaining interior grounds, now more clearly semiprivate, were to be relandscaped and developed with a central recreation complex.

to add the ongoing human services that might have made them viable despite poor design.

In 1972 several buildings in the St. Louis housing project known as Pruitt-Igoe, built only seventeen years earlier with 2,764 modern apartments, were demolished. Widely publicized photos showed the eleven-story towers, their homes now vandalized and vacant, leaning and crumbling into clouds of debris. Whatever the merits of the decision to tear down the project—and there were certainly arguments to be made on both sides—its effect on overall public opinion about high-rise apartment living was negative. Americans who had moved to detached suburban houses spent little time, if any, in these older areas, and made few distinctions between one form of home, or one part of a neighborhood, and another. The image of the deteriorated, crime-ridden housing project came to stand for the potential danger and hopelessness of all older city neighborhoods in the late twentieth century, despite the actual existence of a great variety of home environments.

This sense of hopelessness still translates into a lack of will to try for meaningful improvements in the projects themselves, although they contain thousands of livable modern dwellings at a time when

6-36. A view of the Pruitt-Igoe public housing project in St. Louis, Missouri, shortly after completion in 1955. The complex suffered from crime and vandalism problems from the start; many critics associated these with its vast scale, long corridors, and building entrances under open, unsecured breezeways.

homelessness is widespread. Over the last few years public housing towers in Philadelphia, Chicago, and Newark have also been razed, and many more are scheduled for demolition. The faith that if we just wipe the slate clean we can do it right the next time continues to exceed our regard for current achievements, however flawed, or our patience for adaptive and finely tuned change.

PRIVATE APARTMENTS AFTER WORLD WAR II

The apartment towers constructed as public housing after World War II were perhaps the most literal translation of the European modernists' utopian sketches. Other buildings of the period, however, were also affected by the new design philosophy as well as by changing economics of building construction. New office buildings, stores, factories, schools, and other institutional structures all had simpler shapes, less ornament, and often larger, more continuous windows. They were also more likely to be freestanding and widely separated from other buildings. Not purely the result of aesthetic choice, this reflected the unavoidable need to accommodate ever-growing areas for parking around most structures.

In general, the cost of skilled on-site labor increased after the war relative to the cost of factory-produced materials. Including details such as patterned brickwork or bay windows to break up the flat facade of a modest apartment building thus became more costly. While both architectural journals and mainstream magazines promoted the newest buildings as sleek and elegant, it is probably fair to say that in the eyes of many Americans they were uglier than those of earlier eras. At the same time, however, they represented prosperity and technological convenience. During the 1950s and early 1960s the pace of construction was so rapid and most Americans so involved in the economic boom that criticism of their appearance was not widespread.

A far smaller percentage of the new homes constructed in this era were attached houses and small apartment buildings (up to four units) than had been the case in the first half of the century. In 1950 such low-rise but closely spaced dwellings constituted just over one quarter of all American homes. By 1970 their percentage had declined to 16.2 percent; their actual numbers had also fallen slightly, as more were demolished than built.[18] The explicit criteria of new federal mortgage programs, rising car ownership, tightened local zoning laws, and public sentiment about proper family life all contributed to making the freestanding house a more dominant form than ever before. Of the apartments that were constructed, most were now in large elevator buildings.

Other forms did not disappear, however, and continued to go up, in small numbers, where there was economic logic or an established historical development pattern. Traditional masonry row-houses and semidetached twins, now with stripped-down facades and integral front or rear garages, were still built in outlying sections of the city of Philadelphia. Small two- and three-family houses continued to fill unbuilt lots in the outer boroughs of New York. In Los Angeles, Houston, and other fast-growing cities of the West, where vast acres of undeveloped land were cleared for new ranch houses, freestanding two- and three-story apartment buildings still went up near commercial areas. Small U-shaped apartment complexes with a swimming pool in the central courtyard became a common form.

In cities where land was expensive and apartment living an established tradition, new high-rise buildings were also constructed for

6-37. These middle-class apartment towers built early in the 1960s a block from the Phipps Garden Apartments (shown on page 250) have good views and deep, usable balconies. But cars, rather than gardens, have pride of place between the buildings; parking fills most of the open land.

middle-class and wealthy residents. While almost as plain in appearance as the public housing towers, they were more likely to include small balconies, which added a little three-dimensional interest to their facades. At ground level they had larger, more elegant lobbies, and though frequently set back from the sidewalk, they were generally surrounded by less outdoor open space and had tighter security provisions. Luxury buildings still included a doorman or reception desk with concierge to screen visitors and keep watch on entry areas. Where zoning laws permitted, private developers still built stores or offices at the bases of new towers, as such uses commanded high rents at ground level, where apartments were least desirable. These provided interest and activity along the sidewalk and gave the modern buildings at street level some visual and psychological continuity with the older neighborhoods around them.

Parking was now a major priority—and headache—in the design of middle-class apartments. Sometimes it was included indoors, at the basement or first-floor level, but this solution was

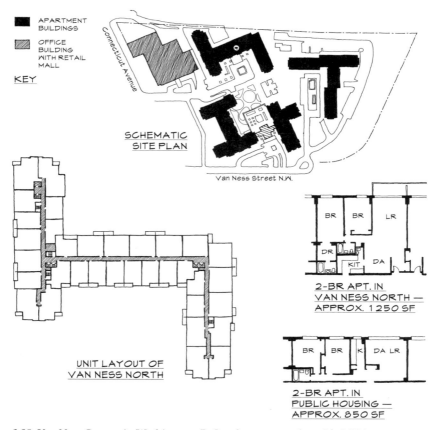

KEY

■ APARTMENT BUILDINGS

▨ OFFICE BUILDING WITH RETAIL MALL

Connecticut Avenue

SCHEMATIC SITE PLAN

Van Ness Street N.W.

UNIT LAYOUT OF VAN NESS NORTH

2-BR APT. IN VAN NESS NORTH — APPROX. 1250 SF

BR BR LR
DR KIT DA

2-BR APT. IN PUBLIC HOUSING — APPROX. 850 SF

BR BR K DA LR

6-38. Van Ness Centre, in Washington, D.C., a luxury complex with 1,524 apartments, two swimming pools, valet parking, doormen, and a separate building of stores and offices, opened in 1964. In Van Ness North, designed by architects Berla and Abel, the apartments, organized along double-loaded corridors, are quite deep. A typical two-bedroom unit has almost 50 percent more floor area but fewer windows and less exterior wall than its counterpart in a public housing tower. The space in the back of the apartments contains multiple bathrooms, windowless kitchens and dining areas, and large dressing rooms.

expensive, so when substantial outdoor space was available in new complexes it was given over largely to paved lots.

In some respects the standards for middle-class and luxury apartment layouts were now lower than those enforced for federal public housing of the same era. As discussed in chapter 3, most local building codes began to allow the substitution of mechanical ventilation for operable windows in bathrooms and kitchens by 1930. After World War II, speculative builders took advantage of this change, which made possible new buildings with less exterior surface area and simpler overall shapes. While the guidelines for public housing still required windowed kitchens or dining alcoves, these spaces in many privately constructed apartments now receded to the dark rear of the unit.

After the struggle around the turn of the century to legislate minimum standards for light and fresh air in homes, one might well ask why, when they represented a real decline in spatial and environmental standards, these code changes were so readily accepted by middle-class Americans. At least part of the reason is that their effects proliferated during the same period in which the technology of air-conditioning was becoming widespread. Through-wall units or building-wide central air systems could make apartments with few windows and no cross-ventilation comfortable, as long as the electric bills were affordable. Moreover, technological conveniences and modern appliances were heavily marketed as substitutes for generous space in homes of all forms, and there was little sentimentality about the recent past. An up-to-date but windowless kitchenette with an eye-level oven and an undercounter dishwasher genuinely looked better, to many eyes, than an older room with mismatched appliances and not enough outlets, but space for a table under the window.

PRESERVATION AND ADAPTIVE REUSE

By the mid-1960s the built environment of the United States had been so transformed and extended by postwar construction that earlier buildings stood in an altered context. In communities decimated by new housing towers, highway construction, and other urban renewal efforts, popular resistance to further large-scale changes developed. Shaken by the rapid deterioration of recently built public housing, residents of older neighborhoods began to feel that the remaining buildings around them were preferable to almost anything new, and to advocate forcefully the renovation of existing structures. Rowhouses, tenements, and other small apartment buildings that once were written off as substandard now were valued for their ornate cornices, continuous facades along the street, or ceiling heights that seemed lofty in comparison with newer homes. Some homes that had been hemmed in and shaded by adjacent buildings now had more light and view because of demolition elsewhere on the block.

Activists in lower-income communities still saw a need for new development as well as preservation, but wanted to ensure more local control over both. During the complex political turmoil of the late 1960s and throughout the 1970s thousands of neighborhood organizations were created across the country. A small number managed to procure the funding and develop the expertise to become effective not-for-profit developers of homes and commercial buildings. Their local origins and clear ties to specific communities were in contrast to philanthropic organizations active in the late nineteenth and early twentieth centuries. These had more often been founded by progressive upper-class white reformers who solicited private capital from "enlightened businessmen." Now that the notion of public involvement in home construction was entrenched, new socially motivated housing organizations worked through and lobbied for government programs rather than appealing directly to private business.

After widespread criticism of the scorched-earth approach taken in earlier public housing efforts, federal programs for the creation of low-income apartments diversified and became somewhat more flexible, often involving neighborhood groups as local sponsors. Design guidelines were revised to allow moderate or gut rehabilitation of older structures in addition to new construction. Vacant buildings, in certain cases already condemned for future redevelopment and in others abandoned by private owners because they were no longer profitable, were now entirely remade from the inside out. Some that had originally contained four or five stories of walk-up apartments were transformed with elevators and altered apartment layouts in addition to new plumbing and wiring. Only the exterior shells remained recognizable. Others were less drastically rebuilt but got modernized bathrooms and kitchens, upgraded mechanical and electrical systems, and tighter, more energy-conserving windows.

As approaches to improving and enlarging the housing stock in urban neighborhoods grew more varied, the scale of construction was also reduced. With some older homes left standing, building lots remaining for new ones were smaller and more irregular. The notion of superblocks lost favor, and existing streets more often

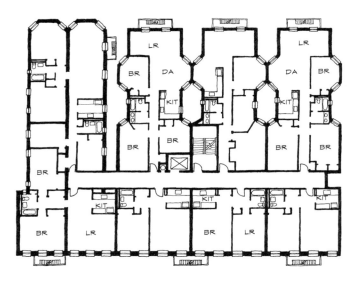

6-39. Typical floor plan, designed by Levenson - Thaler Architects, of a group of five New York "Old Law" tenements, their interiors gutted, rebuilt, and connected to form one building with a new elevator and fire stair. While some rooms still face onto air shafts, overall there are more windows and sometimes more generous and interesting spaces than in conventional post-war apartments.

stayed in place. Even large sites were now frequently broken up into separate parcels, so that the resulting homes were not as repetitive or monolithic.

During the early 1970s innovative housing design was a topic of much interest and debate within the architectural profession. The designers of smaller-scale subsidized developments now experimented with new forms of high-rise apartment organization as well as site layout. These included some buildings of duplex units with skip-stop elevators and others with common exterior galleries instead of interior corridors, both permitting more house-like apartment layouts. In response to the popular emphasis on building and neighborhood preservation, architects attempted to design new homes that were "contextual"—that is, visually compatible with the earlier buildings around them. Certain developments combined both elevator towers and lower walk-up buildings in an effort to provide variety and to blend with the scale of an existing neighborhood. Most designers tried hard to create secure common outdoor spaces that would invite use by residents.

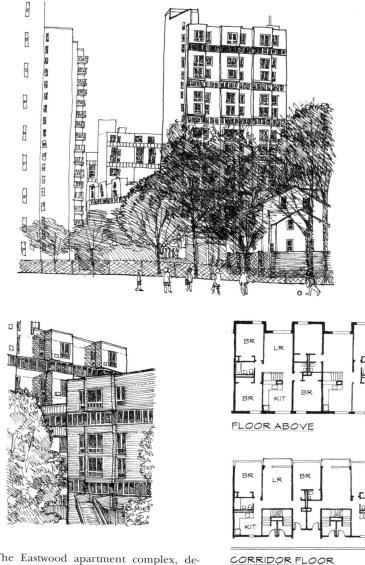

FLOOR ABOVE

CORRIDOR FLOOR

FLOOR BELOW

6-40. The Eastwood apartment complex, designed by Sert-Jackson Associates, was completed in 1976 on Roosevelt Island in New York City, as part of a subsidized, planned new community. The unusual rhythm of windows on the facade reflects the use of skip-stop elevators that stop every third floor and open onto an outdoor corridor. Apartments above and below the corridors are entered from individual stairwells leading up or down, and are floor-through units with family living areas extending from front to back.

Some of these new complexes were highly successful, while others held up less well over time. They were erected during an era when public subsidies were relatively generous, allowing for the inevitable delays and expense of trying to build something unfamiliar. A building with skip-stop elevators and duplex apartments, for instance, may be spatially more efficient than one laid out conventionally, but its layout changes from floor to floor, albeit in a regular pattern. Carpenters and mechanical subcontractors must pay attention and progress more slowly until they get used to the new system and iron out the bugs.

In efforts that paralleled postwar attempts to build prefabricated houses, the federal government also underwrote demonstration projects to develop less expensive apartment construction systems. Through a national program called Operation Breakthrough, established in 1969, architects worked in conjunction with builders on complexes of modular units, somewhat like mobile homes, stacked or arranged irregularly around core elements. They also studied new techniques of high-rise concrete construction becoming common in some European and Communist countries, where large prefabricated panels were used in lieu of walls built in place. In this country, however, discrepancies in local building codes and the resistance of many sectors of the construction industry did not make it any easier to develop such systems on a widespread scale than it had been to build affordable, legal houses in factories. Mobile homes themselves were still looked down on, and proliferated only outside established residential neighborhoods.

Unfortunately, though many alternatives were investigated, lessons learned, and certain projects widely published in architectural journals, all the attention focused on innovative apartment design in the early 1970s never carried over into changes in mainstream private development. Because sites were relatively small, by the standards of the late twentieth century, builders were unable to perfect new techniques and benefit financially from economies of scale. In the first decades of the century, when apartments were a popular and widespread form of home for Americans of all incomes, experimentation took place at all levels. The idea of the garden apartment, for example, was realized in different sizes and degrees of elegance, for wealthy as well as working-class families.

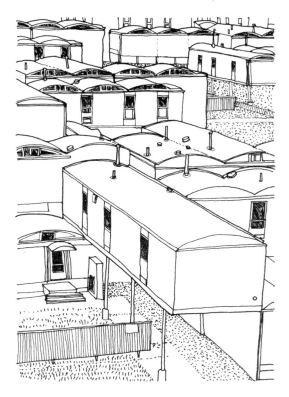

6-41. Oriental Gardens, an apartment complex built in Connecticut using stacked modular units similar to mobile homes. Designed by Paul Rudolph, it was part of the federal initiative Operation Breakthrough, begun in 1969 to develop new, less expensive methods of apartment construction.

With apartments serving a more limited market in recent decades, developers of speculative buildings have stayed with conventional layouts and building techniques, relying on luxurious lobby finishes and lots of bathrooms to market high-priced units.

In the late 1970s and early 1980s, as taxcutting grew in popularity and middle-class support for low-income housing programs waned, the budgets for new subsidized homes grew ever tighter, precluding almost all experimentation with fundamental building organization. The few apartment developments completed were more sensitively designed than those of the 1950s, but they became increasingly plain and conventional, not for lack of architectural effort but for lack of funds.

Not just in poor or declining neighborhoods did the vast scale of postwar demolition and construction lead to an enhanced appreciation of older buildings. While many middle-class families left the city for suburban homes, those who stayed put or moved into older communities also developed a new regard for local structures once taken for granted but now fast disappearing. A growing interest in *historic preservation* took many forms. At an individual level, middle-class families bought old homes and fixed them up with new attention to restoring original finishes and details. A market arose for materials and product styles that had gone completely out of production: stamped tin ceilings, interior plaster ornaments, and freestanding bathtubs with clawed feet. Most renovations were selective in what they preserved or recreated; modern appliances, contemporary kitchen layouts, and increased numbers of electrical outlets coexisted with carefully detailed wood moldings and historically accurate color schemes. Nobody put back the old coal-burning furnace.

Going beyond federal laws protecting a few historic sites around the country, many local governments in the 1960s and 1970s enacted legislation enabling them to impose *landmark designation* on individual buildings or larger portions of existing communities. A landmarked building could not be torn down at will by its owner, and renovations or additions required the approval of a locally appointed panel that included historians or architects. Most designations, especially for homes, applied only to the public face of a building. Because they limited the rights of individual property owners in a new way, beyond zoning ordinances or building codes, these laws were controversial, but their scope widened steadily as interest in preservation grew.

The popular appreciation of older buildings increased during a period in which major shifts in manufacturing technology, transportation modes, and residential patterns left many structures abandoned or underutilized. Multistory factories in industrial areas near rail lines and outdated ports were no longer useful to companies that now needed horizontal plants easily accessible to tractor-trailers. School buildings in cities with fewer young families and steeply declining enrollments were put on the market by financially strapped boards of education. Even churches with dwindling congregations were consolidating, leaving ornate older buildings without a function. Few of these structures were landmarked or widely recognized. Most simply sat empty, available for inexpensive sale or rent. The practice of *adaptive reuse,* through which such obsolescent buildings were rehabilitated to

6-42. A renovated cast-iron warehouse in the Soho section of New York City.

accommodate new uses, grew along with the historic preservation movement.

The most publicized examples of early adaptive reuse, such as the renovation of the Ghirardelli chocolate factory in San Francisco, involved the large-scale renovation of outmoded industrial buildings into highly successful commercial centers. But growing numbers of cheap, vacant buildings were also a resource for individual homesteaders and amateur carpenters, who used them to create new urban apartments without the usual involvement and expense of professional builders and architects. One early example eventually involved an entire neighborhood transformation. Even before 1960, New York City artists, always looking for inexpensive, naturally lit studios, began renting spaces in a run-down Manhattan district of multistory manufacturing lofts with cast-iron facades. The area, known as Soho, was zoned for industrial use, and residences were illegal. With the tacit approval of landlords looking for any tenants they could get, the artists extended wiring and plumbing lines and built dramatic new homes, one by one, within the high-ceilinged, wide-open lofts. Though they were reached only by industrial elevators and single sets of narrow stairs that did not meet current codes, these apartments became increasingly popular as the neighborhood attracted the avant-garde. By the 1970s loft apartments were being custom designed by architects. After periodic crackdowns on illegal loft living, the city revised both its zoning ordinance and building code in 1982 to create special categories for loft conversions, which now extended to other neighborhoods as well. Soho itself by this time had become so expensive that few artists could afford it any longer.

Unlike the individual and often furtive building of artists' lofts, many later conversions of older nonresidential structures into apartments were done on a building-wide basis. In some cases they were sponsored by neighborhood groups using public subsidies. In others, however, they were undertaken by private developers who saw their potential for accommodating market-rate apartments that were more generous, spatially interesting, and individualized than those being constructed even in new luxury buildings. Beginning in the 1970s, it was apartment conversions that had the rich and picturesque quality of homes such as the garden apartments for the wealthy built in Los Angeles in the 1920s. Both movies and commercial advertisements over the last twenty years have increasingly been set in elegant converted apartments, certainly out of proportion to their actual numbers. From the painters' lofts of the 1978 film *An Unmarried Woman* to the corporate lawyer's converted warehouse home in *Philadelphia*, made in 1994, the depiction of them shifted from bohemian to mainstream.

The broadly based historic preservation movement as well as local efforts to preserve low-income neighborhoods began as popular rather than professional initiatives. But while architects did not spearhead these efforts, their design and technical skills were needed, and many became heavily involved. Designers trained according to strict modernist principles found themselves becoming experts in historic styles of ornamentation or in building techniques such as masonry arches and brick corbeling, largely abandoned in new construction.

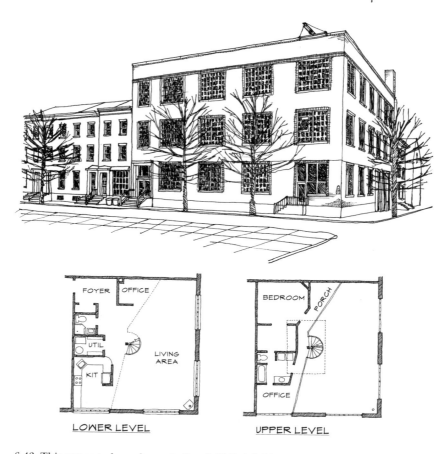

LOWER LEVEL   UPPER LEVEL

6-43. This converted warehouse in South Philadelphia still has its original hoist intact and a builder's shop at street level. Plans show the 1,800-square-foot, two-level corner loft apartment on the third floor. A self-contained home with its own furnace and hot water heater, it has been used as a setting for movies and advertisements.

Adaptive reuse allowed for a more freewheeling combination of old and new design styles and construction techniques than did the historically accurate preservation of landmarks. Nonetheless, it forced architects to familiarize themselves with earlier buildings rather than create new structures that maintained a visual and physical separation from their surroundings. Wading through debris to measure and photograph a long-abandoned factory was a process different from contemplating an undeveloped site or an empty lot. Imagining its possibilities and then shepherding construction through to the creation of new homes tended to change the way designers looked at other existing buildings. It became harder to advocate the demolition of destitute structures even in parts of town where new conversions might not be economically feasible.

Unfortunately, the growing sensitivity of many professionals to the worth and potential of the existing built environment did not arrest the basic economic and political forces that operated throughout the postwar era. Older communities continued to decline, often leading to the emptying and eventual destruction of livable homes even as brand-new ones were built elsewhere.

Although the preservation movement was not able to alter the overall changes taking place across the American landscape, it did have an effect on the surface appearance of many new buildings, especially homes. Mainstream architectural design has been increasingly influenced by the popularity of older building styles. In the mid-1970s, half-round windows, complex gabled roofs, and old-fashioned paneled doors were suddenly common on new condominium apartments and townhouses as well as on custom-built homes. Like much of the actual historic preservation taking place, the stylistic incorporation of historic detail into new buildings focused mostly on public facades and, to a lesser extent, on interior finishes: moldings, paint colors, and traditional-looking cabinetry. The layout and relationships of interior spaces remained contemporary, as did the actual uses of outdoor areas. Thus, a new townhouse complex and a new shopping center might invoke the look of a colonial town—but both would be surrounded by parking lots and strictly separated by modern zoning practice.

A "historic" surface treatment was also applied to large apartment buildings. At the upper end of the market, many of these were designed with exteriors that echoed the luxury elevator towers of the 1920s. Their interior organization, however, remained similar to those of other postwar buildings, using a double-loaded corridor and relying heavily on mechanical ventilation.

For smaller apartment buildings, the study of historic forms as well as surface details produced more varied and inventive results, in homes built for both wealthy and low-income families. California and Texas saw new interpretations of the old form of courtyard apartments. A number of southern cities now have apartment homes, built as public housing, that are modeled on older, closely spaced *side-yard houses:* narrow wood-framed homes with long porches at right angles to the street.

Within the last fifteen years, urban designers and architects proposing new prototypical solutions for both affordable homes and environmentally efficient communities have advocated building forms that resemble the two- and three-family apartment houses built in large numbers around the turn of the century. These are now recognized for their flexibility and economy as well as the ease with which they blend into surrounding neighborhoods of detached houses. However, they have not yet been reinvented as a stock form, built with variations by private developers throughout a region.

Over the century and a half during which apartment houses have been formally defined as a dwelling type distinct from single-family houses, they have been built in a wide variety of sizes and forms across the United States. Changes in technology, social policy, and aesthetic fashion all have affected their design but have not always helped Americans to see them objectively. We have tended to veer wildly from one era to the next, praising and promoting certain forms while condemning others: low-rise or high-rise, freestanding or continuous, oriented to the street or to planted open space. These rushes to judgment have meant not only abrupt changes in home-building practices but also the demolition of many older homes, which we may later come to view more positively.

Perhaps the recent popular interest in building preservation will increase our tolerance and appreciation of the range of ways in which homes may be connected to each other and to the outdoors. We have now built many models to consider: tightly organized towers with privacy, light, and views for densely packed homes on a compact plot; spacious and individualized multilevel units within the basic box of an old factory; straightforward double- and triple-deckers cared for by resident owners but including a mixture of rental units; larger garden apartment complexes organized around gracious courtyards. Homes in apartments need be no less livable or long-lasting than those in individual houses but provide an important variety of environmental and social choices.

7

GROUPING HOMES TOGETHER:
What Makes a Neighborhood?

> There is a Law of Neighborhood which does not leave a man
> perfect master on his own ground.
>
> Edmund Burke

Where do you live?" is a question we can answer at many levels—from galactic, global, national, and local to the specific address that distinguishes a single household from all others. Somewhere in this range, usually smaller in size than the city or town of the legal address but always broader than an individual dwelling, lies the area that we think of as our neighborhood.

Primary dictionary definitions of *neighbor* and *neighborhood* all center on physical proximity. Our neighbors are the people living either adjacent to us or within a certain area around us. Neither of these criteria implies an absolute distance. Next door can be the apartment on the other side of the living-room wall or the farmhouse two miles away. Our neighbors may be the people on the block or everyone within the boundaries of a much larger subdivision.

Secondary definitions relate to the emotional and social ties that, presumably, arise from physical closeness and create a relationship different from those within a family but nonetheless important and binding. Acting neighborly is not the same thing as acting maternally or paternally, but it means watching out for someone else, being available in case of emergency, and working together on common problems. While good neighbors do not have to know our birthdays or agree with our politics, they should call the police if they see someone breaking into our home, help to clear the fallen tree branch that's blocking the street, and perhaps offer to pick up groceries if we're hobbling around with a leg in a cast. At the same time—and this can be a tricky balance—they should be neither too nosy nor too noisy, respecting our needs for privacy and quiet.

The forms of our homes relate straightforwardly to the physical distances involved in defining *neighborhood*. Rowhouse and apartment neighbors are closer than those in freestanding houses, and probably they are also more numerous. How or whether home forms influence the emotional connections of neighborhoods, however, is much less clear. We know where we meet our neighbors and talk with them: the front porch, the stoop, the backyard, a courtyard or playground, a local café, the laundry room, even the elevator. But extrapolating from personal experiences and observations to more "scientific" assertions about neighborhood design has repeatedly proven dubious. Our adaptability is too great and there are simply too many social factors to consider. Cohesive neighborhoods exist in areas with all forms of homes, as do neighborhoods in which residents are indifferent or even hostile to one another. The issue is not that design doesn't matter, or that one neighborhood may not be more livable, friendly, or beautiful than another, but that there are no universal solutions.

Neighborly relationships are not limited to people who live in adjacent or nearby dwellings. They can include those who work in local businesses or public institutions that we use regularly—stores whose owners cash our checks and recognize our children, restaurants or bars where we feel comfortable and are apt to run into friends, schools whose teachers we meet on the street for years after we've graduated. In some settings we also get to know animals, domesticated and wild, around our homes, and regard them in a real sense as neighbors—the birds we watch through the window and perhaps feed in winter, the cat from next door who likes to sit on our front steps.

The term *neighborhood*, then, implies both a defined geographic area of buildings and open spaces, home to a specific set of people, plants, and animals, and an area with some social unity, where those in a variety of relationships behave "like neighbors." Frequently these two definitions, physical and social, don't mesh. We may not even see the person who lives next door to us often enough to know that his or her leg is broken, but bring soup to a sick friend eight miles away.

In the United States, *neighborhood* is almost as emotionally and politically loaded a word as *home*, but its legal and physical meanings are far less defined. Basic standards for neighborhoods are fewer than for dwellings. In fact, we often disagree completely about their most essential components, the types of buildings and outdoor spaces they should contain. Major battles are fought to keep businesses and sometimes even schools and parks from being built in some neighborhoods composed only of private homes. Mingling dwellings of different forms and price levels, whether houses or apartments, can be equally controversial. But in other neighborhoods, just as well loved by their residents, homes of all forms sit side by side not only with stores and restaurants but with factories, offices, sewage treatment plants, and prisons.

Building a neighborhood is, of course, a more shared and ongoing endeavor than erecting a single home. Even communities initially created by a single developer involve both public and private land and responsibilities; all neighborhoods change over time in ways that no single party controls. That their components are more variable than those of a home is therefore not surprising. Less inherently logical is that our minimum legal requirements for safety, basic technology, and functional spaces are all more stringent for the private homes within our neighborhoods than they are for the public spaces that we build together. Today we are over ten times more likely to die in an automobile accident, as pedestrians, passengers, or drivers, than in a fire.[1] Yet the standards for safety along streets in residential areas are far lower than those for fire safety within dwellings. Countless American neighborhoods lack sidewalks or barriers to protect children from high-speed traffic. We not only expect but require that all homes have indoor plumbing and full bathrooms, yet, as mentioned earlier, do not mandate toilet facilities in outdoor public areas. While there are minimum sizes and maximum occupancies for bedrooms and living rooms, there are no such minimums for shared neighborhood spaces such as parks and playgrounds and rarely any requirement that they be provided at all.

These discrepancies are not simply a matter of the cost of public facilities. The technological, spatial, and life-safety standards now governing home construction add a great deal to the cost of housing, in fact putting private legal homes out of reach for many Americans. Rather, we place so much cultural and material importance on our individual homes that we end up feeling that there are few resources to devote to the built environment around them. As the public environment consequently deteriorates or offers us little comfort, we simply focus more, and spend more, on our own private space—a self-perpetuating and costly pattern environmentally, socially, and economically.

PHYSICAL AND SOCIAL BOUNDARIES

Without agreement about the physical components required of a residential neighborhood, defining its extent and boundaries is difficult. The members of even a single household are likely to map the outline of their neighborhood very differently from one another, depending on their daily paths and destinations. Steadily advancing technology and an economy focused on consumer goods have allowed most Americans to bring ever more activities and conveniences inside their homes, reducing day-to-day dependence on their immediate outdoor surroundings, both preexisting and man-made. Underground pipes carry water from distant sources directly indoors; videotapes lessen the allure of a nearby movie theater. With so many indoor comforts, many people no longer rely on their neighborhoods as they did in earlier eras, and hence do not have to be so familiar with them.

Advances in technology, however, have not changed our basic physical and social natures. No matter how much or how little we consciously use them, our neighborhoods are still the beginning of our connection to the world beyond our homes and families. To see a given neighborhood more clearly, it is important to consider how we might define it, even if not all our definitions mesh.

The boundaries of some neighborhoods are very clear. Certain features of the natural landscape, such as a river or a cliff, create a break in the built environment and also give a special visual identity to nearby buildings. (We retain a vivid image of houses on a point jutting into a lake, but would be hard put to describe similar ones in a subdivision across from the supermarket where we shop regularly.) A man-made barrier—for instance, a limited access highway—also can create a definitive edge. Large parks and areas zoned exclusively for factories or office towers separate neighborhoods as well. Some neighborhoods have a uniform architectural style or distinctive street layout that distinguishes them from their surroundings, whether or not they are enclosed with fences and gates.

In a small town or at the edge of a larger one, a neighborhood boundary may simply be where buildings stop and farms or undeveloped lands begin. The United States has grown so quickly, however, that such borders often have not lasted. Towns and cities spread out toward nearby communities until they are no longer separated by open space. When you drive or walk through a continuously developed environment, it is hard to tell one town or neighborhood apart from another; the blocks of "Elmwood" abut those of "Walnut Hill" without a visible dividing line.

Under these conditions, people define their neighborhoods according to social and political criteria as well as clear physical borders. Rich, middle-class, and poor American families most often live in neighborhoods considered separate from one another; usually the sizes and forms of homes in these areas are recognizably different. Frequently, though not always, these economic divisions correspond with government-created boundaries that delineate districts for elections, schools, and services such as garbage collection and policing.

Language, culture, and race can also distinguish neighborhoods even when the types of homes and incomes of the families living in them are similar. If there is overt and systematic discrimination against a given group, the boundary of their neighborhood may be clear and long-lasting. Thus, in many American towns built during the railroad era, African-American communities for several generations truly were limited to one side of the tracks. Other boundaries based on social groupings rather than income are far more fluid and change faster than the buildings themselves. For example, during recent decades Manhattan's Chinatown has expanded beyond the streets that originally defined it, into adjacent areas that still show on tourist maps as Little Italy and the old, once predominantly Jewish Lower East Side. When they developed initially, each of these neighborhoods had similar working-class homes—mostly tenement apartments—but distinct cultural institutions and street-level stores. However, Jewish and Italian residents aged or moved away, and Asian immigration increased. Today the result is a multilayered physical environment where Hebrew letters engraved above the arched entrance of a former yeshiva are framed by banners in Chinese announcing a community center.

Given this variety of possible definitions, many of us could outline several partially overlapping "neighborhoods" that contain our home. In a less complex world, and in many people's ideal surroundings, all boundaries would coincide. Families would know each other, children would go to school together, and those who worked in local businesses would also live there. Such a tightly knit neighborhood would also fall within a single political jurisdiction. The buildings, even if not constructed at the same time, would look harmonious as a group and different from those elsewhere, giving the area a distinct visual identity.

In the United States, which has changed and grown continually since its founding, a desire for this kind of clarity is one reason that we tend to idealize neighborhood life in small towns, whose social and physical boundaries are easier to comprehend. Of course, real country towns, those based on an agricultural economy, do not provide the range of work choices that most of us need or the stores and entertainments to which we are accustomed. However, part of the appeal of suburbs—discrete communities accessible to a city but lying just outside it—is their promise of simpler and more cohesive neighborhoods. Through successive waves of suburban development, many such neighborhoods have actually been quickly engulfed by the city proper. Nonetheless, over the last century and a half, American builders have explicitly advertised and often exaggerated the rural or small-town qualities of these new communities.

TRANSPORTATION MODE AND NEIGHBORHOOD FORM

The population growth and physical spread of American suburbs are historically linked to major technological shifts in transportation. As our available means of daily travel have evolved from walking to trains and streetcars to automobiles, the meaning of being "close to work" has changed profoundly and we have been able to build new home forms. In our individualistic way we have focused largely on these homes—their appearance, comfort, and technology. New forms of transportation we have tended to consider only as changing means to a constant end, that being to live in our "dream house" in a safe and idyllic neighborhood. The ways in which successive transportation modes actually altered the definition and design of new neighborhoods, as well as the functioning of older ones, have not been as widely noted.

The earliest towns and cities in the United States, like those elsewhere in the world, were built mainly around pedestrian traffic. Though some people kept horses for longer trips or for pulling loads, walking was the most convenient and usually the only way to get around on a daily basis. Urban historian Kenneth Jackson estimated that in 1815, 98 percent of Americans lived within a mile of their workplaces.[2] (At that time, of course, in towns as well as on farms, a workplace was commonly part of the home itself.)

As commerce increased, along with the populations of young American cities, both land and buildings were used intensively so that distances could remain small. House lots were narrow and front doors or steps came right to the street. Intermingled with dwellings was a wide range of stores, offices, and artisans' workshops. Only the most foul-smelling and potentially unhealthy businesses, such as tanneries and slaughterhouses, were discouraged and sometimes forced outside of city limits, along with the homes of their workers.

Through the early 1800s, in what Jackson refers to as "walking cities," the desirable place for an affluent, cosmopolitan home in an American metropolis was close to the city center. Such a dwelling was often a sturdily built, attached townhouse in a mixed-use neighborhood with shops and other conveniences. Though by modern standards these neighborhoods were congested and unhygienic, their scale was limited to buildings of just a few stories, workplaces were small and self-contained, and no electric lights or round-the-clock machines disturbed the nighttime quiet. Outdoor spaces—streets, backyards, and small public squares—were heavily used during the day. Because people could walk in all directions, the built environment was evenly and tightly developed. Americans did not enclose their cities with fortified walls, as Europeans had in earlier centuries, but there were still clear edges to urban communities. While interdependent, town and country life were physically and socially distinct.

With the beginnings of the industrial revolution, life in city neighborhoods changed rapidly. Individual businesses expanded and many kinds of production moved out of home-based shops. Both noise and air pollution increased dramatically. The growing concentration of industry also generated new wealth for factory owners and merchants, so that at least some city dwellers' expectations for their homes rose while conditions around them grew more chaotic. Out of this mixture of turmoil, prosperity, and advancing technology came both new visions and actual possibilities for larger houses in quieter, more secluded neighborhoods. Over the course of the nineteenth and early twentieth centuries, the notion of the home as a sheltered retreat from the workplace grew steadily. Initially a concept that was realistic only for the wealthy, it gradually became a national ideal.

A secluded home setting is practical, however, only if one can get back and forth to it as necessary. The first suburban neighborhoods in this country all depended on some alternative to walking. By the early 1800s there was sufficient traffic across the rivers or harbors bordering cities such as New York, Philadelphia, Boston, Cincinnati, and Pittsburgh to support commercial ferries, which took daily passengers back and forth.[3] Regular boat service fostered the development of new towns on the opposite bank, where well-to-do city dwellers built quieter and more spacious homes than those they could afford on the other side. Robert Fulton's invention of the steamboat, which began operating as a ferry in 1814 between Manhattan and Brooklyn, made service faster and increased the carrying capacity of individual boats, enabling these towns to grow rapidly. In some cases, like that of Camden, on the Delaware River opposite Philadelphia, and, later, Oakland, across the bay from San Francisco, they eventually became cities in their own right. The number of possible ferryboat suburbs, however, was limited by natural geography.

It was the development of new land-based transportation systems, which could extend in nearly any direction, that allowed for

7-1. The Kenwood station and stationmaster's cottage, built in 1859 south of Chicago along the main line of the Illinois Central railroad. By 1871 the city limits had expanded to within a mile of the station, and by the turn of the century the area was part of the city proper.

the growth of suburban neighborhoods around virtually all sizable American cities. During the 1830s railroad tracks began to be laid for trains pulled by new steam-powered locomotives, initially linking major cities in the East and Midwest. Though their primary purpose was the hauling of freight and passengers over long distances, railroad entrepreneurs were hungry for all the business they could get. Along their routes they erected stations at small towns that lay within about an hour's ride of major terminals. These offered new residential options to those who could afford the high fares and the time for what was at first a somewhat unreliable commute.

Early railroad suburbs quickly developed neighborhoods of wealthy homes. The most elaborate mimicked country estates of the British gentry, though they rarely included much real farming. Others were less formal but still spacious houses on lots within easy walking distance of the new stations. However, most of these towns or "villages," as they were self-consciously called, also developed small neighborhoods, sometimes just pockets, of closely spaced and modest homes, perhaps a few blocks of rowhouses or semi-

7-2. By 1873, suburban towns such as Morgan Park, also south of Chicago, were being established by real estate developers and served by branch commuter lines. This sketch, based on a promotional rendering, shows the essential elements of such communities: a steam-powered train, a small commercial center close to the station, and an idealized "country house" within walking distance.

attached cottages. Such dwellings housed servants, tradesmen, and construction workers, who could not afford the time or expense of the train but provided essential services to wealthier families (often in addition to their live-in staff). Thus, many of the earliest suburban enclaves of the rich, like those in Westchester County north of New York City, or along the Main Line of Philadelphia, were actually, of necessity, economically and sometimes also racially mixed.

As the potential of daily commuting by rail became apparent, short-run train lines were built in a radial pattern extending outward from the largest cities. These commuter lines brought service to areas off the main long-distance freight and passenger routes. By the second half of the century, real-estate speculators and railroad entrepreneurs, working hand in hand, were creating new suburban towns from previously undeveloped or agricultural land. Inter-railroad competition, in combination with improving technology, caused fares to drop, making train commuting affordable for more middle-class families. New suburbs containing blocks of smaller and more closely spaced houses were now built in addition to those for the wealthy. Regardless of who lived there, however, the growth of railroad suburbs was constrained by steam engine technology: stops had to be spaced far enough apart to allow the locomotive to gather momentum and then slow down again, generally a couple of miles. This created a self-limiting physical pattern of distinct and separated nodes along the train lines. As commuters were not willing to walk more than a half-mile or so to the station, open land or large estates remained between and around these new communities, reinforcing a small-town atmosphere.

Concurrent with the development and spread of steam-powered trains, the alternate technology of the streetcar made possible a more continuous pattern of new neighborhood growth. In its first incarnation, originating in France in the 1830s, the streetcar was simply a large horse-drawn carriage, known as an *omnibus*, that traveled along a regular route and allowed passengers to get on or off every few blocks. Only slightly faster than walking, it provided a bumpy ride along cobbled or dirt streets. In 1852 came the invention in the United States of slotted rails laid flush with the street surface. These enabled a horse to pull its carriage on level tracks without impeding other traffic, providing a smoother and faster ride than earlier wheeled carriages, at an average speed of six to eight miles per hour.[4] Unlike the steam-powered train, the new "horse railway" could make stops as frequently as necessary, so homes and businesses extended evenly in a corridor on either side of the avenue where the tracks ran. Horsecar lines thus allowed the building of new homes for the affluent toward the outskirts of many cities, without necessarily defining separate towns. In most cases they were part of the gradual enlargement of the city itself.

By the end of the 1880s, streetcars powered by overhead electric lines had begun to replace those drawn by horses. Popularly known as *trolleys*, their name derived from the device that connected them to wires above. A major technological advance, electric streetcars almost doubled the speed of travel, held more passengers, and freed streets of horse droppings. They were also less expensive per passenger to operate than horse cars; riding the streetcar became affordable to factory workers and others with low-wage jobs.

Trolley lines were a powerful tool for real-estate development. With amazing rapidity, private entrepreneurs across the United States secured operating franchises from local governments. According to a federal study, a total of about 7,500 miles of streetcar track existed nationwide in 1890, most of it still for horse-

7-3. Electric streetcar lines were relatively easy to build along existing streets; they allowed small cities and towns to expand rapidly. This view of Atchison, Kansas (population about 16,000), in 1909, shows the trolley running alongside horse-drawn carriages and wagons down a prosperous and newly electrified main street, with greener and more residential areas just up the hill.

drawn vehicles. Thirteen years later, in 1903, this had grown four-fold to 30,000 miles, 98 percent of it electrically powered.[5] Unlike the earlier commuter railroads, these lines opened up land not just for more middle-class neighborhoods but for new working-class homes as well. Many families could now leave overcrowded tenements in built-up factory districts and move to modest homes farther from work, some still within the city and some outside.

The forms of these new homes varied according to land values and local building customs. Elaborate but closely spaced late-Victorian houses, smaller single-family "cottages," bungalows, row-houses, double- and triple-deckers, and other small apartment buildings were erected along blocks surrounding the trolley lines. In general, however, homes for different income groups were not intermingled. As the scale of home construction increased and people traveled greater distances to work, neighborhoods became more economically and culturally stratified. The members of a single factory's workforce, for example, could now live much farther apart from one another. An owner might travel by trolley to the train station and from there to an exclusive suburban town. Foremen and workers could ride to distinct neighborhoods with differing lot sizes and home forms. And though they all paid about the same amount of rent, Polish, Italian, and Jewish laborers might go in separate directions as well, to blocks inhabited by those of similar backgrounds, with nearby stores and services reflecting their distinct culture.

While streetcars enabled most American cities and towns to expand with relative economy and speed, this new transportation mode still did not meet the needs of those metropolitan areas with the most concentrated commercial downtowns and the largest populations. In Boston by 1889, for example, trolley cars lined Tremont Street, a major artery, for a continuous half-mile during rush hour; pedestrians were said to be able to walk along their roofs.[6] Alternate forms of transportation that relieved this congestion were elevated or underground electric train lines. Though far costlier to build, both moved passengers more quickly than the trolleys and left streets free for other vehicles and pedestrians.

Starting in the late 1800s, subways and "els" were constructed in a few cities in the United States, among them Boston, New York, Chicago, and Philadelphia. Like the streetcar lines, they precipitated new home construction but at a higher density, often in the form of large apartment buildings or continuous blocks of rowhouses. These train lines, however, proved far more durable than the trolley tracks, which disappeared almost completely by the mid-twentieth century. Today the neighborhoods around the subways and elevateds, while complex and often struggling, provide some of the few opportunities in this country for viable car-free living.

Changing transportation technologies throughout the nineteenth century thus allowed progressively more Americans to move outward to neighborhoods that lay beyond walking distance of where family breadwinners worked. Though the economically self-sufficient country town was still invoked as an image, especially for wealthy railroad suburbs, the actual conception of a

7-4. The extension of elevated trains and subways into New York City's outer boroughs in the early 1900s spurred the development of new, high-density neighborhoods. The 82nd Street stop on the #7 train still serves the garden apartment community of Jackson Heights, Queens (including the Chateau, see page 249). Clustered around the station are neighborhood commercial services such as branch banks, pharmacies, food stores, and restaurants.

"good" residential neighborhood became one that excluded most modern workplaces—that is, large factories and offices.

Through the 1920s, however, all new neighborhoods, whether suburban or in outlying sections of the city, still included nonresidential buildings. Wealthy and working-class families alike needed convenient access to stores that sold food, dry goods, or hardware, and to services such as shoemakers and tailors. Quite a few of these establishments delivered along residential streets, first by horse-drawn wagon and later by truck, but many errands were still done on foot by women and children at home during the day and by wage earners on their way home from the train or trolley. Additional neighborhood entertainments and services such as theaters, restaurants, and lawyers' offices tended to locate in these same business areas.

One way of defining a neighborhood, therefore, was around an accessible commercial and social center. Most often this was close to a train station or along an avenue where the trolley ran. During the first few decades of this century, even as car ownership grew and builders added garages next to new high-end homes, the same pattern continued. Americans initially used the new vehicles, which were still somewhat unreliable, more for recreation than as daily transport. Moreover, many people had not yet learned to

7-5. This mixed-use shopping center, with 25 stores, 12 offices and 28 apartments, was built in the 1920s close to the train station in Lake Forest, Illinois, still a prosperous Chicago suburb. Designed by a resident, architect Harold Van Doren Shaw, it served rail commuters, pedestrians, and automobile drivers.

drive, and parking was often unavailable on busy main streets. In this period, when apartments and attached houses were widely constructed as middle-class homes and before they were strictly limited by local zoning ordinances, many established suburbs also saw the construction of garden apartments or semiattached twin houses around the fringes of their commercial centers. These concentrated new homes on land close to existing transportation lines, providing alternatives to older city neighborhoods for those who wanted to live in a suburban setting without the cost or maintenance of a freestanding house. Of course, the increased population in these alternative forms of homes also expanded the customer base of local stores, allowing more specialty shops to flourish along established commercial streets.

In 1947, just after World War II, William Levitt and his sons began the construction of 17,400 modest freestanding houses on what had been Long Island potato fields. Though the property they purchased was far from any train station or trolley line, their site plan was in many ways modeled on older suburbs. Determined to create not just homes but "community," they subdivided the

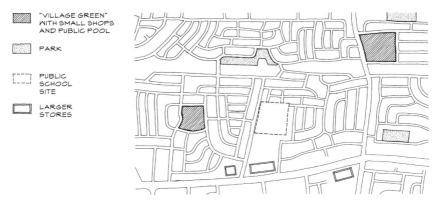

"VILLAGE GREEN"
WITH SMALL SHOPS
AND PUBLIC POOL

PARK

PUBLIC
SCHOOL
SITE

LARGER
STORES

7-6. Street layout of a section of Levittown, Long Island, showing two of the seven "village greens" dispersed within the curving blocks of small ranch houses. Additional larger stores were located along Hempstead Turnpike, a regional thoroughfare that bisected the development.

development into seven sections. Each was centered around its own "village green," with a park, a public swimming pool, and a commercial center of small stores. As in many older and wealthier suburban towns, streets curved gently and trees were planted to create a casual and bucolic atmosphere. The setting was "natural" but tame, and also included some pleasures of town life; residents could walk to the village center after dinner, along continuous sidewalks, for ice cream and conversation with their neighbors.

This first Levittown, an unprecedented experiment in large-scale home-building, was dramatically successful. Despite skepticism on the part of social critics and city planners, demand for the houses was high and many residents remained satisfied over the years, by most accounts getting to know their neighbors and feeling that they had gotten good value for their investment.[7] The only parts of the development that did not turn out as profitably as expected were the village stores. The Levitts were annoyed when it became apparent that a single larger shopping center, not built by them, was drawing business away from their planned neighborhood commercial areas. The next two Levittowns, in Pennsylvania and New Jersey, still included playgrounds, parks, swimming pools, and sidewalks, but each contained only one large cluster of shops at the edge of the development, accessible by major roads to other communities as well.[8] If not already in the freezer, ice cream after dinner was now a car trip, and sidewalks were quieter.

Postwar suburban development spread rapidly during the 1950s and 1960s. Some large-scale builders, like the Levitts, continued to include community facilities and public open spaces in their developments. Many more, however, simply purchased land around the fringes of existing suburban towns and covered it with private lots and houses. Thus boundaries blurred and one residential area edged into another, without any regular pattern of parks or commercial streets to break them up. Except where they were required by local ordinance, sidewalks were no longer built as a standard feature along new blocks of houses; all coming and going was now assumed to be by car. With the closing down of trolley service in many localities, foot traffic dropped off substantially in older neighborhoods as well.

The lesson learned from the weak performance of the first Levittown's village stores was not an isolated one. As the spatial logic of car-oriented business retailing became apparent, retailers located new stores on land near highways or major through-streets rather than within or right next to newly built tracts of homes. It was now more important to be visible to drivers and to provide ample space for parking than to occupy prime space amidst a ready-made neighborhood marketplace. The flexibility of the car made comparative shopping easier than it had been on foot or by trolley, especially with purchases to lug home. This gave new advantage to large businesses that could offer volume discounts. Even in older towns people began to buy their food in supermarkets that were perhaps ten or fifteen minutes beyond the smaller local grocery store because supermarkets offered better prices and greater choice.

The growing use of cars visibly affected newly built homes and neighborhoods. Streets were wider, both houses and businesses generally lower and farther apart from one another, garages and parking lots now part of the main routes leading indoors. Existing neighborhoods, however, also underwent gradual but profound changes. Trains, streetcars, and subways had all, in effect, been intermodal, involving a transfer from walking to riding. While enabling people to live in new forms of housing, they did not

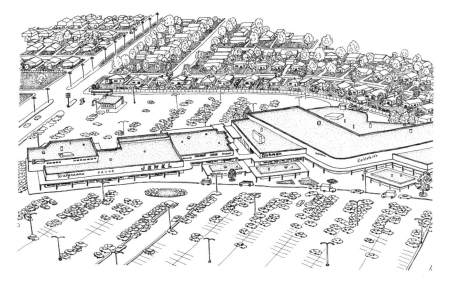

7-7. A 1950s shopping center on the outskirts of Chicago. Typical of new commercial developments of the era, it abutted growing neighborhoods of single-family tract houses, but was located along a local highway and designed to be reached by car.

directly alter the physical environment around and between these homes, which were still approached on foot. The blessing and the curse of the passenger automobile was that it came right up onto private property. As cars became increasingly necessary for most Americans, they affected older neighborhoods in myriad ways, both physical and social.

The same new shopping centers that attracted residents from developments such as Levittown also drew customers away from the smaller stores clustered around train stations in nearby suburbs and along the commercial streets of older towns and outlying sections of the city. All over the country, connections between local stores and the homes surrounding them weakened. Americans who grew up in older neighborhoods during the 1950s or 1960s frequently have vivid memories of a particular shop close to their home, often bearing its proprietor's name, put out of business by the opening of a mall some distance away.

Most people living in these neighborhoods valued the low prices and variety available in the new stores, not to mention the ease of parking, but were saddened at the same time by the decline of nearby shopping areas where they had personal ties.

Established business interests, naturally, were also threatened. Striving to help them compete, local town and city governments spearheaded changes along older streets. They tore down buildings to create municipal parking lots, and altered traffic patterns to improve the flow of cars. Because their costs and constraints were almost always greater than those involved in building on open land, however, many commercial districts failed to remain competitive despite these interventions. Shopping streets that had been the focus of neighborhood life now became troubling voids of shuttered stores, even when the homes surrounding them were sound and fully occupied.

Older commercial streets that did survive often went through ongoing physical changes. Continuous rows of storefronts developed new gaps for rear parking access. Banks bought the lots next door and demolished neighboring structures to put up drive-in teller booths. Gas stations took over choice corner sites, replacing solid buildings with a mixture of pump kiosks and lighted signs. When the fast-food chains arrived, they built according to a new pattern, set back from the street and surrounded by paving on all four sides. Other new stores imitated their success. Gradually, sometimes over the course of several decades, commercial areas grew more fragmented. Buildings and patterns of outdoor uses from different eras appeared to intermingle at random. As nearby homes were also modified to accommodate cars, residents also became less apt to do their errands on foot. The increasing discontinuity of sidewalks, therefore, was not necessarily seen as a problem.

Although these circumstances are not universal, they have become increasingly widespread. The sets of physical places and personal and business connections that in the past constituted discrete neighborhoods are now, for many people, more individualized and scattered. We may live in "Cedar Heights" but habitually shop ten miles away in "Yorktown Center" because it's on the way to work or because we like the stores there (or, in some cases, because we used to live there and the car gives us the choice to maintain that connection). Our next door neighbor, who works half an hour in the other direction, has a completely different set of routine destinations. If we have a dog to walk we may know well, at a small scale, the buildings, plants, squirrels, cats, and other dogs around our own block; otherwise we rarely venture on foot beyond the end of the driveway, and are familiar by quick glance only with neighboring blocks past which we drive regularly. For entertainment away from home there are restaurants, movie theaters, and clubs in two kinds of locations: one a busy, gaudy commercial strip of individual businesses, most surrounded by their own parking areas, and the other a large but more visually sedate mall, with acres of parking surrounding a more compact group of retail businesses. Both of these cater to people from many surrounding neighborhoods, so the likelihood of seeing someone we know is not great unless we arrange it ahead of time.

In communities where the built environment spreads in all directions and we depend on cars to get from one place to another, are we in fact any worse off than in the more walkable neighborhoods of densely built-up cities, or in clearly defined small towns surrounded by open land? There are optimists and pessimists among those who design, build, and write about the American environment. Suburban sprawl, which extends ever outward and also exists within the boundaries of many contemporary cities, has been lamented by critics ever since automobiles became widely available to middle-class Americans. It has been condemned for destroying the countryside, whether farms or undeveloped land, for the alleged sterility and ugliness of its homes, businesses, and parking lots, for promoting social bigotry and insularity, for its absence of old-fashioned neighborhood connections and cultural institutions, and for turning us into a nation of overweight, underexercised drivers and passengers. One of the most virulent attacks from the design community was published in 1963 by the architects Christopher Alexander and Serge Chermayeff, in *Community and Privacy:*

> The view from the picture window is of the other man's picture window. The individually owned and independently maintained outdoor spaces lap around the house and dribble miserably over curb edges into the gutters of the street. The bare unused islands of grass serve only the myth of independence. . . . Countless scattered houses dropped like stones on neat rows of development lots do not create an order, or generate community. Neighbor remains stranger. . . . The housewife, or mother, for whom the suburb was intended, has become its greatest victim.[9]

Notwithstanding such multilayered criticism, ongoing since the 1950s, new car-dependent homes and businesses continue to go up and are successfully marketed. Some of the problems raised, such as the isolation of housewives at home during the day, have been at least partially solved in ways unanticipated, or not thought economically possible, in the decades after World War II. Today even moderate-income families typically have multiple cars for greater individual mobility. A vast new array of home entertainment and communications devices—VCRs, electronic game systems, computers, and modems—have both broadened the ways we can amuse ourselves at home and made it possible to do many kinds of paying work there as well. And middle-class women have entered the paid workforce in droves, often using the second car to get to their job. Boredom and loneliness are not the main complaints today of most suburban mothers.

The ongoing vigor and popularity of new car-oriented developments, both residential and commercial, imply that they must be doing something right, that although certain positive aspects of older neighborhoods are indeed missing, the new built environment must be meeting our human needs for connection and social interaction in a different way. John Brinckerhoff Jackson, an influential essayist who wrote from the 1950s to the early 1990s about changes and patterns in what he called the "vernacular landscape," described how he saw our new dependence on car travel changing neighborhoods:

> The question which insists on an answer is, What kind of small or local community can we hope to have? . . . What seems to bring us together in the new landscape is not the sharing of space in the traditional sense but a kind of sodality based on shared uses of the street or road, and on shared routines.[10]

He also found much to admire visually in the changing commercial areas commonly reviled by architects and social critics:

> [T]he highway strip is developing a remarkable aesthetic of its own. Its lighting effects . . . are often extremely handsome; so are the bright clear colors of the buildings and installations; so are the open spaces, even though they are not coordinated. It often seems that

America is evolving a taste for a new kind of beauty: clean-cut geometric forms, primary colors, vast smooth surfaces and wide spaces uninterrupted by any detail.[11]

One may or may not admire suburban houses, or find exciting the large-scale forms and bright signage of commercial buildings designed to be seen from the highway. After fifty years of intense car-oriented development, however, the original condemnations of what are now a majority of American neighborhoods sound overwrought, reminiscent of nineteenth-century descriptions of the depravity of life in the early tenements. In the same way they combine actual physical observations, aesthetic judgments, and sweeping generalizations about human behavior into a critique that sounds forceful but is all too easy to dismiss when one piece of the argument proves inaccurate.

The critics of the 1950s and 1960s were reacting in part to a new scale of construction rather than to the content of what was built. Old photographs show that partially built blocks of speculative rowhouses and apartments around the spreading fringes of cities such as Chicago or New York in the late nineteenth and early twentieth centuries looked equally raw and out of place. In comparison with the houses of post–World War II suburbs, however, there just weren't as many of them at once. Over time, many originally identical suburban houses have been individually altered and landscaped to create more visual variety; recently completed complexes that now look stark and awkward will no doubt also soften as they age. Socially, while many new neighborhoods are indeed economically and racially homogenous, others have become as diverse as some in older towns and cities—where, of course, certain neighborhoods are also exclusive.

EDGE CITIES: THE END OF PHYSICAL NEIGHBORHOODS?

By the 1970s, as early postwar houses were starting to age and neighborhoods were turning over and diversifying, new building types began to appear along some highways. In addition to the freestanding houses, retail strips, and malls, which came first, builders put up large office buildings and corporate parks—totally sealed structures despite their often self-consciously planted and wooded surroundings. Along with them, inevitably, came additional acres of parking. As these workplaces appeared and suburban land grew more scarce and expensive, it became harder to build affordable tract houses. In a few restricted locations, some towns began to permit the construction of apartments and townhouse complexes, again with ample parking. Regions that include clusters of office space as well as stores and a new variety of home forms have recently come to be referred to as *edge cities*, a term coined as the title of a 1991 book by journalist Joel Garreau.[12] They are now the fastest-growing part of our national built environment.

Millions of Americans have settled in or relocated to these edge communities. New cultural institutions have emerged to serve them and some existing ones moved with their audiences: regional theaters, art museums, even alternative music clubs. Not just corporate executives but violinists and performance artists can be found living in sprawling ranch houses and two-story Colonials. Even the small-scale entrepreneurship often associated with dense urban neighborhoods flourishes through catering to customers who come by car. While corporate-owned chain restaurants may predominate in the newest commercial developments, unpretentious, family-owned ethnic restaurants do exist in the more run-down malls and highway strips, anywhere traffic is sufficiently heavy and the rents sufficiently low.

Thus, most of the physical and social elements that together make up traditional cities and their individual neighborhoods are now present, if not always in the same ratios, within the more dispersed residential and commercial areas of this country still generally referred to as suburban—an increasingly inaccurate term. For many people the geographic disunion of these elements may not matter. They have a network of social and business connections and daily destinations with which they feel familiar and comfortable. One could argue that their choices of workplace, entertainment, and housing are greater than in either a more densely built or a more isolated environment. Whether or not they even regard the area around their home as a neighborhood to which they are personally connected is simply another choice.

This is not to say that the components and layout of the neighborhoods around our homes are no longer important, only that deterministic assertions and, even worse, predictions, of the relationship between our built environment and our social behavior or well-being are often oversimplified. Humans are amazingly adaptable, and many have adapted quite thoroughly to the car.

This very adaptability, however, probably makes it harder for us to appreciate the enormous changes that have in fact occurred with the dominance of automobiles. Some of these are well documented; figures on gasoline consumption and the steadily increasing miles per family that we have been driving over the last fifty years, mostly for routine, everyday purposes, are easy to obtain.

It is more difficult to get a firm grip on the actual area of land that we and our automobiles occupy. In *Edge City,* Joel Garreau dismisses the issue of the consumption of land by car-oriented development:

> The noise of this conflict is greater than might seem justified. . . .
> After all, if you housed every household in the United States in that
> beloved suburban "sprawl" density of a quarter acre lot each, that
> would still take only around twenty-three million acres—1.22 percent of all the land in the United States even if you leave out
> Alaska.[13]

Calculations such as this, reflecting only the individual plots of land on which our homes sit, do not begin to take into account the real amount of space we use, or the extent to which the car has increased it. Most office parking lots are empty at night, so a household of two car-dependent commuters takes up two parking spaces and a proportion of the access lanes outside their workplaces on a full-time basis in addition to their driveway and garage at home. The same household must also be considered to occupy some portion of all the lots around all the stores, schools, churches, and other routine destinations of its residents. Many of these are vacant for much greater stretches of time than the office lot; thus, if a church builds one space for each parishioner family expected to attend on an average Sunday, that's another full-time space for the household even if it is used only once a week.

Safe and convenient designs for car travel, moreover, require far more land than that actually covered by paving. Earlier we saw how usable outdoor land around homes of diverse forms tended to become leftover strips, with a little ornamental planting at best, after the car was accommodated. As vehicles go faster than in a residential driveway or parking lot, they become even less nimble and more dangerous, requiring greater room to turn, accelerate, and slow down. This means wider buffer zones between high-speed roadways and areas where people might actually be walking around. At the scale of highways and interchanges, even within densely built-up communities, these required leftover areas are huge, although we may be unaware of their size as we travel past them at high speeds or are stalled in traffic, surrounded by other vehicles. Only when we break down or run out of gas and have to walk down a cloverleaf exit ramp for help do we realize both how long it is and how much space it actually encloses.

NEIGHBORHOODS AND ACCESSIBILITY

When in 1966 J. B. Jackson described the "remarkable aesthetic" of the highway strip and commented that Americans were developing a taste for "vast smooth surfaces and wide spaces," he may have been writing accurately about the way we perceive and enjoy the outdoors through a windshield. Writers like Jackson and Garreau, however, who seem to view the changes in the American landscape as both inevitable and largely positive, do not discuss them from the point of view of those who don't drive. For adults who have adapted completely to getting around by car, what is perhaps hardest to appreciate about these changes is how they affect people of all ages who can't get behind the steering wheel. Considered collectively and estimated conservatively, nondrivers make up more than a third of the total population.[14] They include able-bodied adults who can't afford a car or one dependable enough for regular use, those who do not drive for physical or emotional reasons, particularly the elderly, and children.

For people in these groups, daily connections cannot be individually selected and pieced together from a network of widely spaced choices. Depending on the public transportation available and the variety of destinations within walking distance, they may live, effectively, in neighborhoods far more physically and socially circumscribed than those of an earlier era. In other cases they must adapt to a state of dependence on family or friends to get around. Children may simply take this situation for granted, but adults sometimes find themselves left dangerously in the lurch.

Low-income workers who do not own cars are excluded from many job opportunities, particularly in the commercial and residential areas of prosperous communities accessible only by highway and zoned only for expensive houses. At best they must make do by commuting long hours on roundabout and infrequent bus routes for trips that would take only minutes by automobile. But even in developed suburban regions where public transportation is relatively extensive, buses do not serve the more remote and leafy neighborhoods and corporate parks. Those who would willingly take low-paying jobs in such areas must often turn them down for lack of access.[15]

People who can afford cars are still without alternative ways of getting around when necessary. The more affluent elderly who have long lived in or retired to spacious suburban environments now depend on driving even when health problems make it risky. Accident statistics show that drivers over age seventy-five have more accidents per mile, but as one Florida state official explained in 1997 to a *New York Times* reporter, "You can't live down here without driving. You can't go to the grocery store, the doctor, the hospital. You can't go anywhere."[16] Like other recently built homes, many retirement communities are situated on the fringes of sprawling edge-city development and linked to nonresidential areas only by highway. Though they include recreational and social facilities, these rarely meet all practical everyday needs, and the food at the on-site coffee shop can get boring. Even when special van or car services exist, driving oneself is far more convenient, and giving it up often means a traumatic loss of independence. For some, losing the ability to drive is a major factor in a regretful decision to move within retirement—from an active community organized around a golf course, for example, to a building for frail elderly or to a nursing home.

Children and younger adolescents comprise the largest group of nondrivers, and adult attitudes toward their mobility can be complicated. For almost 150 years, a major marketing theme for suburban developments has been the notion that freestanding private houses with large yards and plenty of greenery are the best possible, most natural setting for raising families. This thinking holds that children, to grow up healthy and happy, need to run around outdoors and play on their own but at the same time be protected from the adult world of factories and offices as well as from the dangers of traffic, crime, and corrupting social influences. Critics of this attitude, of course, have been around for just as long; some are themselves products of such communities. In their view this insulation from the "real world" is not only boring but harmful, stifling adventure and delaying real maturity. However, the undeniable appeal of the country house image—complete with kids playing on the lawn—endures to this day and still underlies many American families' decisions about where to live.

After World War II, when suburbanization increased dramatically and cars became the main way to get around within new communities, it was widely noted and somewhat lamented that a major role of mothers was now that of chauffeur. Movies and popular songs also attested to the new symbolic and real importance of cars for teenagers' freedom. As the Beach Boys sang in the 1960s, "She'll have fun, fun, fun till her daddy takes the T-bird away."

Less attention was paid to the ways in which these idealized suburban environments actually changed, for younger children, as a result of the automobile. The disappearance of sidewalks, the growth in traffic volume, the increased separation of stores and commercial entertainment from residential districts, and the relentless development of previously vacant land into private home sites combined to limit the scope of their physical independence and exploration. As single-story ranch houses became a standard form and the size of an average individual lot at least doubled, the distances between homes and other basic facilities such as parks and schoolyards grew proportionately. These greater distances were not usually seen as problems because far more homes now had yards and driveways of their own. A basketball hoop mounted above the garage door was initially almost always more appealing, to parents and children alike, than a larger court several blocks away.

Increasingly, however, children had to rely on parents or other adults for transportation around even their immediate neighborhoods. With desirable destinations—friends' houses, movie theaters, ballfields, even libraries—ever more distant and the streets ever less pedestrian- or bicycle-friendly, reason was greater to negotiate for a lift in the car. In many new neighborhoods it was in fact the only realistic option. Patterns of adult mobility, of course, were changing at the same time. Everyone was walking less, and as long as most mothers were home on a full-time basis children simply got used to, and as often as not preferred, being driven. But today, sadly, their independence is often measured not in terms of how far they can go on their bike or when they can take the bus on their own but by whether or for how long they can stay alone at home without adult supervision. Sometimes this isolation is tempered by newly sophisticated home technology, which provides absorbing role-playing adventures on the screen or allows getting together on-line with friends.

We should consider the environmental as well as the social and developmental implications of these changes. For many children, the experience of wandering freely outside, whether through a largely man-made or undeveloped environment, is no longer associated with the neighborhood surrounding their own homes. When available, opportunities for outdoor exploration are now more often in large parks or legally protected wilderness tracts some distance away by car. A major priority of contemporary environmental groups is the creation and preservation of such areas, which are important not just in protecting regional biodiversity but also in providing hiking trails and stretches of car-free landscape for our own enjoyment and recreation. These human uses of so-called wilderness areas, though not always helpful to the survival of other species, give popular strength to land conservation efforts. But they also focus our attention away from the physical constrictions and environmental problems of our own neighborhoods. They may help children to develop a real appreciation for non-human life-forms and natural geography, but not a familiarity with or sense of stewardship for the outdoors through which they travel daily.

In the second half of this century, the ever-growing dominance of car travel led to changes in our built environment that cause major problems of accessibility for many more people than those whom we define as physically handicapped. At the same time, in seeming contradiction, cars have vastly increased most Americans' access to places that were previously remote. Typically, middle-class adults and families travel more widely around the country and see distant friends and relatives more often today than they did in earlier eras. But at a neighborhood level, the automobile's effect has been to inhibit and in some places render almost impossible getting around by any other means. Even in communities where walking or biking is feasible, the zoning of homes far away from other building uses can make it hard for people to fulfill their most basic daily needs (including earning a living, the most basic of all) without a car.

Only over the last twenty-five years has accessibility for the physically handicapped, within and immediately around individual buildings, been accepted—first as a goal and then as a legal standard. While improving, most structures are still not fully compliant or barrier-free; each existing building presents slightly different conditions requiring a unique set of modifications. We associate accessibility standards with specific features in limited areas: ramps at building entrances, and restricted blue-lined parking spaces at the front of lots. But their intention is far more comprehensive: that the construction of new buildings and the alteration of existing ones allow disabled Americans as much independence and productivity as possible. For designers, this means considering all parts of a building and its site, not just the places where handicapped modifications are visible.

Accessibility standards, especially as embodied in the 1990 Americans with Disabilities Act, represent the creation of new civil rights. They came about not only because of changing social attitudes but also because of modern technologies such as elevators, well-engineered wheelchairs, and new communications devices. Today they enable disabled and elderly persons to function more productively and with greater independence than was previously feasible. At a larger scale, however, problems of physical isolation and lack of mobility present barriers to all nondrivers as great as stairs do to wheelchair users.

One strategy to improve the connections between homes and other essential parts of the built environment might be the extension of accessibility standards to cover more aspects of neighborhood design and planning. In order to meet the needs of residents of all ages as well as all physical abilities, such additional regulations would have to address three separate issues. Most straightforward would be new mandates for a broadening of transportation choices: adding sidewalks, providing safe bikeways, and expanding public transportation networks wherever possible. Under existing laws such facilities are or soon will be required to be handicapped-accessible if they are built. Sidewalks must have ramped curb cuts, for instance, and, under a phased schedule, all new buses must within a few years accommodate wheelchairs. But requirements that alternatives to driving be created in the first place are far less clear-cut; within private residential neighborhoods they are most often nonexistent.

Equally important to improving connections would be a relaxation and revision of local zoning codes that regulate both the separation of building uses and the separation of home forms and sizes. Enabling people to become and remain independent as they grow up and then age would mean creating closer physical links between homes, community facilities, commercial centers, and workplaces. Because we typically no longer live within extended families, accessible neighborhoods where we could choose to stay over our lifespan would have to include either homes in a range of sizes and forms or those that could be easily and legally subdivided and recombined to meet changing needs.

Such recommendations are hardly new. To one degree or another all have been advocated by environmentalists, transportation planners, architects, and urban designers. But discussions about neighborhood design still take place on a wholly different level from those about individual buildings. Over the last century Americans have first wrestled with and then created minimum standards for homes and other structures that essentially supersede issues of immediate costs and benefits. While early housing reformers tried hard to show that affordable city homes with adequate light and air could also be profitable, the legal standards finally enacted simply required certain levels of ventilation and sunlight whether or not they might allow for profit. When the use of electrical wiring transformed middle-class household life to the point where its absence made homes seem backward and underdeveloped, the government undertook the electrification of rural dwellings from which no initial return was made. This use of public funds made possible new electrical standards for all homes. More recently, the Americans with Disabilities Act mandated sometimes costly features in all public and commercial buildings, regardless of the frequency with which any given structure might actually be used by those with specific handicaps.

None of these regulations, of course, is enacted without some consideration of the costs involved; unrealistically high or narrow standards are unenforceable and get diluted over time. But each represents consensus about the public interest in the quality of buildings that transcends individual choices or rights to profit. Because we lack such consensus about neighborhoods, proposed improvements are more often met with skepticism or with resentment of the costs involved. We do accept the need for basic public health provisions such as sewers and for road improvements to facilitate driving. But while public corridors within buildings must now comfortably accommodate the small number of people in wheelchairs along with the vast majority of those on foot, we don't apply the same logic to our outdoor built environment. On public streets we do not require a means for the minority as well as the majority to get around safely. When compared with amenities such as elevators and ramps, sidewalks are not terribly expensive, yet they are lacking along most new residential streets as well as major thoroughfares, even those with bus routes and stops.

Many of the ways that our neighborhoods have changed over the last half-century are really technological byproducts of a new transportation mode rather than deliberate choices. The automobile is now the tail that wags the dog. While most American parents today worry more about safety than they might have in earlier eras, they don't actually prefer that their school-age children be confined to the house and yard and know that the home computer is not a substitute for the outdoors. Most people who are not yet elderly sympathize wholeheartedly with aging relatives who want to remain independent, feeling conflicted even while negotiating with them to give up driving or to move out of their present home into someplace more "suitable" but often far away. After reductions in public welfare support, the problems of getting to work for those who can't afford cars are increasingly apparent; ignoring these obstacles does not serve the interests of either the poor or the wealthy.

Reducing the negative side effects of our dependence on automobiles can seem a daunting proposition. Most parts of our built environment are already too dispersed, and their components too rigidly separated, to be easily knit back together solely with sidewalks and improved public transportation systems. Even in older communities, along blocks originally built around trolley lines, restoring the service would not meet the same needs it once did. From these homes neighbors used to ride together downtown, where jobs were concentrated. Now they go to work in several directions and make their way home doing errands or picking up children along individualized routes of stores and day-care centers. In more recently built communities, adding sidewalks in front of homes might encourage a little more walking by all residents and certainly make it safer for young children to ride bikes or to get from one house to another. It would not by itself, however, create other accessible, interesting, or useful destinations. The whole notion of revising zoning codes to permit a greater mixture of home forms, or some variety of land uses intermingled with homes, is extremely controversial.

With homes now so spread apart, and our patterns of land use so entrenched and wasteful, it is tempting to contemplate only the possibilities for creating alternative neighborhoods from the ground up rather than to consider modifying what we already have. The notion of brand-new and better-planned communities that are both tightly knit and modern is seductive. At least in theory they could accommodate cars more comfortably than existing congested cities yet increase our transportation choices by providing a greater variety of homes and other uses than today's typical subdivisions. Proposals for new towns are always fascinating. The problem is that they rarely get built in their entirety and are never self-contained; at a certain point they must intersect with, rather than replace, the older environment. And our experience with demolishing large numbers of homes to rebuild from scratch, as we did after World War II, was sobering. Today many of the older homes once deemed substandard are seen in a more positive light than those that replaced them.

Part of the power of the minimum standards enacted in the past was their transforming effects on existing homes as well as new ones. They guided the gradual modification of nineteenth-century rowhouses, and even tenements, from dark and sooty rooms with pungent backyard privies into brighter, warmer, and cleaner homes with modern plumbing and rear gardens. They reduced the frequency of fires, as well as the rate of deaths from those that do occur, in houses from the Victorian era as well as in split-levels from the 1950s.

It is easy to appreciate the scope of these changes looking back over a long period, but harder to see the force of those in progress. While upgraded standards are quickly and fully realized in new construction, their application to older buildings can seem half-hearted or illogical. Thus, when elevator apartments are individually renovated today in New York City, the bathroom door often ends up wider than the main entrance to the unit because only spaces that are altered must conform to new accessibility standards. Such anomalies frustrate current residents trying to make the most of tight living quarters and may or may not be the most efficient route to change. Over time, however, progressively more of the indoor environment is indeed becoming navigable by wheelchairs. Eventually the dimensions that accommodate them will seem normal rather than oversize, just as plumbing and electrical wiring are now standard in homes from all eras.

In many American neighborhoods, the major housing problems we now face are not unsafe or primitive indoor conditions but connections outward from the front door. Distances to work, social institutions, and essential stores have all grown to the point where many people, for a variety of reasons, are left isolated. The custom of widely separating different forms and sizes of homes through zoning now means that as people's needs change over their lifespan they must often move from one community to another. Minimum standards to knit our neighborhoods back together would have to be met by adapting existing buildings and outdoor spaces as well as incrementally adding new ones. Like other gradual changes to the built environment, this process would not be as clean or efficient as building completely anew.

Efforts now underway to broaden transportation options and build a greater variety of homes are supported by those with both social and environmental priorities. These do not always mesh perfectly. In some communities zoning laws are being challenged to permit the construction of more affordable homes, while in others more closely spaced forms are encouraged not to make them less expensive but to preserve open land. Certain choices that might solve the transportation problems of poor people, such as subsidizing individual car ownership, do not meet the environmental goals of energy efficiency and improved air quality.

For residents of many established communities, proposals either to add public transportation systems or to allow new forms and sizes of homes raise fears of undesirable social change as well as issues of visual incompatibility. Even sidewalks can be seen as inviting unwanted intrusion and a loss of privacy. But the physically simplistic neighborhoods we build now not only exclude others—they fail to serve many of their residents as well. While using the logic of improved accessibility to establish new standards for neighborhood design would not meet every social and environmental goal, it might be more widely accepted than other rationales on the basis of long-term self-interest. We invest a great deal in establishing both the social and physical connections that ground us in our homes and neighborhoods. Though Americans may move more often than people in many other countries, such dislocations carry many costs. When people do move, it is certainly better if they do so out of choice rather than necessity.

Regardless of the exact ideological basis on which we justify planning for our neighborhoods, fundamental change depends at least in part on our learning to see the environmental and social worth of "real" homes in a range of forms. Looking back on the imaginative variety of livable homes already built in this country should help us think flexibly about what to do next. We need to conceive of a possible apartment complex at the end of the block not automatically as a threat or an intrusion but as an option that might benefit the neighborhood, not least by providing choices for those within our own families. Then we can argue about what it should look like.

Notes

Introduction

1. William Cronon, "The Trouble with Wilderness," in *Uncommon Ground: Rethinking the Human Place in Nature,* ed. William Cronon (New York: Norton, 1996), 85.
2. Sym Van der Ryn and Stuart Cowan, *Ecological Design* (Washington, DC: Island Press, 1996), 29.

Chapter 1

1. This is the primary and most inclusive definition in the *Shorter Oxford Dictionary;* subsequent entries limit the term to mean only structures considered or intended as "fine art."
2. Jane Brody, "Facing Up to the Realities of Sleep Deprivation," *The New York Times,* March 31, 1998.
3. Amos Rapoport, *House Form and Culture* (Englewood Cliffs, NJ: Prentice Hall, 1969), 70.
4. Judith Heerwagen and Gordon Orians, "Human, Habitats, and Aesthetics," in *The Biophilia Hypothesis,* ed. Stephen Kellert and Edward Wilson (Washington, DC: Island Press), 151.
5. June Fletcher, Behind Walls, Millions Seek Safe Havens," *The Wall Street Journal,* February 2, 1996.
6. Roger S. Ulrich, "Biophilia, Biophobia and Natural Landscapes," in *The Biophilia Hypothesis,* ed. Stephen Kellert and Edward Wilson (Washington, DC: Island Press, 1993), 90.

7. For a full discussion of land use conflicts between Indians and early colonists in New England, see William Cronon, *Changes in the Land: Indians, Colonists, and the Ecology of New England* (New York: Hill and Wang, 1983).

Chapter 2

1. Quoted in Anthony Jackson, *A Place Called Home: A History of Low Cost Housing in Manhattan* (Cambridge: MIT Press, 1976), 134.
2. Minutes of the Common Council of New York City, 1675–1776, quoted in Richard Plunz, *A History of Housing in New York City* (New York: Columbia University Press, 1990).
3. Harold M. Mayer and Richard C. Wade, *Chicago: Growth of a Metropolis* (Chicago: University of Chicago Press, 1969), 106–16.
4. See Constance Perin, *Everything In Its Place: Social Order and Land Use in America* (Princeton, NJ: Princeton University Press, 1977), 259, Table 8.
5. Plunz, *History of Housing*, xxxii.
6. Ibid., 3.
7. Charles Haswell, quoted by Anthony Jackson, *A Place Called Home: A History of Low Cost Housing in Manhattan* (Cambridge: MIT Press, 1976), 33.
8. *The New York Times*, 7 April 1856, quoted by Anthony Jackson, *A Place Called Home*, 18.
9. Benjamin Marsh, *An Introduction to City Planning*, quoted by Seymour Toll, *Zoned American* (New York: Grossman Publishers, 1969), 123–24.
10. Alfred Bettman, quoted by Toll, ibid., 268.
11. Kenneth T. Jackson, *Crabgrass Frontier: The Suburbanization of the United States* (New York: Oxford University Press, 1985), 242.
12. Ibid.
13. Toll, *Zoned American*, 281.
14. David E. Nye, *Electrifying America: Social Meanings of a New Technology* (Cambridge: MIT Press, 1990), 296–304.
15. Quoted by Nye, ibid., 304.
16. Plunz, *History of Housing*, 227.
17. Ibid., 208.
18. U.S. Bureau of the Census, *Statistical Abstract of the United States, 1996*, 116th edition (Washington, DC, 1996).
19. Ibid.

Chapter 3

1. Bureau of the Census, *Statistical Abstract of the United States, 1996*, 58.
2. The basis for most local and national laws on handicapped accessibility is a document published and periodically updated by the American National Standards Institute, Inc. Often referred to simply as ANSI 117.1, its full title is *American Standard for Buildings and Facilities—Providing Accessibility and*

Usability for Physically Handicapped People. It is available from the American National Standards Institute at 1430 Broadway, New York, NY 10018.

3. Department of Housing and Urban Development, *Cost Containment and Modest Design Requirements for the Section 8 and Section 202 Programs* (H.U.D. memorandum dated November 1981, issued as an update to the H.U.D. Minimum Property Standards).

4. Amos Rapoport, *House Form and Culture* (Englewood Cliffs, NJ: Prentice-Hall, 1969), 61–62.

5. U.S. Bureau of the Census, *Statistical Abstract of the United States, 1996,* 721.

6. Ibid.

7. U.S. Bureau of the Census, *Statistical Abstract of the United States, 1991,* 111th edition (Washington, DC), 730.

8. Ibid.

9. This analogy is presented in more detail by Esmond Reid in *Understanding Buildings: A Multidisciplinary Approach* (Cambridge: MIT Press, 1984), 129–30.

10. U.S. Bureau of the Census, *Statistical Abstract of the United States: 1996,* 582.

Chapter 4

1. Lester Walker, *American Shelter: An Illustrated Encyclopedia of the American Home* (Woodstock, NY: Overlook Press, 1996).

2. Clifford Edward Clark, Jr., *The American Family Home 1800–1960* (Chapel Hill: University of North Carolina Press, 1986).

3. Constance Perin, *Everything in its Place: Social Order and Land Use in America* (Princeton, NJ: Princeton University Press, 1977), 259.

4. U.S. Bureau of the Census, *Statistical Abstract of the United States: 1996,* 116th Edition (Washington, DC, 1996), 719.

5. Stewart Brand, *How Buildings Learn: What Happens After They're Built* (New York: Viking Penguin, 1994), 7.

6. Andrew Jackson Downing, *The Architecture of Country Houses* (D. Appleton & Co., 1850; reprint, New York: Dover, 1969).

7. William Cronon, *Changes in the Land: Indians, Colonists, and the Ecology of New England* (New York: Hill and Wang, 1983), 48–50.

8. Hugh Morrison, *Early American Architecture* (New York: Oxford University Press, 1952; reprint, New York: Dover, 1987), 49.

9. Ibid., 103.

10. Ibid., 13.

11. Ibid., 22.

12. Clark, *The American Family Home 1800–1960,* 60.

13. Andrew Jackson Downing, *The Architecture of Country Houses,* Preface, 1.

14. Youmans, George, "The Higher Education of Women" *Popular Science Monthly* (April 1874) quoted in Clark, *The American Family Home 1800–1960,* 104.

15. Catherine E. Beecher and Harriet Beecher Stowe, *The American Woman's Home: or Principles of Domestic Science* (New York: J. B. Ford, 1870).
16. Clark, *The American Family Home 1800–1960,* 162.
17. Gwendolyn Wright, *Building the Dream: A Social History of Housing in America* (Cambridge: MIT Press, 1983), 172 and Clark, *The American Family Home 1800–1960,* 167.
18. Clark, *The American Family Home 1800–1960,* 162–63.
19. Aladdin Company, *"Built In A Day" House Catalog, 1917* (Bay City, Michigan: The Aladdin Company, 1917; reprint, New York: Dover, 1995), 17.
20. Allan D. Wallis, *Wheel Estate: The Rise and Decline of Mobile Homes* (New York: Oxford University Press, 1991), 54–55.
21. Ibid., 94.
22. Elmer Frey, president of Marshfield Homes, quoted in Wallis, *Wheel Estate: The Rise and Decline of Mobile Homes,* 130.
23. Wallis, *Wheel Estate: The Rise and Decline of Mobile Homes,* 167–71.
24. Ibid., 105–8.
25. Kenneth T. Jackson, *Crabgrass Frontier: The Suburbanization of the United States* (New York: Oxford University Press, 1985), 234.
26. D. J. Waldie, *Holy Land: A Suburban Memoir* (New York: Norton, 1996), 1.
27. Wallis, *Wheel Estate: The Rise and Decline of Mobile Homes,* 108.
28. Perin, *Everything in its Place: Social Order and Land Use in America,* 259.
29. Jackson, *Crabgrass Frontier: The Suburbanization of the United States,* 202–3.
30. U.S. Bureau of the Census, *Statistical Abstract of the United States: 1996,* 714.
31. Levitt advertisement, quoted in *Newsday,* September 28, 1997 "The Pioneers of Suburbia: Levittown at Fifty," H15.
32. U.S. Bureau of the Census, *Statistical Abstract of the United States: 1996,* 714.

Chapter 5

1. U.S. Bureau of the Census, *Statistical Abstract of the United States: 1996*, 116th Edition (Washington, DC, 1996), 719.
2. Hugh Morrison, *Early American Architecture* (New York: Oxford University Press, 1952; reprint, New York: Dover, 1987), 137.
3. Gwendolyn Wright, *Building the Dream: A Social History of Housing in America* (New York: Pantheon, 1981), 25.
4. Kenneth T. Jackson, *Crabgrass Frontier: The Suburbanization of the United States* (New York: Oxford University Press, 1985), 90–91.
5. Sally Lichtenstein Berk, *The Richest Crop: The Rowhouses of Harry Wardman (1872–1939), Washington, DC ,Developer* (master's thesis, George Washington University, 1989), 88–89.
6. Beth Yanofsky, "Tranquil Setting for Frank Lloyd Wright Contemporary" *Main Line Times,* July 27, 1995, and earlier undated local news clippings from the files of the Lower Merion Historical Society.

Chapter 6

1. Andrew Jackson Downing, *The Architecture of Country Houses* (1850; reprint, New York: Dover Publications, 1969), 110.
2. See Judith Heerwagen and Gordon Orians, "Humans, Habitats, and Aesthetics" in *The Biophilia Hypothesis*, Stephen Kellert and Edward Wilson, eds. (Washington, D.C.: Island Press, 1993), 151–52.
3. Richard Plunz, *A History of Housing in New York City* (New York: Columbia University Press, 1990), 37.
4. Harold M. Mayer and Richard C. Wade, *Chicago: Growth of a Metropolis* (Chicago: University of Chicago Press, 1969), 256.
5. Plunz, *History of Housing*, 22–23.
6. Jane Holtz Kay, *Lost Boston* (Boston: Houghton Mifflin, 1980), 125.
7. Bernard Newman, quoted in Gwendolyn Wright, *Building The Dream: A Social History of Housing in America* (Cambridge: MIT Press, 1981), 150.
8. James M. Goode, *Best Addresses: A Century of Washington's Distinguished Apartment Houses* (Washington, D.C.: Smithsonian Institution Press, 1988), 8–10.
9. Stefanos Polyzoides, Roger Sherwood, and James Tice, *Courtyard Housing in Los Angeles: A Typological Analysis* (Berkeley: University of California Press, 1982).
10. Plunz, *History of Housing*, 208.
11. Allan D. Wallis, *Wheel Estate: The Rise and Decline of Mobile Homes* (New York: Oxford University Press, 1991) 103.
12. Plunz, *History of Housing*, 272.
13. Ibid., 268.
14. Le Corbusier, *Looking at City Planning*, trans. Eleanor Levieux (1946, as *Maniere de Penser L'Urbanisme*, reprint, New York: Grossman Publishers, 1971), 48–49.
15. U.S. Bureau of the Census, *Statistical Abstract of the United States: 1996*, 719.

Chapter 7

1. U.S. Bureau of the Census, *Statistical Abstract of the United States: 1996*, 116th Edition (Washington, D.C., 1996), 101.
2. Kenneth T. Jackson, *Crabgrass Frontier: The Suburbanization of the United States* (New York: Oxford University Press, 1985), 15.
3. Ibid., 33.
4. Ibid., 39.
5. Ibid., 111.
6. Jane Holtz Kay, *Lost Boston* (Boston: Houghton Mifflin, 1980), 249.
7. For detailed accounts of the design, construction, and marketing of Levittown, L.I., and the criticism accompanying its development, see Clifford Edward Clark, Jr., *The American Family Home, 1800–1960* (Chapel Hill: The University of North Carolina Press, 1986), chapter 8.

8. Herbert Gans, *The Levittowners: Ways of Life and Politics in a New Suburban Community* (New York: Pantheon Books, 1967), 5.

9. Christopher Alexander and Serge Chermayeff, *Community and Privacy* (Garden City, NY: Anchor Books, Doubleday, 1963), 62–63.

10. J. B. Jackson, *A Sense of Place, A Sense of Time* (New Haven, CT: Yale University Press, 1994), 10.

11. J. B. Jackson, *Landscapes* (Amherst: University of Massachusetts Press, 1970), 149.

12. Joel Garreau, *Edge City: Life on the New Frontier* (New York: Anchor Books, Doubleday, 1991).

13. Ibid., 390.

14. U.S. Bureau of the Census, *Statistical Abstract of the United States: 1996,* 116th Edition (Washington, D.C.), 33. Using national population figures for 1995 broken down by age, this estimate includes 95 percent of children age 0 to 17, 7 percent of adults from age 18 to age 64 (a low percentage of poverty, physical handicaps, and inner-city residence are all taken into account), and 35 percent of adults 65 and over. With these percentages, the rough total of nondrivers comes to about 34 percent of the U.S. population. The actual total is probably much higher.

15. Jane Gross, "Poor Without Cars Find Getting to Work Can Be a Job," *New York Times,* 18 November 1997, A1.

16. Sara Rimer, "An Aging Nation Ill-Equipped for Hanging Up the Car Keys" *New York Times,* 15 December 1997, A1.

Illustration Credits

All illustrations are original and were drawn by the author except as here noted. All interpretation of source material was solely the responsibility of the author. Elizabeth Newman drew perspective views constituting all or part of the following illustrations: 4-2, 4-3, 4-5, 4-11, 4-18, 4-19, 4-20, 4-22, 4-23, 4-24, 4-25, 4-27, 4-28, 4-29, 4-30, 4-32, 4-33, 4-34, 4-35, 5-5, 5-6, 5-8, 5-9, 5-15, 5-17, 5-18, 5-19, 5-20, 5-24, 6-13, 6-14, 6-19, 6-20, 6-21, 6-24, 6-25, 6-27, 6-29, 6-30, 6-40, 6-42, 6-43, 7-1, 7-2, 7-3.

Source material for individual illustrations:

2-1: Photo from Historic American Building Survey, reproduced in *Building The Dream*, by Gwendolyn Wright (Cambridge, Mass.: MIT Press, 1983), 28.

2-2: Photos in *The Tenements of Chicago*, by Edith Abbott (Chicago, Ill.: The University of Chicago Press, 1936)

4-2: *Japanese Houses and Their Surroundings*, by Edward S. Morse (reprint edition, New York: Dover Publications, Inc., 1961)

4-3: *The Architecture of Country Houses*, by A. J. Downing (reprint edition, New York: Dover Publications, Inc., 1969), 78–82.

4-6, 4-7, 4-8, and 4-9: *Early American Architecture*, by Hugh Morrison (reprint edition New York: Dover Publications, Inc., 1987), 21– 57.

4-12: *Ozark Vernacular Houses*, by Jean Sizemore (Fayetteville: The University of Arkansas Press, 1994), 53, 67.

4-13: *A Field Guide to American Houses*, by Virginia and Lee McAlester (New York: Alfred A. Knopf, Inc., 1984), 134–136.

4-14: *Early American Architecture*, 245–246.

4-15: *Great Georgian Houses of America, Vol. I*, by the Architects' Emergency Committee (reprint edition New York: Dover Publications, Inc., 1970), 39–42.

4-17: *The Architecture of Country Houses*, 78–82.

4-18: *The American Woman's Home*, by Catherine E. Beecher and Harriet Beecher Stowe (New York, J. B. Ford and Company, 1870).

4-19: *Bicknell's Victorian Buildings*, by A. J. Bicknell & Co. (reprint edition New York: Dover Publications, Inc., 1979), plates 3 and 4 and following specifications.

4-20: photo in *Gritty Cities*, by Mary Procter and Bill Matuszeski (Philadelphia, Temple University Press, 1978), 238.

4-21: *A Field Guide to American Houses*, 90–91.

4-22: *Aladdin "Built in a Day" House Catalog*, by the Aladdin Company (reprint edition, New York: Dover Publications, Inc., 1995), 17, 51.

4-23: *Your Future Home*, by the Architect's Small House Service Bureau, (reprint edition, Washington, D.C.: AIA Press, 1992).

4-25, 4-26, 4-29: *Wheel Estate*, by Allan D. Wallis (New York: Oxford University Press, 1991), 72, 106, 137, 144, 158.

4-30: *Newsday*, September 28, 1997, H28.

5-13: *Early American Architecture*, 136–37.

5-14: *Bricks and Brownstone*, by Charles Lockwood (New York: Abbeville Press, 1972), 16.

5-16: *Victorian City and Country Houses*, By Geo. E. Woodward (first published as *Woodward's National Architect, Vol II*, in 1877. Reprint edition, New York: Dover Publications, Inc., 1996), 66–68.

5-18: Builder's advertisement reproduced in *Philadelphia: Portrait of an American City*, by Edwin Wolf 2nd (Philadelphia: The Library Company of Philadelphia, 1990), 277.

5-19: *Toward New Towns for America*, by Clarence S. Stein (Cambridge, Mass: MIT Press, 1957), 78–81.

5-25: Magazine cover reproduced in *Building The Dream*, 187.

6-7: A similar section, with raised front porches, was used in the Riverbend apartment complex built in New York City in 1976, designed by the architectural firm of Davis and Brody.

6-11, 6-12: *A History of Housing in New York City*, by Richard Plunz (New York: Columbia University Press, 1990), 13.

6-14: Photo in *Chicago: Growth of a Metropolis*, by Harold M. Meyer and Richard C. Wade (Chicago: The University of Chicago Press, 1969), 365.

6-15, 6-16: *A History of Housing in New York City*, 32, 49.

6-17: *Sears, Roebuck Catalog of Houses, 1926* (reprint edition, New York: Dover Publications, Inc., 1991), 95.

6-18: *The Richest Crop: The Rowhouses of Harry Wardman (1872–1939), Washington, D.C. Developer* by Sally Lichtenstein Berk (master's thesis, George Washington University, 1989), 218.

6-19: Photo in *Lost Boston*, by Jane Holtz Kay (Boston, Houghton Mifflin Co., 1980), 125.

6-22: *Best Addresses: A Century of Washington's Distinguished Apartment Houses* , by James M. Goode (Washington, DC: Smithsonian Institution Press, 1988), 8–9.

6-23: *New York's Fabulous Luxury Apartments,* by Andrew Alpern (reprint edition, New York: Dover Publications, Inc., 1987), 20–21.

6-24: Advertisement reproduced in *Chicago: Growth of a Metropolis,* 322.

6-25: *New York's Fabulous Luxury Apartments,* 26–27, and N.Y. C. Land Map, Sanborn Company, Plate 134, 1906.

6-26: Promotional material for Alden Park courtesy of the Philadelphia Historical Commission.

6-27: *American Apartment Houses, Hotels, and Apartment Hotels of Today,* by Randolph William Sexton (New York: Architectural Book Publishing Co., Inc., 1926), plate XIX.

6-28: *Jackson Heights: A Garden in the City,* by Daniel Karatzas (New York: Daniel Karatzas, 1990), 59, and *A History of Housing in New York City,* 143.

6-29: *Toward New Towns for America,* by Clarence S. Stein (Cambridge, Mass: MIT Press, 1957), 90, 113.

6-30: *Courtyard Housing in Los Angeles: A Typological Analysis,* by Stefanos Polyzoides, Roger Sherwood, and James Tice (Berkeley: University of California Press, 1982), 78–79.

6-31: *Best Addresses: A Century of Washington's Distinguished Apartment Houses,* 339.

6-32, 6-33: *A History of Housing in New York City,* 244, 265, 266.

6-35: *The Form of Housing,* edited by Sam Davis (New York: Van Nostrand Reinhold Co., 1977), 49.

6-36: *Defensible Space,* by Oscar Newman (New York: The Macmillan Co., 1972), 57.

6-38: *Best Addresses: A Century of Washington's Distinguished Apartment Houses,* 447–48.

6-39: *A History of Housing in New York City,* 327.

6-40, 6-41: *The Form of Housing,* 29, 226.

6-43: Floorplans courtesy of Tom Miles.

7-1, 7-2: *Chicago: Growth of a Metropolis,* 72, 165.

7-3: *Hometown U.S.A.,* by Stephen Sears, Murray Belsky and Douglas Tunstell (New York: American Heritage Publishing Co., Inc., 1975) 16–17.

7-5 and 7-7: *Chicago: Growth of a Metropolis,* 87, 425.

Acknowledgments

The author is grateful to the following for permission to quote from copyright material:

From *The American Family Home* 1800–1960 by Clifford Edward Clark, Jr. copyright © 1986 by the University of North Carolina Press. Used by permission of the publisher.

Excerpt from *The Architecture of Country Houses* copyright © 1969 by Andrew Jackson Downing reprinted by permission of Dover Publications.

Granted with permission from *The Biophilia Hypothesis*, Stephen Kellert and Edward Wilson (Eds.), copyright © Stephen Kellert and Edward Wilson, 1993. Published by Shearwater Books, Washington D.C. and Covelo, California.

Excerpt reprinted by permission of The Feminist Press at The City University of New York, from Paule Marshall, *Brown Girl, Brownstones* (New York: The Feminist Press at The City University of New York, 1981), copyright 1959, 1981 by Paule Marshall.

From *Community and Privacy*, by Serge Chermayeff and Christopher Alexander. Copyright © 1963 by Serge Chermayeff. Used by permission of Doubleday, a division of Bantam Doubleday Dell Publishing Group, Inc.

Excerpt from *Crabgrass Frontier: The Suburbanization of The United States* copyright © 1985 by Kenneth T. Jackson reprinted by permission of Oxford University Press.

Down in the Depths (On The 90th Floor), by Cole Porter © 1936 (Renewed) Chappell & Co. All Rights Reserved. Used by permission, WARNER BROS. PUBLICATIONS U.S. INC., Miami, FL. 33014.

Index